Endangered Wildlife and Plants of the World

Volume 6
IGU–MAN

Marshall Cavendish
New York • London • Toronto • Sydney

Marshall Cavendish Corporation
99 White Plains Road
Tarrytown, NY 10591-9001

Created by Brown Partworks Ltd.
Editor: Anne Hildyard
Associate Editors: Paul Thompson, Amy Prior
Managing Editor: Tim Cooke
Design: Whitelight
Picture Research: Helen Simm
Index Editor: Kay Ollerenshaw
Production Editor: Matt Weyland
Illustrations: Barbara Emmons, Jackie Harland, Tracy Williamson

Library of Congress Cataloging-in-Publication Data

Endangered wildlife and plants of the world
p.cm.
Includes bibliographical references (p.).
ISBN 0-7614-7194-4 (set)
ISBN 0-7614-7200-2 (vol. 6)
1. Endangered species--Encyclopedias. I. Marshall Cavendish Corporation.

QH75.E68 2001
333.95'22'03--dc21
99-086194

Printed in Malaysia
Bound in the United States of America
07 06 05 04 03 02 01 00 7 6 5 4 3 2 1

Photo Credits

Cover: Kristi Du Bois
Title page: Corbis, Susan Middleton & David Liitschwager
Contents page: National History Photographic Library:
Kevin Schafer

American Fisheries Society: William N. Roston 823; J.R. Shute
840, 841; Peter Arnold Inc.: Yann Arthus-Bertrand 830; Asad
813; Fred Bavendam 855; B.I.O.S. 802; John Cancalosi 735,
814, 831; David Haring 800; Kevin Schafer 737, 806; Ted
Schifman 798; Bruce H. Bauer: 837; Biological Photo Service:
819; Kristi du Bois: 780; California Native Plant Society: Rick
York 811; Bruce Coleman Inc.: Kenneth W. Fink 788; Michael
Freeman 853; Frank W. Lane 771; Bruce Coleman Ltd.: Hans
Reinhard 757; Rod Williams 801; Suzanne L. Collins & Joseph
T. Collins: 838; Corbis: Ray Bird 727; Darrel Gulin 808;
Susan Middleton & David Middleton 809; D.R.K. Photo:

Stephen J. Krasemann 816; Friends of the Roanoke River:
Noel Burkhead 843; Rob Meinke: 850; Robert & Linda
Mitchell: 803; Natural History Photographic Library: Kevin
Schafer 770; Oxford Scientific Films: Max Gibbs 777; B.
"Moose" Peterson: 818; Glen Smart: 765; Tom Stack &
Associates: Bob McKeever 726; Larry Tackett 754; Dave Watts
755; Warren D. Thomas: 729, 733, 775, 781, 782, 795, 796,
832, 834; VIREO: H Cruikshank 764; C. Heideker 738;
Wildlife Conservation Society (H.Q. at the Bronx Zoo): 856;
D. Demello 761; Zoological Society of San Diego: 828, 846;
Ron Garrison 785, 789, 799, 804, 826, 827, 858, 860; Ken
Kelley 769

Cover: Ute ladies' tresses. Kristi Du Bois
Title page: Florida perforate cladonia. Corbis: Susan
Middleton & David Liitschwager
Contents page: Klipspringer. NHPL: Kevin Schafer

TABLE OF CONTENTS/VOLUME 6

ESA and IUCN

In this set of endangered animals and plants, each species, where appropriate, is given an ESA status and an IUCN status. The sources consulted to determine the status of each species are the Endangered Species List maintained by the U.S. Fish and Wildlife Service and the Red Lists compiled by IUCN–The World Conservation Union, which is a worldwide organization based in Switzerland.

ENDANGERED SPECIES ACT

The Endangered Species Act (ESA) was initially passed by the U.S. Congress in 1973, and reauthorized in 1988. The aim of the ESA is to rescue species that are in danger of extinction due to human action and to conserve the species and their ecosystems. Endangered plants and animals are listed by the U.S. Fish and Wildlife Service (USFWS), which is part of the Department of Interior. Once a species is listed, the USFWS is required to develop recovery plans, and ensure that the threatened species is not further harmed by any actions of the U.S. government or U.S. citizens. The act specifically forbids the buying, selling, transporting, importing, or exporting of any listed species. It also bans the taking of any listed species in the U.S. and its territories, on both private and public lands. Violators can face heavy fines or imprisonment. However, the ESA requires that the protection of the species is balanced with economic factors.

The ESA recognizes two categories of risk for species:

Endangered: A species that is in danger of extinction throughout all or a significant part of its range.

Threatened: A species that is likely to become endangered in the foreseeable future.

RECOVERY

Recovery takes place when the decline of the endangered or threatened species is halted or reversed, and the circumstances that caused the threat have been removed. The ultimate aim is the recovery of the species to the point where it no longer requires protection under the act.

Recovery can take a long time. Because the decline of the species may have occurred over centuries, the loss cannot be reversed overnight. There are many factors involved: the number of individuals of the species that remain in the wild, how long it takes the species to mature and reproduce, how much habitat is remaining, and whether the reasons for the decline are clear cut and understood. Recovery plans employ a wide range of strategies that involve the following: reintroduction of species into formerly occupied habitat, land aquisition and management, captive breeding, habitat protection, research, population counts, public education projects, and assistance for private landowners.

SUCCESS STORIES

Despite the difficulties, recovery programs do work, and the joint efforts of the USFWS, other federal and state agencies, tribal governments, and private landowners have not been in vain. Only seven species, less than 1 percent of all the species listed between 1968 and 1993, are now known to be extinct. The other 99 percent of listed species have not been lost to extinction, and this confirms the success of the act.

There are some good examples of successful recovery plans. In 1999, the peregrine falcon, the bald eagle, and the Aleutian goose were removed from the endangered species list. The falcon's numbers have risen dramatically. In 1970, there were only 39 pairs of falcons in the United States. By 1999, the number had risen to 1,650 pairs. The credit for the recovery goes to the late Rachel

Carson, who highlighted the dangers of DDT, and also to the Endangered Species Act, which enabled the federal government to breed falcons in captivity, and took steps to protect their habitat.

Young bald eagles were also successfully translocated into habitat that they formerly occupied, and the Aleutian Canada goose has improved due to restoration of its habitat and reintroduction into former habitat.

IUCN–THE WORLD CONSERVATION UNION

The IUCN (International Union for Conservation of Nature) was established in 1947. It is an alliance of governments, governmental agencies, and nongovernmental agencies. The aim of the IUCN is to help and encourage nations to conserve wildlife and natural resources. Organizations such as the Species Survival Commission is one of several IUCN commissions that assesses the conservation status of species and subspecies globally. Taxa that are threatened with extinction are noted and steps are taken for their conservation by programs designed to save, restore, and manage species and their habitats. The Survival Commission is committed to providing objective information on the status of globally threatened species, and produces two publications: the *IUCN Red List of Threatened Animals*, and the *IUCN Red List of Threatened Plants*. They are compiled from scientific data and provide the status of threatened species, depending on their existence in the wild and threats that undermine that existence. The lists for plants and animals differ slightly.

The categories from the *IUCN Red List of Threatened Animals* used in *Endangered Wildlife and Plants of the World* are as follows:

Extinct: A species is extinct when there is no reasonable doubt that the last individual has died.

Extinct in the wild: A species that is known only to survive in captivity, well outside its natural range.

Critically endangered: A species that is facing an extremely high risk of extinction in the wild in the immediate future.

Endangered: A species that is facing a very high risk of extinction in the wild in the near future.

Vulnerable: A species that is facing a high risk of extinction in the wild in the medium-term future.

Lower risk: A species that does not satisfy the criteria for designation as critically endangered, endangered, or vulnerable. Species included in the lower risk category can be separated into three subcategories:

Conservation dependent: A species that is part of a conservation program. Without the program, the species would qualify for one of the threatened categories within five years.

Near threatened: A species that does not qualify for conservation dependent, but is close to qualifying as vulnerable.

Least concern: A species that does not qualify for conservation dependent or near threatened.

Data deficient: A species on which there is inadequate information to make an asssessment of risk of extinction. Because there is a possibility that future research will show that the species is threatened, more information is required.

The categories from the *IUCN Red List of Threatened Plants*, used in *Endangered Wildlife and Plants of the World*, are as follows:

Extinct: A species that has not definitely been located in the wild during the last 50 years.

Endangered: A species whose survival is unlikely if the factors that threaten it continue. Included are species whose numbers have been reduced to a critical level, or whose habitats have been so drastically reduced that they are deemed to be in immediate danger of extinction. Also included in this category are species that may be extinct but have definitely been seen in the wild in the past 50 years.

Vulnerable: A species that is thought likely to move into the endangered category in the near future if the factors that threaten it remain.

Rare: A species with small world populations that are not at present endangered or vulnerable, but are at risk. These species are usually in restricted areas or are thinly spread over a larger range.

Mona Iguana
(Cyclura stejnegeri)

ESA: Threatened

Length: 3–4 ft. (0.9–1.2 m)
Clutch size: Average, 12 eggs
Diet: Omnivorous, prefers the toxic Manzanillo fruit
Habitat: Most common along major escarpments and slopes
Range: Mona Island, Greater Antilles

THE MONA IGUANA is the largest Puerto Rican lizard. It is a heavy-bodied lizard, with a large head and a robust, laterally compressed tail. It has a jowl under the jaw that can be quite pronounced in large, mature males, and a small horn on the snout just in front of the eyes. There is a crest on its back, extending from head to tail, and the general color of the lizard is olive to olive gray, with some individuals displaying intermittent blue and brown hues. Mona iguanas may grow between 3 and 4 feet (0.9 and 1.2 meters) in length.

Mona Island

This iguana is restricted to Mona Island—a small limestone island located midway between Puerto Rico and Hispaniola in the Greater Antilles. Large parts of the island are covered by outcrops of solid limestone, where mostly dry and semideciduous scrub vegetation of low trees and shrubs or cacti grow.

The Mona iguana eats both plants and animals. Fecal samples determined that at least 71 plant species and 12 animal species make up its diet. A favored food is the fruit from the toxic Manzanillo tree. All the plant species that iguanas eat are also eaten by the island's goats, which reduces the amount of food available to iguanas.

Mona iguanas do not need to use much energy to forage. They are most apt to eat what is readily available. They tend to be slow movers that stay close to their burrows. Outside of mating season, almost all of their time—an

The Mona iguana has probably been a food source for native people on Mona Island since pre-Colombian times.

estimated 94 percent—is spent resting. The remaining time is spent foraging and eating; travel is reserved for food searching, although the female will travel to search for nesting grounds.

Reproduction

The breeding season begins in mid-June and ends in November when the eggs hatch. Males begin the process by establishing a territory that includes female retreat burrows. Males will defend their territory aggressively, and fights usually involve head-bobbing, tossing, or pushing, although biting rarely occurs. Females seldom move from retreat burrows within male territories during breeding. Afterward, they migrate to nesting grounds, and egg laying occurs two to four weeks after mating.

Only a small portion of Mona Island offers soils deep enough for iguana nesting, and gravid or egg-bound females are often forced to migrate great distances searching for optimal nesting sites. These sites are at a premium. Sometimes a female will inadvertently destroy the nest

The Bahama Island rock iguana, *Cyclura cychlura*, is listed as vulnerable by the IUCN–The World Conservation Union.

and eggs of a prior nesting female in her own attempt to nest. Once a spot has been located a female will dig for about two hours, retreating occasionally to cool off, and continuing to dig until a hole large enough to accommodate the whole animal has been excavated. Once the nest is ready, she lays her eggs, and the clutch size averages 12. The female covers the egg chamber once the eggs have been laid, but leaves an air space above them. She will guard the nest for 10 days. Three months later, the young emerge by digging out from the nest chamber. The young receive no parental care.

Status

Prior to 1972, little was known about the populations of the Mona iguana. Threats to the species have probably been intro-

duced relatively recently. These would include non-native predators such as cats, dogs, mice, and rats that were introduced by early colonists. Animals such as goats, burros, and pigs have also had adverse effects on the iguana because of changes they cause to the native vegetation.

Pig problem

Pigs are a serious threat, as they are known to dig up nests and eat iguana eggs. One estimate suggests that there are about 2,000 iguanas on Mona Island but there is an apparent scarcity of immature individuals. However the major cause of the Mona iguana's decline is human-related activities. Introduction of mammals, hunting, agriculture, deforestation, and recreational activities have all posed threats to iguana adults, juveniles, and

MONA IGUANA
Caribbean

eggs, limiting its population growth and stability.

Privacy is essential for the iguana's mating and egg laying, and human activities interfere with this. For example, humans have trampled nest chambers. Iguanas are also quite often accidentally killed by vehicles as they attempt to cross roads.

Improved protection

Little was done for the Mona iguana until the Department of Natural Resources was established in 1973. This department has managed the island since then, protecting its natural wildlife and vegetation.

From 1973 to 1976, one resident biologist was assigned to the island, improving the enforcement of protective legislation.

Elizabeth Sirimarco

Black-faced Impala

(Aepyceros melampus petersi)

ESA: Endangered

IUCN: Vulnerable

Class: Mammalia
Order: Artiodactyla
Family: Bovidae
Weight: 88–176 lb. (40–80 kg)
Diet: Leaves, twigs, and grasses
Longevity: 12–15 years
Habitat: Open woodland to scrub
Range: Southwest Angola and Northwest Namibia

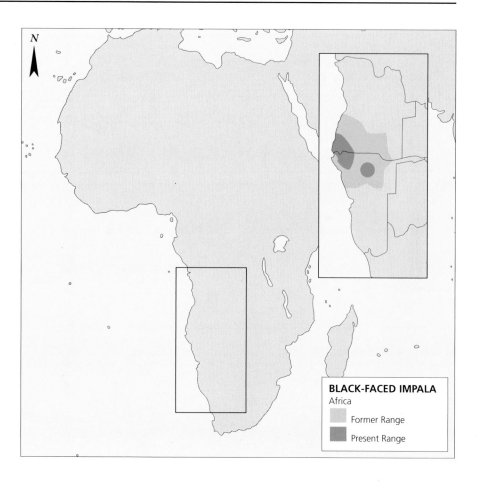

BLACK-FACED IMPALA
Africa

Former Range

Present Range

THE IMPALA IS ONE of the most graceful four-legged animals. It is an antelope, part of the same group of animals that includes hartebeests and wildebeests. An impala's fawn-colored coat, curved horns and graceful movements make it a very beautiful animal to observe.

While the impala does inhabit scrub bush country and open grassland, it prefers areas that have some cover near a constant water source. An impala is a sociable animal, and is often found in the company of other African plains animals. Its social habits, however, are very fixed, with two common groupings: male bachelor groups and families made up of one dominant male and 15 to 20 females. While this may seem like a pleasant situation for the male, it is actually one of constant work; he must round up the females continually, because they tend to wander. He must also fight off other males who try to take over his harem. A male keeps his dominant status for only a few years before he is replaced by a younger, stronger male. Once a male is cast out, he becomes solitary and is preyed on by leopards, lions, cheetahs, and hyenas.

The impala is a browser, eating leaves, twigs, young shoots, and especially the acacia plant. It has good vision and smell and is wary of humans who approach too closely, unless it has become accustomed to people, for instance, in a wildlife park.

One species in danger

The one endangered subspecies of impala is the black-faced impala. Growing to a height of 37 inches (95 centimeters) at the shoulder, this particular impala is so-called because of a dark patch on its face. Otherwise, its col-

oration is much the same as the common impala.

The animal is found in Angola and Namibia, and its numbers in Angola are seriously diminished because of competition with domestic animals, heavy hunting, and the devastation that has been caused by a very long civil war.

This impala is fairly stable in Namibia's Etosha National Park, but elsewhere in that country its numbers have dwindled. There are perhaps only between 1,000 to 2,000 of these animals left. Impalas do well in captivity and

The black-faced impala is the only form of impala that is endangered. Few of this species exist in captivity.

there is a healthy population of the common impala. A few black-faced impalas exist in captivity, but the gene pool (that is, the number of individuals that are unrelated) is too small.

The gene pool needs to be broadened if captive breeding is to produce healthy animals that will enable this species to recover in the wild.

Warren D. Thomas

IMPERIAL-PIGEONS

Class: Aves

Order: Columbiformes

Family: Columbidae

Imperial-pigeons grow to be quite large and heavy. Many of them sport knobs at the base of the upper half of the beak. Two species inhabit portions of eastern India and range into Southeast Asia, while two others live in northern and eastern Australia. Otherwise, the imperial-pigeons are birds of the Pacific islands and the East Indies. They are closely related to the fruit-doves, and their genus (*Ducula*) accounts for the third largest number of species in the pigeon family. Those species that live in areas easily accessible to ornithologists have been moderately well studied. Some of the more remote species have not been studied at all.

Giant Imperial-pigeon

(Ducula goliath)

IUCN: Vulnerable

Length: 20 in. (50.8 cm)

Weight: Unknown

Clutch size: 1 egg

Incubation: Unknown

Diet: Fruits

Habitat: Montane forests

Range: New Caledonia and the South Pacific

A GREAT BOOMING call thunders down through the trees of New Caledonia. To the uninitiated, the call sounds like the bellow of a bull or some other great mammal. It is, however, the call of the giant imperial-pigeon, a bird that is unique to the New Caledonian forests.

A large, dark bird, the giant imperial-pigeon has a blackish head, back, wing, tail, and breast band. A band around the throat

Imperial-pigeons belong to the genus *Ducula*, a group that makes up the third largest number of species in the pigeon family.

and neck is more slate gray in color. A chestnut band across the mid-tail and a chestnut belly patch highlight an otherwise drab bird. Its bright red foot, toe, and beak add a splash more color. Being a fruit-eating bird, the giant imperial-pigeon has a sweet, tender meat that has made it a favorite with hunters.

For many years the species thrived in the primary forests of remote mountain slopes and valleys. No observations or research evidence indicate that the bird uses secondary forest or other habitat types. The effects of human progress on New Caledonia now threaten the survival of the giant imperial-pigeon.

Almost 200,000 people live in New Caledonia's 6,530 square miles (16,978 square kilometers). They grow coffee, tobacco, bananas, and pineapples, but nickel mining is the most important part of the economy. Mining activity directly destroys the habitat of the imperial-pigeon. Mining roads built into remote mountain areas also open new access roads for people. The improved access has already increased the number of hunters coming to the region. Hunting is allowed only one month each year, but illegal hunting is not vigorously discouraged.

If the giant imperial-pigeon is to survive, measures to preserve its habitat must be undertaken now. Someday, New Caledonia will mine its last nickel deposits.

GIANT IMPERIAL-PIGEON
New Caledonia

MARQUESAS
IMPERIAL-PIGEON
Polynesia

The New Caledonian people may find that they have no nickel, forests, or giant-imperial pigeons.

Marquesas Imperial-pigeon

(Ducula galeata)

IUCN: Critically endangered

Length: 22 in. (56 cm)
Clutch size: 1 egg
Diet: Large fruits
Habitat: Forests and woodlands
Range: Nukuhiva Island in the Marquesas Archipelago, French Polynesia

THE PEOPLE OF Nukuhiva Island once fed themselves on the flesh of other people. So long as the people lived as cannibals, the Marquesas imperial-pigeon thrived. As Western civilization overtook the Nukuhiva people, both cannibalism and the imperial-pigeon declined together. The phenomena are not linked, but they share a common cause.

Shiny green back

The Marquesas imperial-pigeon is a large, stout bird with broad wings and long tail. It has a dark, shiny green back and tail with a dark gray head, neck, and underparts. The undertail is a reddish-brown color. The cere, which is a fleshy area at the base of the beak, extends forward to near the beak's tip. The cere is covered with small white feathers.

This bird may have lived on other islands in the Marquesas group, but it now survives only in the western valleys of Nukuhiva.

The Marquesas are an archipelago of 11 islands in French Polynesia, which is part of France's overseas territories in the South Pacific. Together the islands cover about 1,544 square miles (4,014 square kilometers). Once called Marquesas Island, Nukuhiva is the largest island at 127 square miles (330 square kilometers). Oceanic explorers of Melanesian ancestry settled on the islands, probably around C.E. 200. Thirteen centuries passed before Spanish sailors explored the islands in 1595. This first meeting of two cultures was violent and disastrous for the native islanders. Captain Cook rediscovered the islands in 1774. During the many European struggles for power in the 18th and 19th century, France won control over many South Pacific islands, including the Marquesas.

Europeans seeking territorial conquests carried with them the diseases from their own countries. They introduced smallpox, tuberculosis, syphilis, and leprosy into a human culture that had never experienced any of these diseases. A native population of more than 100,000 people dropped to less than 3,000 by the 1960s. The native people on some Marquesas Islands disappeared altogether. Intent on using distant territories as a source of wealth for the mother country, the French people brought African and Asian laborers to the Marquesas to work on the sugarcane plantations.

Changing landscape

As European culture replaced the indigenous culture, enormous changes took place. Most significantly, forests and woodlands were chopped down for building materials and to make room for agriculture and livestock grazing. The Marquesas imperial-pigeon seems to be unique to the Marquesas Archipelago, if not to Nukuhiva. This species had no outlying populations on other atolls or island groups, where it could survive if catastrophic events occurred on Nukuhiva.

Low numbers

Population estimates in 1993 ranged from 150 birds to 300 individuals. Despite the low numbers and a hunting ban imposed by France in 1967, islanders still hunt the birds as food. The combination of the human population growth on Nukuhiva; the continued emphasis on agriculture; the persistent grazing by both domestic and feral pigs, goats, sheep, and cattle; and the lax enforcement of the hunting ban have had serious repercussions for the imperial-pigeon. If anything, conditions are likely to steadily worsen.

Ornithologists have tried their best to save endangered island birds by establishing them on other islands where they do not encounter such severe problems. While this idea has its merits, it also threatens the survival of other species. Many island birds are endangered because introduced species have out-competed them in their own habitat. If these birds are transported to other islands, it is possible that they will cause similar problems in the new habitat.

Despite this problem the Marquesas imperial pigeon has been recommended as a candidate for such a relocation program.

Kevin Cook

Simien Jackal (Ethiopian Wolf)
(Canis simensis)

ESA: Endangered

IUCN: Critically endangered

Class: Mammalia
Order: Carnivora
Family: Canidae
Weight: 15–33 lb. (7–15 kg)
Longevity: Up to 10 years, 16 years in captivity
Range: The Simien and Bale Mountains, Ethiopia

ANUBIS, A GOD OF ancient Egypt, was depicted as having the head of a jackal. That he was the god responsible for leading souls to the underworld makes sense. As highly visible carrion eaters, jackals must have seemed like logical escorts to the spirit world, where Egyptians believed they would go after death. Since then, people have come to understand the role of jackals a little differently, but humans still have an uneasy feeling about this animal.

Little is known about the Simien jackal. Until recently, it seemed to be a creature of too many names and too few appearances. It was known as the Abyssinian wolf, the Simien fox, the Simien dog, and the Ethiopian Wolf.

Only the threat of extinction has sparked some scientific agreement. The Simien jackal is too small and light to be a wolf, too high at the shoulder and too long-legged to be a fox, and its face is too pointed to be a true dog. Increasingly rare, it is still believed by many to be a subspecies of the similar and more numerous golden jackals found throughout much of northern and eastern Africa and southwestern Asia.

Appearance

The Simien jackal has a long slender muzzle and a light yellowish-to-reddish brown coat that becomes darker toward the middle of the animal's back. The tail is black with a white tip. This jackal attains a height at the shoulder of between 15 to 24 inches (38 to 60 centimeters).

Where once the animal was visible at lower elevations, increased persecution by humans (and perhaps by hyenas and other carnivores) has driven it into remote areas of the Simien and Bale Mountains of Ethiopia. These mountain ranges are separated by several hundred miles of flat, developed land over which the animals do not range. This suggests that the jackals represent the last survivors of two disappearing population groups. The Simien Mountains jackals are smaller in size and their coats are red to reddish yellow in color. Those in the Bale Mountains are larger, with darker red coats.

Hunting practices

The jackal hunts its favorite prey, grass rats, mainly by patrolling, investigating holes and burrows, lying in wait for the rodents to appear, and then dashing after them and pouncing. Rodent hunting tends to be a solitary activity, although the jackal hunts its other prey in cooperative packs. Larger game is usually located by scent, pursued until it is exhausted, then killed by the more powerful adults in the pack.

While most jackals are somewhat nocturnal, the Simien jackal is diurnal. They prefer to hunt grass rats by day, when the rats are easily seen and their escape routes can be easily cut off. Unlike many of its fellow jackals, the Simien jackal often sleeps in the open or in places with slightly longer grass, even under cold conditions. Generally, the animal appears to tolerate the presence of others of its kind very well.

Social carnivores

This jackal seems to have a clan-based society. Around dawn and dusk, adult jackals usually gather together in groups of up to seven members. On such occasions there is much friendly action and noise. The strange utterances of jackals do not closely resemble those of wolves or foxes. They often seem to use high, whining howls, repeated at short intervals, to keep in contact. Other noises include a bark of annoyance and a yipping cry. Short barks and whines near pups have been reported.

Jackals appear to pair off in January, but births do not occur until May or June. Both sexes mature after about one year, but sexually mature pups often stay on with family groups, remaining with the group to help their parents raise a second litter. This behavior enables the jackals to combat what seems to be a high rate of pup mortality. Pups are nursed for about eight weeks and then they are introduced gradually to solid food through regurgitation. At about six months pups are introduced to hunting practices.

Researchers who have examined this jackal's droppings have found that no traces of wool or livestock appear, yet native shepherds and other people continue

Until recently, the jackal was known by a variety of names, including the Abyssinian wolf, the Simien fox, and the Simien dog. Scientists did not agree that the animal was, indeed, a jackal until it became endangered.

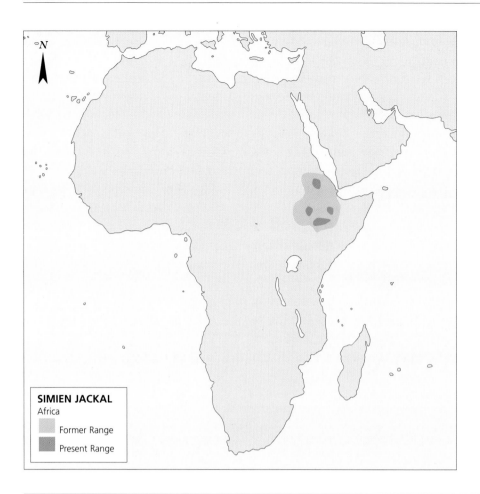

SIMIEN JACKAL
Africa

Former Range

Present Range

to kill these animals because they consider them to be pests, sometimes shooting them on sight. Farmers and shepherds have increasingly brought domestic dogs into the jackals' habitat, applying further pressure to a diminishing population. Eagles also prey upon jackals. Granted minimal protection from the Ethiopian government, even national park lands have been made available for grazing, thus further endangering this jackal.

The Simien jackal is protected by law and is classified as endangered by both the IUCN, and the U.S. Fish and Wildlife Service, but the numbers of this animal continue to dwindle. One authority in the mid-1980s suggested that as few as 500 Simien jackals remained in the wild.

Renardo Barden

Jaguar
(Panthera onca)

ESA: Endangered

IUCN: Lower risk

Class: Mammalia
Order: Carnivora
Family: Felidae
Size: 44–61 in. (112–185 cm)
Weight: 80–350 lb. (36–158 kg)
Diet: Deer, monkeys, peccaries, tapirs, and aquatic animals
Range: Formerly southern United States through Central America to South America into northern Argentina

THE JAGUAR VARIES from a pale yellow color to a reddish brown with black spots, which form rosettes. Some spots may merge to form lines. Black or melanistic color is not uncommon, but the spots can be seen even on these darker cats. The jaguar prefers forests and savanna, but is also found in drier areas, sometimes even desert, though not far from fresh water. It is rarely found at altitudes above 3,280 feet (1,000 meters).

Subspecies
There are eight recognized subspecies of the jaguar. They tend to be solitary animals and mark their territories with urine, much like other cats. They are good swimmers and climbers. These cats hunt at dawn, dusk, or during moonlit nights, and their food consists largely of aquatic animals, including capybaras, turtles, caiman, and fish. Jaguars also feed on a number of animals up to the size of deer.

The jaguar was once common from Mexico to northern Argentina, and it occurred as far north as the southern United States at the turn of the century. Today, the animal is extinct in Uruguay and virtually extinct in the United States, most of Mexico, and Central America. Unfortunately, this cat has been killed within much of its former range. However, it is still found over most of South America.

Persecuted as predators
The number of jaguars has declined almost everywhere due to their role as predators of cattle. Predation on livestock by big cats occurs in ranching areas throughout the world, resulting in attempts to destroy the cats,

JAGUAR
North and South America

Former range

Current range

regardless of whether or not they have actually killed livestock. Even today, near cattle ranches the jaguar is treated as a pest, and ranch owners may still pay large sums of money, equivalent to the price of two cattle, for the extermination of a jaguar.

Poaching

Jaguars are often shot by poachers who are looking for other animals that reside in the jaguar's habitat. One scientist who works in Venezuela reports that of all the exterminated jaguars examined from that country, 75 percent of the suspected cattle killers had previous wounds to the head or body. A specialist in

Jaguars are beautiful, sleek animals that have long been admired for their attractive appearance. This admiration has played a role in the animal's decline, since the jaguar's fur was once a very popular commodity.

Belize found that 40 percent of the cats there had gunshot wounds that damaged their sight and/or their teeth.

Fortunately, there are ranchers who want to preserve the wild cats while bringing predation to acceptable levels. One Venezuelan rancher who raises about 15,000 cattle notes that his losses amount to some 200 head a year, mainly calves and juveniles. Nonetheless, he sees the jaguar as a big attraction to tourists and an important part of the country's natural history, and has outlawed all jaguar shooting on his 270-square-mile (700-square kilometer) ranch, even if predation occurs. A group of cat specialists is hoping to sponsor a study of jaguar and puma predation on livestock at this ranch to develop management recommendations that may be enlisted on other ranches too.

Fur trade

In addition to this problem, jaguars have also been hunted for sport, and the skins of these cats once commanded high prices in the fur trade. The demand for the fur of Latin American spotted cats was high in the 1960s, when an estimated 15,000 jaguars were killed annually in the Brazilian Amazon alone. Known exports of the skins dropped by 1969, however, when new conservation restrictions were introduced.

Unfortunately, hunting and export is still allowed in some Central American countries, and restriction in others is poorly enforced. Even where hunting is prohibited, the import of skins originating from elsewhere is often allowed. Habitat loss is also greatly responsible for the decline of the jaguar. The construction of highways in the Amazon Basin is a threat to cats as well as all to other wildlife. Conversion of forest into cattle pasture, and clearing for timber, firewood, cropland, and plantations have greatly reduced the jaguar's habitat, as has the construction of airstrips for mining and oil exploration. The development of these once remote areas has also made them much more accessible to hunters. Restrictions have been placed on commercial trading of the jaguar, and though enforcement is hard, improvement has been noted. A few national parks in South America protect limited cat populations, and several protect isolated pairs or families.

Reserves needed

Studies of the population densities and the ecology of the jaguar need to be conducted to protect the species, and illegal hunting and trade in skins must be stopped. Its survival depends largely on habitat preservation, and a few reserves have been proposed. Unfortunately, this has been opposed because the areas are valuable as potential pasture.

Elizabeth Sirimarco

Texas Jaguarundi

(Herpailurus yaguarondi cacomitli)

ESA: Endangered

ESA: Endangered

Class: Mammalia
Order: Carnivora
Family: Felidae
Size: 21¾–30⅓ in. (55–77 cm)
Tail length: Up to 26 in. (60 cm)
Shoulder height: 14 in. (35 cm)
Weight: 10–20 lb. (4.5–9 kg)
Gestation period: Usually 63–70 days
Diet: Various animals including frogs, birds, and small mammals
Range: Southern Texas and Mexico

THE JAGUARUNDI differs from all other types of cat due to the form of some of its chromosomes, and by the number of chromosomes—there are 36 instead of the 38 found in other cats. While it is often considered part of the genus *Felis*, some scientists consider it the sole member of the genus *Herpailurus*. The jaguarundi is widely distributed from the extreme southern United States through Central and South America. There are eight subspecies of the cat, including the Texas jaguarundi, and the distribution of these varying types is patchy. Four of these subspecies are listed as endangered by the U.S. Fish and Wildlife Service, while only the Texas jaguarundi is listed as endangered by the IUCN–The World Conservation Union.

The jaguarundi is quite different from Old World cats, particularly in the structure of its skull. The most conspicuous features are the projections of the frontal bones of the head that support and protect the eye sockets. These are directed toward the back of the head, which gives the jaguarundi a streamlined shape.

This cat is characterized by a slender, elongated body and a small, slim head; small, round ears; and a long tail. The forearms are slightly shorter than the hind limbs, and it is slightly larger than the domestic cat. It is almost uniform in color, being black, gray, or reddish brown, with no spots or bands, although the kittens are said to have spots for a short time. This has led scientists to believe that the jaguarundi may be closely related

JAGUARUNDI (ALL)
North and South America

TEXAS JAGUARUNDI
North America

humans, it also preys on domestic poultry, which has, in turn, made the jaguarundi prey for angry ranchers. Most scientists refer to the animal as a lowland forest dweller, and it seems to favor clearings and forest edges. Its body seems to be highly adapted to living in areas of thick undergrowth, as its shape allows it to maneuver swiftly through thick vegetation. The Texas jaguarundi lives in a habitat of dense, thorny shrublands of cacti and other spiny forms of vegetation. In the past, this prickly habitat provided an almost impenetrable barrier to the jaguarundi's main enemies—dogs and humans. However, this safety is threatened by habitat destruction and in Texas this jaguarundi subspecies is now only found in Cameron, Hidalgo, Starr, and Willacy counties.

The jaguarundi is more cursorial (adapted to running), than arboreal, unlike other New World

to the panther, though the skull structure and chromosomes do not support this theory. Individuals with red coats were thought to be a separate species, but it is clear that red, gray, and black animals can occur in one litter.

The habitat requirements of the jaguarundi are not well known, but it is normally thought to be a lowland species. It appears to inhabit areas of thick undergrowth, preferably near water, and is reputedly a good swimmer. Frogs and possibly fish make up a portion of its diet, together with birds and small mammals. In areas inhabited by

A uniformity in color has led scientists to believe that the jaguarundi may be closely related to the panther, although the skull structure and chromosomes do not support this view.

small cats. Scientists believe it may hunt its prey as a cheetah does, using a quick speed burst to capture prey rather than chasing it for a long time.

Reproduction

Little is known about reproduction in jaguarundis, but mating in Paraguay was recorded in September through November and in Mexico in November through December. It is possible that there are two litters per year. In captivity the gestation period is between 63 and 70 days. Although the cat appears to be predominantly solitary, pairs have been seen sharing their territory—an unusual habit for cats. They also have very complex vocalization, which scientists believe may indicate a high level of social activity. The fur of the

jaguarundi apparently has little commercial value, and the species does not appear to have been subjected to the intense hunting that has affected other American small cats such as the ocelot and margay.

Indiscriminate hunting

When traps are used, animals that are not necessarily desired by hunters are often captured. So even though the jaguarundi may not be particularly desirable to the fur industry, it may still become the victim of indiscriminate hunting. There is limited trade of live animals, primarily for zoos, but there has been some demand for the cat from the pet trade. The biggest threat is from hunting and habitat destruction.

Jaguarundis have certainly declined, but it is difficult to

know exactly how much they have been affected by hunting. Jaguarundis occur in the majority of Central and South American countries, but they are not recorded in Chile; and if they occurred in Uruguay, they are now extinct in that country. There is a lack of data describing past population numbers, and very little data about current numbers. Trade in jaguarundis is now subject to strict regulation, and trade for any commercial purpose is virtually banned. A number of jaguarundi are held in captivity, and the animal breeds well in these circumstances. There have been no studies of animal behavior in the wild. Until such studies have been done, the status of the jaguarundi will remain uncertain.

Elizabeth Sirimarco

JAYS

Class: Aves

Order: Passeriformes

Family: Corvidae

Jays make interesting animals for study. They live active, busy lives filled with unusual behavior, and they are bold and curious birds.

They store food when it is readily available, then retrieve it when supplies are harder to find. These food caches may also help parent birds keep themselves fed while they raise their young.

Their searches often bring them across objects for which they have no particular use but which they stockpile anyway. Jays are the bird world's equivalent of the pack rat.

Perhaps their most fascinating behavioral feature is one they share with their cousins the

crows: offspring help their parents at the nest.

Nest helpers are either adult or immature birds that remain in their parents' territories. They help build nests, defend against predators and intruders, and feed their younger siblings from later nestings. Not all 105 species in this family exhibit nest-helping behavior. However, those birds that do use helpers enjoy greater nesting success, measured in terms of the number of nestlings that survive to adulthood.

The jay and crow family also includes magpies, treepies, and nutcrackers, and around 45 species in 13 genera carry the English name "jay."

At least a half-dozen jays are considered to be jeopardized by habitat loss. One is listed as threatened by the U.S. Fish and Wildlife Service while several others are listed by IUCN–The World Conservation Union.

Florida Scrub Jay

(Aphelocoma coerulescens coerulescens)

ESA: Threatened

Length: 12 in. (30.5 cm)

Weight: 3 oz. (82 g)

Clutch size: 3–6 eggs

Incubation: 15–17 days

Diet: Acorns, insects and other invertebrates, small lizards

Habitat: Shrub lands

Range: Scattered localities in peninsular Florida

PEOPLE KNOW THE mid-Atlantic coast of Florida as the launching pad of America's space program. However, Cape Canaveral and the adjoining Merritt Island also shelter the largest surviving population of the rapidly dwindling Florida scrub jay. In the early 1990s the population of this species at Kennedy Space Center was estimated to be around 2,100 individuals.

A round head with no crest and a dark blue wing and tail with no white immediately distinguish the Florida scrub jay from the more abundant and common blue jay (*Cyanocitta cristata*). The Florida scrub jay appears hooded. A sky-blue rear crown, nape, and cheek are offset by a pale bluish gray forehead and a grayish white chin and throat. A sooty smudge extends from the base of the beak, through the lore, and past the eye. Another smudgy line, running across the breast, separates the biblike whitish chin and throat from the dingy gray breast and side. The upper back is dingy gray but fades to a blue rump. The stout, blackish beak ends with a tiny hooked tip. Feathers at the base of the beak project forward, covering the nostrils, which are typical of birds in the jay and crow family.

Scrub homes

Florida scrub jays display the characteristic curiosity of their family. They can be quite tame around people. Tolerance and curiosity have probably cost the jays less than their dependence on a habitat that people have often viewed as worthless. In fact, the bird derives its name from that habitat. The term *scrub* refers to plants that grow large but never attain the stature of trees. In general usage, *shrub land* and *scrub* refer to similar habitat. Shrub lands of oaks (*Quercus* sp.), pines (*Pinus* sp.), wax myrtle

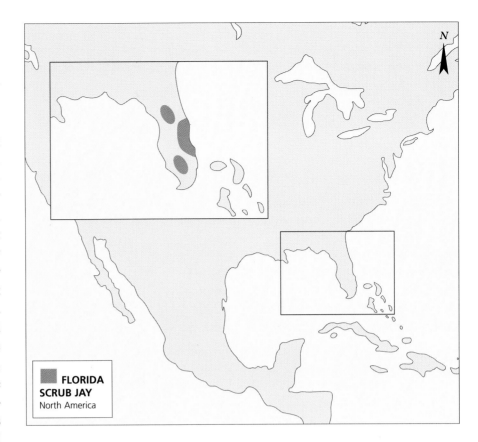

FLORIDA SCRUB JAY
North America

(*Myrica pumila*), and saw palmetto (*Serenoa serrulata*) harbor the last of these jays.

The jays nest in the shrubbery and find much of their food in it. They also eat larger insects, spiders, millipedes, snails, and even the eggs and nestlings of other birds. They like seasonal food, such as acorns and the fruits of the saw palmetto, as well as other fruits and seeds. They bury excess acorns in soil and sand, to be recovered and eaten later.

Habitat destruction

Important as the shrub lands are to the Florida scrub jay, people have disregarded the bird's needs. They have cut and burned the inland shrub lands to open up land for cattle grazing and citrus orchards. Coastal shrub lands have been cleared for oceanfront development. More than half of the Florida scrub jay's habitat has been lost. The jay's population

has fallen from 50,000 in the 1880s to less than 22,000 in 1984. The rate at which habitat was lost in the 1980s showed a decline in the population of the Florida scrub jay. Many ornithologists expected only a few jays to survive into the 2000s.

The human population in Florida grew tremendously in the last decades of the 1900s, from fewer than one million people in 1930 to more than 13 million people in 1990. Many people find the climate pleasant for retirement. Others find it suitable for growing vegetables and fruit or for grazing cattle. Inevitably, human ambitions for the Florida landscape require vast alterations that leave little native plant growth, and therefore little habitat for the Florida scrub jay.

Scrub jays do not migrate, and they are not known to wander; therefore, the Florida scrub

jay constitutes an isolated subspecies. This means that the Florida population cannot be bolstered by individuals who wander in from other parts of the species' range.

Some ornithologists believe that the Florida scrub jay will disappear entirely because so much of the species' habitat is on private land. Suitable habitat for jays remains in Ocala National Forest, which is between Gainesville and Orlando and on Merritt Island National Wildlife Refuge. It is quite likely that at least small populations will continue to persist in these areas.

Sichuan Jay
(Perisoreus internigrans)

IUCN: Vulnerable

Habitat: Dense coniferous woodlands
Range: Southeastern Qinghai, western Gansu, northern Sichuan, and eastern Xizang provinces of China

PEOPLE CANNOT SAVE what they do not know they have lost. The Sichuan jay has become increasingly rare in recent years, yet virtually nothing is known about this bird. It could slip into extinction before anyone even bothers to record how long it is or how much it weighs.

The Communist rulers of the People's Republic of China have not favored research on a wildlife species such as the Sichuan jay, which is seen to have no value to the people. Nearly all wildlife research in this country has been conducted from an economic perspective. Wildlife species that possess value or cause problems have captured all the attention. Many U.S. travelers to China have returned with stories of never having seen a rabbit or a squirrel, even in the rural areas. One traveler remarked that he had been in China for a week before he realized that he had not heard a single bird singing.

Roughly two-thirds of China consists of mountains and deserts, and only one-tenth of the land supports crops. More than one billion people now live there. Most of these people live along the coast, while the Sichuan jay lives in China's mountainous interior. It inhabits pine (*Pinus* sp.) and spruce (*Picea* sp.) woodlands and inhabits fairly high elevations, probably to the timberline. It has been described as slightly larger than a gray jay (*Perisoreus canadensis*), which measures 11½ inches (29 centimeters) and weighs 2½ ounces (70 grams). It has plain gray plumage, highlighted only by a black head and throat. Some

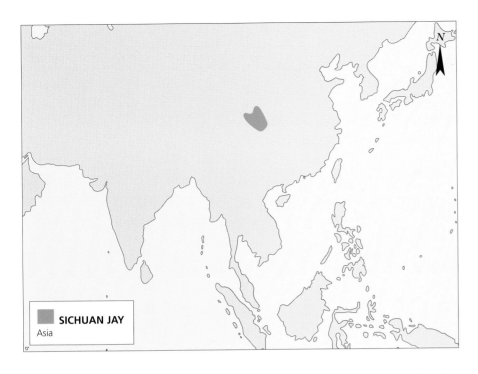

SICHUAN JAY
Asia

eats insects, carrion, and various small fruits, as well as conifer seeds. After building a nest up to 20 feet (6 meters) above the ground, it probably lays three to five eggs that require around 19 days of incubation. Lacking particular information about its habitat needs, no definite reasons or events can be cited as the exact cause for the decline of the species. Presumably, habitat loss has some effect. The cutting down of forests to provide lumber products may also be an important factor. Unless authorities within mainland China take a particular interest in the Sichuan jay and investigate what its requirements are for survival, no meaningful actions can be recommended that will halt its decline and aid its preservation.

Kevin Cook

observers report that the jay mimics other birds' calls. No other information is available on this species, but if the behavior of the Sichuan jay is similar to that of its relative the Siberian jay (*Perisoreus infaustus*), ornithologists can assume a little more. If it is similar to the Siberian jay, then the Sichuan jay probably

---

Juil Ciego

(Rhamdia reddelli)

IUCN: Vulnerable

Class: Actinopterygii
Order: Siluriformes
Family: Pimelodidae
Length: 4⅓ in. (11 cm)
Reproduction: Egg layer
Habitat: Cave streams and stream pools
Range: Cave at Cañada San Antonio, Mexico

WHEN WE THINK of caves, we think of creatures like bats, large insects, or other animals that shun bright light. In the dark, cool recesses they can prey on unsuspecting victims groping through the darkness. However,

we seldom consider that many caves hold water, or are completely filled with water, and that fish might live in these underground recesses, pools, and streams. Indeed, many fish have evolved exclusively underground in the absence of light. Caves offer conditions that are very different from those at the surface. Cave-dwelling animals live in total darkness in an energy-poor environment. Caves cannot sustain green plants that capture sunlight and turn it into food for other plants and animals. Because of their isolation from the surface, subterranean fish depend on the movement of food items from the surface to their underground domain. In addition to the absence of light, caves have very stable temperatures. Cave temperatures vary little, if

at all, and usually correspond with the average yearly temperature at the surface.

In response to their unusual environment, cave-dwelling fish have developed unique physical characteristics. These fish lack eyes and are totally blind. Eyes would not only be useless in the dark cave recesses, but could also be damaged by the darkness and would require energy to develop and maintain. As a replacement for eyes, the exterior of these fish is packed with other sensory organs—touch, taste, and smell are extremely important. A less obvious feature of cave-dwelling fish is their lack of skin pigmentation; all of these fish are albino—that is, white and pink in color. This is because subterranean animals do not need camouflage to protect them from

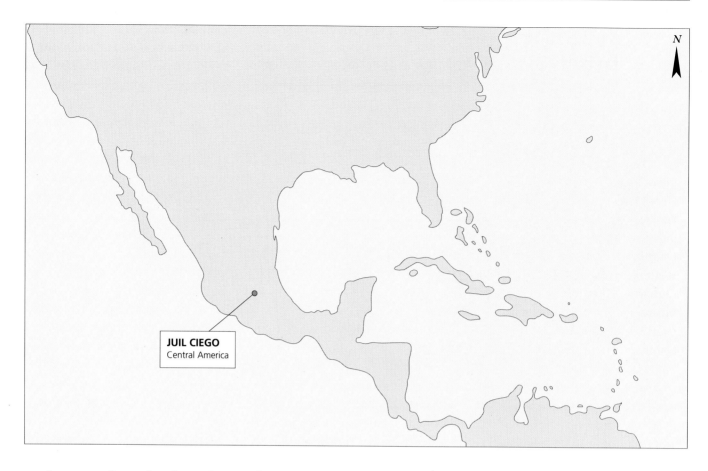

JUIL CIEGO
Central America

predators or from the damaging rays of the sun. To cope with the reduced availability of food, these fish have a slower metabolism than many others and have larger fins for more efficient swimming. In addition, cave-dwelling fish are able to store fat more efficiently during times of plenty. All blind catfish, such as the juil ciego, lack a swim bladder, an organ used by most fish to regulate their buoyancy. Instead, these fish rely on their stores of fat to provide buoyancy, as well to provide an energy supply when food is hard to find.

Creatures of both the surface and subterranean world, bats play an important role in the lives of some of these fish. In caves that are not completely filled with water, bats are one of the transport mechanisms that support fish populations. Solid wastes, such as bat guano and dead bats, are key sources of food for cave fish and other inhabitants of the cave ecosystem. Aquatic plankton, fungus, decaying organic material, small amphibians, and other fish are also important foods.

Limited range

The juil ciego can be found at the cave at Cañada San Antonio, southeast of Mexico's capital of Mexico City. The main threat to the juil ciego is the limited extent of its range. The cave is only about three miles in length, and the water supply is a single groundwater source. If the water supply becomes severely polluted, the population of juil ciego could be lost.

This small blind fish is ideally built for life in a cave. From the side, the head of the juil ciego appears somewhat flattened, so that it can more easily fit into tight spaces. The dorsal fins on the back, while average in their length, extend from behind the head to the base of the tail. This makes swimming more efficient.

The tail fin is forked, and the sensory barbels (whiskers) on the face are unusually long, a trait of the family Pimelodidae.

Given the thin margin between death and survival for the juil ciego, it is unsurprising that little energy remains available for reproduction. Consequently the fish does not breed regularly, and depending on the food supply, the fish may not breed at all during the year. When breeding does occur, few eggs are produced.

An important adaptation of the blind catfish is its ability to protect newly hatched fish by holding them in its mouth, decreasing the likelihood of a predator feasting on offspring.

William E. Manci

Guadalupe Junco

(Junco insularis)

IUCN: Critically endangered

Class: Aves
Order: Passeriformes
Family: Emberizidae
Subfamily: Emberizinae
Length: 6¼ in. (15.9 cm)
Weight: About ¾ oz. (20 g)
Clutch size: 4 to 5 eggs
Incubation: 12–13 days
Diet: Seeds, insects
Habitat: Forests, woodlands
Range: Guadalupe Island, west of Baja, Mexico

NO ISLAND IN THE eastern Pacific Ocean has been more brutalized than Guadalupe. The natural plant and animal communities of the island have been destroyed, and one species after another has vanished. The Guadalupe junco may be the next victim of extinction. It is now only to be found in the north of Guadalupe island and it is thought that only 100 birds still survive.

Unique species

A small bird on a medium-sized island, the Guadalupe junco closely resembles the juncos of the North American mainland. It has a light belly and pinkish tan side that highlight an overall gray plumage. The bird sports white outer feathers on an otherwise gray tail, as do all juncos. It also bears the ivory-colored beak and black lore characteristic of this group. Originally considered a distinct species from the mainland dark-eyed junco (*Junco hyemalis*), the bird was regarded for many years as just a subspecies. Opinion has swung back to treating it as a species unique to Guadalupe Island.

Guadalupe itself resembles many other islands along the Pacific coast of the continent. The island sits 157 miles (251 kilometers) off the Baja Peninsula, roughly 250 miles (400 kilometers) southwest of San Diego, California. Isolated by that expanse of open ocean, over time a few species on Guadalupe developed unique characteristics that set them apart from their mainland ancestors. Among them were about 30 plants found only on Guadalupe, and another 24 that were scattered across a few other islands. Roughly 60 birds have been recorded on Guadalupe, and three of them are (or were) unique species, with six others classified as unique subspecies.

Two of the three unique species of these birds are now extinct, and several of the subspecies have also disappeared or have been drastically reduced.

Old problems

Spanish sailors found Guadalupe in 1565 and again in 1602. A string of sea travelers stopped at the island throughout the 1700s. Guadalupe was uninhabited by people and difficult to negotiate for ships. Many ships passed it by; few stayed for long. Russian sealers found the island as they explored the Pacific Coast in quest of sea otters and fur seals in the early 1800s. By 1895 the Guadalupe fur seal (*Arctocephalus townsendi*) was extinct. The northern elephant seal (*Mirounga angustirostris*), once believed extinct, survived and was rediscovered on Guadalupe in 1954.

As the seals and fur seals declined on Guadalupe, so did the plants and the birds. They were each lost for different reasons, however. For example, several unique plants were grazed into extinction by feral goats, and those native plants which did survive were badly depleted. Goats were introduced to Guadalupe by sailors who planned future trips at sea. When the old sailing ships stopped at islands to take

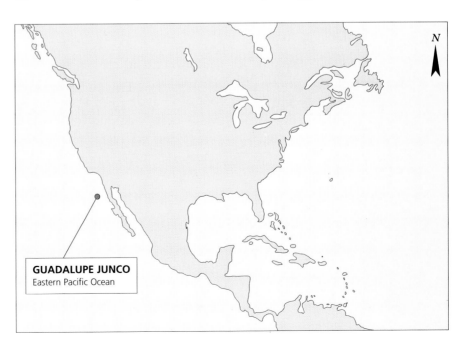

GUADALUPE JUNCO
Eastern Pacific Ocean

on firewood and water, goats were shot as a source of fresh meat, but their introduction to Guadalupe proved disastrous for the island's natural species.

Because they were unchecked by natural population controls, the goats multiplied. The Guadalupe cypress (*Cupressus guadalupensis*) and Guadalupe palms (*Erythea edulis*) are native to the island and were severely depleted by the hungry goats. As they dwindled, habitat for unique birds such as the Guadalupe ruby, crowned kinglet (*Regulus calendula obscurus*), and the Guadalupe flicker (*Colaptes cafer rufipileus*) disappeared. The flicker is extinct and the kinglet's numbers are drastically reduced.

Sailors also released cats on the island. Cats were routinely kept aboard sailing ships to catch rats and mice. It is likely that these cats had litters, and that the sailors put the excess cats ashore when possible. The cats killed birds for food. They undoubtedly caused the extinction of the Guadalupe storm-petrel (*Oceanodroma macrodactyla*), a small seabird that nested in island burrows. This bird was only discovered in 1887, but was extinct by 1912. The Guadalupe caracara (*Polyborus lutosus*) suffered the same fate, becoming extinct within 25 years of its discovery.

Special protection

In 1922 the Mexican government declared that the wildlife of Guadalupe Island should be protected. Soldiers were garrisoned on the island, but the move came too late. Undaunted, the Mexican government decided to commercially process goat meat and a meat cannery was duly established. Production continued for many years before failing after World War II. Canned goat meat did not find a big market, but the overgrazing problem has been solved and the goat population removed. Exotic plants have replaced much of the native vegetation, which degrades habitat for the island's birds.

Unlike islands such as New Zealand and Mauritius that have also been ravaged by humans, Guadalupe does not have a resident culture. The only people on the island are peasant fishers.

Ornithologists are aware of the plight facing the Guadalupe junco, but at present they are powerless to protect it.

Kevin Cook

Kagu

(Rhynochetos jubatus)

ESA: Endangered

IUCN: Endangered

Class: Aves
Order: Gruiformes
Family: Rhynochetidae
Length: 20–22 in. (51–56 cm)
Weight: 2 lb. (860 g)
Clutch size: 1 egg
Incubation: 36 days
Diet: Snails, worms, insects
Habitat: Montane forests
Range: New Caledonia, South Pacific

GREAT TREASURES lie hidden in the islands of the Pacific Ocean. In the forests of these islands live unique plants and animals that are found in no other places on Earth. Among these is a bird called the kagu.

The kagu's upperparts are the pale gray-brown color of old barn wood. Below, it is the dingy color of a whitewashed picket fence. A shaggy crest adorns its crown. Its beak, foot, and toe are the color of seasoned straw. A bold pattern of black and white bars streaks across the flight feathers in the wing, but the pattern is hidden when the wing is folded.

The only member of its family, the kagu leads a secretive life. It prowls the forest floor, where it finds various worms and insects, but snails (*Placostylus bavayi*) are its favorite food. Hitting the mollusk with its beak, the kagu smashes the shell, then shakes off the fragments before swallowing the snail. Ornithologists long suspected that the kagu is nocturnal and terrestrial. However, those few birds in captivity busy themselves by day and, occasionally, people report seeing a wild kagu perched in a tree.

Wild kagus call noisily by night, making a loud yelping and barking sound. The nights on New Caledonia have grown quieter as the kagu has dwindled away. A narrow island 248 miles (397 kilometers) long and 31 miles (49.6 kilometers) wide, New Caledonia is about 930 miles (1,488 kilometers) east of Queensland, Australia. The island was already inhabited by people when Captain James Cook discovered it in 1774.

By 1989 just under 200,000 people were settled in New Caledonia's 6,530 square miles

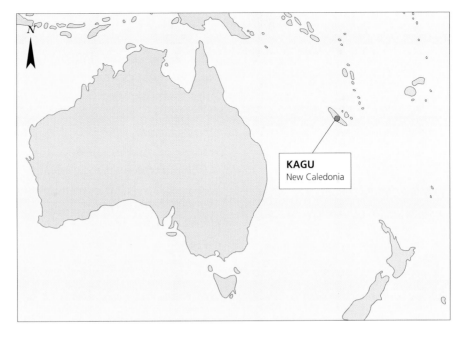

(16,978 square kilometers). They raise cattle and grow many different crops, including some for export, such as coffee, tobacco, bananas, and pineapples. Most farming occurs on the plains that lie between the coast and the mountainous interior. Once heavily forested, New Caledonia's mountains have been stripped of their trees to develop grazing land, later mined for metals. Nickel is an important source of wealth for the island.

Changing landscape

Mining leaves the land uninhabitable for the kagu. Once distributed throughout New Caledonia, the kagu now survives only in the southern third of the island. There a few valleys have escaped the axe and still feature primary forests. The kagu easily eludes those who want to study

The kagu makes its home on the exotic island of New Caledonia in the South Pacific, a region that is rich in natural wonders.

it, so population figures are difficult to estimate. Considering the extent of habitat loss and the habitat available, ornithologists suspect that only 500 to 1,000 kagus now survive in the wild. As the bird's population continues to decline, other factors besides habitat loss aggravate its potential for survival. Exotic mammals may finish off what deforestation has started.

People brought more than coffee and tobacco to New Caledonia. Dogs and pigs came along as pets and livestock. Rats (*Rattus* sp.) probably arrived as uninvited hitchhikers. No terrestrial mammals were native inhabitants of New Caledonia. Consequently, the kagu developed in a landscape that was free of significant predators. However, exotic mammals posed an immediate threat. Dogs, of course, can find adult birds and their chicks. The domestic pig (*Sus scrofa*) eats not only table scraps and feed, but also small animals. Ground-nesting birds, such as the kagu, are very vulnerable to pigs. As habitat destruction reduces the kagu population, the effects of predation by exotic mammals become more critical. Small populations are vulnerable to extinction.

After New Caledonia's forests are cut down and its ores mined, the island will be a different place. If protective measures are not taken soon, New Caledonians will have no forests left, no precious metals and no kagus.

Kevin Cook

Kakapo

(Strigops habroptilus)

ESA: Endangered

IUCN: Extinct in the wild

Class: Aves
Order: Psittaciformes
Family: Psittacidae
Subfamily: Strigopinae
Length: 22–26 in. (56–66 cm)
Weight: Males, up to 8 lb.
(3.5 kg); females, up to 3⅓ lb.
(1.5 kg)
Clutch size: 1–2 eggs, rarely 3
Incubation: Approximately
30 days
Diet: Mostly plant materials
Habitat: Forest and grassland
Range: Offshore islands of
New Zealand

A STRANGE BOOMING sound drifts down from the ridge tops and disturbs the night. Again and again the booming can be heard. This eerie noise once filled the New Zealand mountains. The origin of these sounds was the kakapo, a giant parrot, which used the sound as a mating call. The settling of people in New Zealand, however, nearly caused this distinctive bird to become extinct.

The presence of humans on New Zealand disrupted an ancient plant and animal system. Polynesians first arrived in New Zealand some time before C.E. 1000. Some historians believe that Polynesian immigrants even settled in the islands on more than one occasion. In any case, although the kakapo can live for 60 years or more, many of the birds became extinct even before European explorers arrived in the region. Britain eventually claimed the islands and began settling on them in 1840.

The native Maori, descendants of Polynesian immigrants, resisted British colonization and fought bitterly against them. The presence of the Maori drastically affected New Zealand birds, and this endangerment continued with the British. Colonists started what were known as acclimatization societies to alter the plant and animal communities of New Zealand. Their goals were to diversify the available species but, more important, to recreate the character of the flora and fauna of their homeland. These societies operated by importing plant and animal species and releasing them in order to establish wild populations. Many native plants and animals were overwhelmed by these exotic species and suffered as a result. Birds were particularly vulnerable to predatory mammals such as rats (*Rattus* sp.), house cats (*Felis sylvestris*), and weasels (*Mustela erminea*). The combined predation by these mammals nearly drove the kakapo into extinction, but other factors also contributed to its gradual demise.

Early naturalists, eager to acquire peculiar and bizarre examples of animal species, found the kakapo irresistible. They collected specimens for stuffing and mounting. Specimen collecting alone would not have driven the kakapo into extinction but, combined with some other problems, it reduced numbers.

A flightless bird

One of seven parrots unique to New Zealand, the kakapo long ago lost its powers of upward flight. Living on an island with no terrestrial mammalian predators meant that flying was unimportant. Once predators arrived, the kakapo was powerless to protect itself; it could run, but not very swiftly. Adults, immature animals, nesting animals, and eggs

One of the largest parrots, the kakapo, was hunted as food by both the Maori and by British colonists in New Zealand.

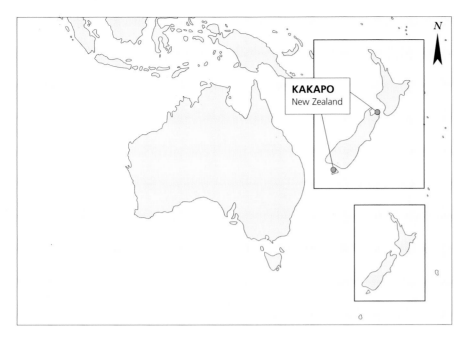

KAKAPO
New Zealand

New Zealand wildlife specialists has saved the kakapo from dying out. Its population has slowly recovered, so that extinction is now not as imminent. Still, there were known to be only 50 live birds in 1985, and by 1989 the kakapo was extinct on South Island. Between 1987 and 1992, all 37 birds that were known to remain on Stewart Island were relocated to three predator-free islands: Codfish, Maud, and Little Barrier Island. The birds on Little Barrier Island have since been moved to other islands.

In 1996 a successful recovery plan was initiated; the 1999 population consisted of 56 adults, made up of 22 females and 34 males, on six offshore islands, and a record number of six chicks were being raised.

Kevin Cook

were equally vulnerable. With such aggressive predation, the kakapo failed to reproduce, and its population rapidly dropped. By about 1970 the kakapo was believed to be doomed to extinction because the only known surviving birds were all males. Fortunately, a small kakapo population that included females was discovered on Stewart Island in 1976. Aggressive protection by

KANGAROO RATS

Class: Mammalia

Order: Rodentia

Family: Heteromyidae

Kangaroo rats (genus *Dipodomys*) are members of the family Heteromyidae, a category they share with kangaroo mice and pocket mice. The genus *Dipodomys* contains 21 species, and its members are found in semi-arid habitats from the southern plains of Canada south to central Mexico. Although many species of kangaroo rats seem to have experienced population decline, it is in the Californian region that the situation is most alarming.

Kangaroo rats are distinguished from other rodents by their hairy tails. The tail is longer than the entire body and has a tuft of hair at the end. They also have skulls formed of thin bone. Kangaroo rats and kangaroo mice are distinguished from pocket mice by their means of locomotion. Rather than running around on four legs as most rodents do, they hop on their hind legs, hence their common name. They also use their tails for balance when moving and as a prop when standing. The small forelegs are used mainly for manipulating food and cleaning their external, fur-lined cheek pouches.

High-speed, long distance travel by kangaroo rats involves jumps that can be over 6 feet (2 meters) in length. Because they can move rapidly, kangaroo rats prefer open areas with sparse brush or grass that allows both a clear view and room to jump.

Kangaroo rats have excellent hearing, which also helps them avoid predators. Studies have shown that these little rodents are able to detect the low frequency sounds made by flying owls and by rattlesnakes just before they strike.

Kangaroo rats are mostly nocturnal. They prefer areas with well-drained soil in which they can dig their burrows. Individuals make food caches. They collect food materials in their cheek pouches and bury them in or near to their burrows.

Habitat loss is the major factor affecting all endangered species of kangaroo rats. Drought complicates their survival. Another concern is that many methods used to control the squirrel population will kill kangaroo rats as well.

Fresno Kangaroo Rat
(Dipodomys nitratoides exilis)

Tipton Kangaroo Rat
(Dipodomys nitratoides nitratoides)

ESA: Endangered

IUCN: Critically endangered

Weight: Up to 1½ oz. (40 g)
Body length: 4–4⅓ in. (9–11 cm)
Diet: Seeds, plant material, some insects
Gestation period: 32 days
Habitat: Sparsely vegetated scrub, especially saltbush scrub and arid grassland with alkali sinks
Range: San Joaquin Valley, California

All kangaroo rats are primarily granivorous, or seed eating. They tend to reduce breeding when drought causes a drop in seed production.

WHEN FIRST DISCOVERED in 1891 the Fresno kangaroo rat probably ranged over 250,000 acres (101,000 hectares). It inhabited areas located east of Fresno, California, between the San Joaquin River and the Kings River, living on open grasslands that contained alkali sinks.

The Fresno kangaroo rat is a dull yellow color above and white below. Its gestation period is about a month, and because the animals breed year-round, females are able to bear three litters yearly, each with up to five offspring. Little else is known of the life history of the Fresno kangaroo rat, but it is probably similar in many ways to that of its relative, the Tipton kangaroo rat.

This animal was historically indigenous to over 1.7 million acres (695,000 hectares) in parts of four California counties. Its habitat occurred in the Tulare Lake Basin, where the soft basin floor did not experience the seasonal flooding common to other parts of the region. This species does not like wet conditions.

The Tipton kangaroo rat is a dark tannish-brown color above with a white underside. It has a white stripe across each flank, down both sides of the tail. The rat grows to 4⅓ inches (11 centimeters) in length. Its main breeding season is December to August, when the climate is suitable. As many as three litters a year of up to five offspring may result. The young, which are born blind, open their eyes when

they are 10 to 11 days old, leave the burrow after 18 to 21 days, and are weaned after 21 to 24 days.

Civilization spells trouble
For both of these subspecies, population decline began soon after their discovery. This was due to habitat loss from agricultural activities, and it continued during the first half of the 20th century, with residential development destroying more of the habitat. It was believed that the Fresno kangaroo rat had become extinct until a population was discovered in 1933. By then, the area of suitable habitat was down to about 100,000 acres (41,000 hectares). By the summer of 1985, the Tipton kangaroo rat's range was only 63,400 acres (25,700 hectares), a reduction of over 96 percent from its estimated range early in this century. At the close of the 1990s its habitat was reduced to slightly over

6,000 acres (2,400 hectares), which have been adversely affected by heavy livestock grazing. Habitat conversion is still a threat to this subspecies, as most of its remaining habitat occurs on small fragments of private property surrounded by agricultural land. About 10 percent of the remaining Tipton kangaroo rat habitat is administered by local, state, and federal agencies, and appears secure from threat.

As of 1988, these areas contained low to moderate populations of Tipton kangaroo rats, but there is concern that these areas are too small to ensure long-term population survival.

Significant species

Tipton kangaroo rats dig shallow burrows near shrubs where winds deposit fine soil. The burrows aerate the soil and serve as refuges for other species in the region, including the blunt-nosed lizard (*Gambelia silus*). Like many other small rodents in the region, this kangaroo rat is prey for the endangered San Joaquin kit fox (*Vulpes macrotis mutica*). If both subspecies of this kangaroo rat are wiped out, the kit fox will have one less species that it can prey on, and another species may become endangered.

It is essential that suitable habitat areas of adequate size be preserved. Experts say this would mean at least 800 to 3,000 acres (325 to 1,214 hectares) for the Tipton kangaroo rat. Today, few of the secure areas in California's San Joaquin Valley are of this size, and continued pressure from farming, as well as commercial and residential building, threatens to wipe out what is left of both subspecies.

Giant Kangaroo Rat

(Dipodomys ingens)

ESA: Endangered

IUCN: Critically endangered

Weight: 6–6⅓ oz. (170–180 g)
Body length: 5–6 in. (12.7–15.2 cm)
Diet: Seeds, fresh vegetation
Gestation period: About one month
Habitat: Arid, open, native grassland
Range: South-central California

AS ITS NAME SUGGESTS, this is the largest of the kangaroo rats. Its large size, however, has not protected it from the activities that threaten other species of kangaroo rat. Like its relatives found in central and south-central California, this species has suffered greatly from intense agricultural development.

Accounts from the early 20th century estimated the range of the giant kangaroo rat at anywhere from 1 to 2.5 million acres (0.5 to 1 million hectares). This range was spread out over six counties in southern California: Fresno, Kings, Merced, San Benito, San Luis Obispo, and Santa Barbara. By 1980 the species was found in scattered colonies over areas totaling less than 77,000 acres (32,000 hectares). Its range has continued to decrease, and has been reduced over 50 percent since 1980. As of 1990 this kangaroo rat has been eliminated from one county, has stayed in a few isolated colonies in three other counties, and found suitable habitat in four other counties.

The giant kangaroo rat is about 14 inches long (35.5 centimeters), including its 8-inch (20-centimeter) tail. It is medium brown in color on the back and sides and white below. Females bear two to four young after a gestation of about one month, and the young are weaned when they are about one month old.

Food storage

Like many of the other kangaroo rats, giant kangaroo rats store food in their burrows when they have more than they need. They do this in order to survive during periods of sparse rainfall. Burrows are shallow, but deep enough to prevent food spoilage due to the seeping of water caused by infrequent rains.

These rodents forage above ground for 20 minutes each night, searching for food they can stuff in their cheek pouches and take to their storage places. Forage areas are less than an acre (4 hectares) in size, and they occur in annual grasslands with well-drained, sandy loam soils and sparse vegetation. However, this type of habitat has been in great demand for agriculture.

Human use of the habitat

Although some populations are found within protected areas, others are threatened by human activities. Besides habitat loss to agriculture, oil-related activities have taken their toll. An oil spill in 1986 resulted in the death of 14 individuals—a small number, but for an endangered species, every loss can be critical. Other populations could be at risk from seismic exploration for oil reserves, because the explosion of dynamite charges could cause burrows to collapse.

As with so many other species that occur in the rapidly developing regions of California, it is hard to tell what the future holds for the highly endangered giant kangaroo rat.

San Quintin Kangaroo Rat

(Dipodomys gravipes)

IUCN: Endangered

Weight: 2¾–3 oz. (80–90 g)
Body length: 5 in. (13 cm)
Diet: Seeds
Habitat: Flat, arid coastal plain with short, sparse vegetation
Range: A 12½-mile-wide (20-kilometer) coastal strip from San Telmo to El Rosario, Baja California

ONE OF THE BIGGER kangaroo rats, the San Quintin species has large-boned hind feet. First described in 1925, this species has suffered from the crop cultivation that has occurred in its native Mexican habitat.

There appears to be a totally separate southern population occupying a different geographic region that seems to have somewhat different habitat traits. This population, situated near El Rosario, apparently does not have any contact with the northern populations and, therefore, is reproductively isolated. This El Rosario population is composed of individuals which are, on average, larger than the individuals to the north.

Throughout its range, the San Quintin kangaroo rat is found in flat and sparsely vegetated habitats mainly at low elevations. The upper body of the San Quintin kangaroo rat is a pale, pinkish buff color and has occasional black hairs. The underside of its body, including the forelegs and the upper surface of the hind legs, is white. There is also a white spot above each eye and a white stripe down both sides of the tail. The soles of the hind feet are black. The San Quintin kangaroo rat is not very large: its body grows to a length of about 5 inches (12.6 centimeters).

Birth patterns

There have been few studies of the natural history of this species, and there is little data concerning its reproductive biology. One study indicates that while young are born during several months of the year, there appear to be distinct peak birth periods in winter and spring.

While kangaroo rats eat seeds, they do not eat enough to cause much economic hardship to farmers. Still, any rodent this size is thought to be a pest by farmers and is often dealt with accordingly. The changes in their habitat expose kangaroo rats to other predators, but it is cultivation that has been the primary cause of this species' decline

Since the San Quintin kangaroo rat lives in an area where human populations are placing increasing demands on land use, if nothing is done to ensure some protected habitat, this species may soon be known only through museum specimens.

Stephens' Kangaroo Rat

(Dipodomys stephensi)

ESA: Endangered

IUCN: Lower risk

Weight: 2⅓–2½ oz. (65–68 g)
Body length: 4½–4¾ in. (11.3–12 cm)
Diet: Seeds and other plant material
Gestation period: About one month
Habitat: Coastal sage scrub and annual grassland
Range: Southwestern California

IT IS POSSIBLE that no other species of kangaroo rat has been as consistently put at risk as the Stephens' kangaroo rat. It is thought to have been widespread throughout several California counties (western Riverside, southwestern San Bernardino, and northwestern San Diego) early in the 20th century. But this species' range, and its future, is of serious concern today. It has experienced a decrease in suitable habitat from an estimated 308,000 acres (125,000 hectares) in the early 1900s to approximately half that area in 1984. Most of the remaining habitat occurs in isolated fragments. Once habitat loss was attributable to agriculture; however, in recent years residential development and off-road vehicle use have posed the greatest risk.

The Stephens' kangaroo rat can be distinguished from other kangaroo rats by its pale tannish brown fur above and the white fur on its underside. It has dusky,

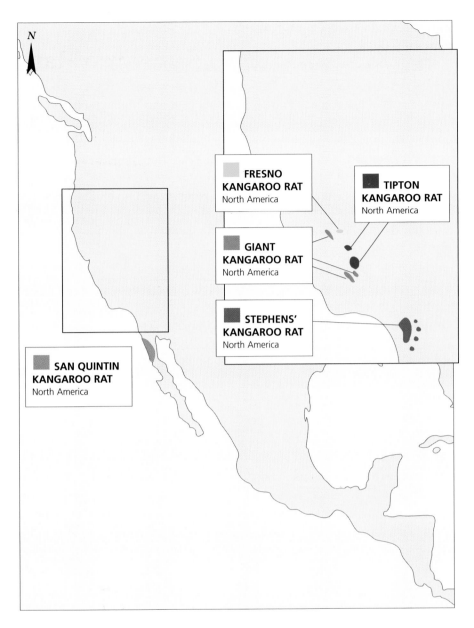

FRESNO KANGAROO RAT
North America

TIPTON KANGAROO RAT
North America

GIANT KANGAROO RAT
North America

STEPHENS' KANGAROO RAT
North America

SAN QUINTIN KANGAROO RAT
North America

this may be an indicator of the strict habitat requirements of this species. For example, trapping programs have made high catches in open areas, while adjacent areas of light chaparral yield few kangaroo rats.

Forced by agricultural development from low-lying areas to the edges of fields, this species is currently found in sparsely vegetated, gently rolling habitat with graveled soils—the kind of lands residential developers look for in southern California. The areas that were previously disturbed by the growth of off-road vehicle recreation have been further fragmented by housing and commercial development.

It is currently believed that only about 6 percent of the land within the remaining range of this species will remain safe. Much of this safe area occurs in fragments which may be too small for long-term population support. Furthermore, there are reports of developers and private landowners grading areas suspected to contain kangaroo rat habitat. Conservative estimates put the total habitat destroyed in this manner at over 1,000 acres (400 hectares). It is even thought that rodent poisons have been set out to destroy the kangaroo rat. People do this to avoid restrictions on the land use that might be imposed under the Endangered Species Act.

Such practices involving the habitat loss of endangered species illustrate the need for increased scrutiny of areas set aside for rapid development, where species like the Stephens' kangaroo rat are being squeezed out of existence.

Terry Tompkins

rather than dark, soles on the hind feet and its fur appears grizzled due to the presence of shafts of dual-colored hair. It also has a narrower white tail band and a smaller number of white hairs in the tuft at the end of the tail than other kangaroo rats.

Breeding

The breeding season appears to be in late spring and early summer. The young are born hairless and blind. The average litter size is two or three, but up to five have been reported. The young grow a dark olive-brown coat at about nine days and molt at about three months. Their eyes open at two weeks, and two months after they are born they are nearly adult in size.

Population densities vary from 3 to 23⅓ per acre (7.5 to 57.5 per hectare), and the home range area varies from 500 to 1,915 square yards (420 to 1,699 square meters). It has been noted that when population levels go up, home range sizes go down. This reduction probably means that individuals are reluctant to disperse into surrounding areas during population increases, and

Texas Kangaroo Rat

(Dipodomys elator)

IUCN: Vulnerable

Head-tail length: Average 12½ in. (31.7 cm)
Weight: Unknown
Longevity: Unknown
Gestation period: Unknown
Diet: Oat seeds, grass seeds, and other plant material
Habitat: Short-grass areas with exposed patches
Range: North-central Texas

THIS RODENT is found in north-central Texas, from Cottle and Mottley Counties in the west to Montague County situated in the east. The range of the Texas kangaroo rat is restricted to the specific habitat of mesquite grassland. This is characterized by an abundance of the leguminous shrub, *Prosopis*, which possesses nutritious pods. The opening to the Texas kangaroo rat's burrow is often found at the base of a small mesquite bush.

Appearance

Compared to the 20 other extinct species of kangaroo rat, the Texas kangaroo rat is a rather large animal, which measures a total length averaging 12½ inches (31.7 centimeters). The upper fur is buff in color and is tinted with a darker blackish pigmentation, while its underparts are white. The most striking features of this species are its large hind feet, its four toes, and its tail. The thick tail of the Texas kangaroo rat is much longer than its actual body and it displays a conspicuous white banner of long fluffy hairs on the very tip.

This rare rodent feeds on the seeds, stems, and leaves of a number of different grasses, forbs (herbs other than grass), and perennials. In cultivated areas the Texas kangaroo rat has been shown to prefer the seeds of the cultivated oat (*Avena*) and Johnson grass (*Sorghum*). Also selected, but to a lesser degree, are the annual forbs such as stork's bill (*Erodium*), broomweed (*Xanthocephalum*), and bladderpod (*Lesquerella*). The Texas kangaroo rat does not eat many shrubs or insects.

After successfully foraging, the Texas kangaroo rat gathers its meal and uses its small forefeet to transfer the food matter into its cheek pouches. The rodent then transports all its food to a convenient feeding location. Like other kangaroo rats, this species is able to store food when it is scarce.

All kangaroo rats, including the Texas kangaroo rat, are highly nocturnal and therefore activities such as foraging and burrow construction are only conducted under the cover of darkness. Darkness is so important to this species that it reportedly ceases activity on moonlit nights. Unlike other kangaroo rats, the Texas kangaroo rat does not plug the entrance to its burrow before it sleeps inside during the daytime.

Social interaction

The Texas kangaroo rat is not particularly sociable. Only one adult is found per burrow. The burrow and the surrounding home range are fiercely guarded by its occupant. This can result in savage battles if an occupant is challenged for its territory.

While the Texas kangaroo rat is not particularly vocal, it does occasionally generate a thumping or drumming sound. This may function as an alarm call to alert predators that they have been spotted or as a warning to possible intruder kangaroo rats to keep out of another's territory. Potential predators of this species include owls, coyotes, bobcats, foxes, and large snakes.

Breeding

Very little is known of the Texas kangaroo rat's breeding habits, but it is thought that it is capable of breeding all year round, with a noticeable peak in reproductivity during the spring and again in the late summer. The resultant offspring reach sexual maturity quickly, producing an average of three embryos following successful conception.

Kangaroo rats that reside close to cultivated grainfields may carry away a small proportion of the crop seeds produced. However the Texas kangaroo rat does not generally have any significant effect on the overall crop yield. Thus this species is generally harmless to the interests of human populations.

The reverse is not true however and the habitat preferences of this small rodent, combined with the clearing of mature mesquite bushland, have had a negative effect on the viability of this species' population. The population of the Texas kangaroo rat has been in decline within its small range. During one of the last population surveys, the species could not be located in Oklahoma or in five of the nine Texas counties where it had originally been found.

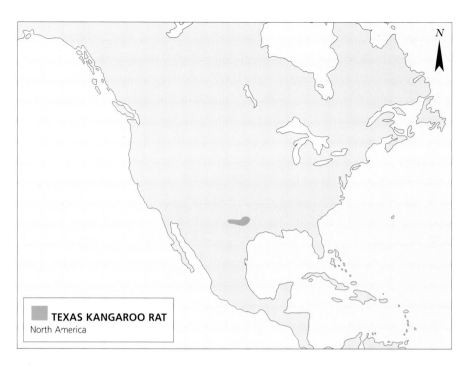

TEXTAS KANGAROO RAT
North America

However, recent research does suggest some hope for the survival of the species. This study has shown that the Texas kangaroo rat can, in certain situations, exploit human-made terraces and mounds for burrow sites.

Alternative habitats

It has been revealed that the Texas kangaroo rat exhibits a preference for the heavily grazed short-grass areas with exposed earth that result from heavy vehicle and livestock use. This indicates that the species may well be able to take advantage of the alternative habitats created by humans. If this proves to be true, habitat modification could possibly be used in the future as a survival aid where the ideal habitat has been destroyed.

Adrian Seymour

Bushland damage

The factors that cause depletion of the mesquite bushland are its conversion to pasture for grazing, conversion to various types of crops, and the gradual sprawl of urbanization. In addition, bush control projects have destroyed the food sources and cover required by this species.

Mauritius Kestrel

(Falco punctatus)

ESA: Endangered

IUCN: Endangered

Class: Aves
Order: Falconiformes
Family: Falconidae
Length: 11½ in. (29.2 cm)
Weight: Males, 4½–5 oz. (123–142 g); females, 6¼–7⅓ oz. (173–204 g)
Habitat: Primary evergreen forests, and secondary forest and scrub

TWO SMALL FALCONS have earned fame for vastly different reasons. The American kestrel achieved general recognition because it is the most abundant and widespread bird of prey in North America. The Mauritius kestrel became a celebrity because, for many years, it was the rarest bird on earth. In 1974 only four Mauritius kestrels were known to exist. The circumstances that brought the species to near extinction are not unique to the kestrel nor to Mauritius Island. Similar events also affected birds of Hawaii and New Zealand.

The people of Mauritius did no more to promote the extinction of a species than other people have done. Americans were responsible for the tragic fate of passenger pigeons (*Ectopistes migratorius*) and Carolina parakeets (*Conuropsis carolinensis*), and have yet to fully understand the impact of these losses. But three centuries of modern-day extinctions began in Mauritius when the last dodo (*Raphus cucullatus*) was seen there in 1680.

Mauritius lies about as far to the south of the equator as the island of Hawaii lies to the north. Mauritius is 500 miles (800 kilometers) east of Madagascar, and because of its situation, it often experiences violent cyclones born at sea. Portuguese sailors probably found Mauritius in 1507, but no one claimed the uninhabited island until the Dutch landed in 1598. The French and the British then took turns colonizing it. Mauritius became independent in 1968.

Over the centuries, people cut down the island's forests partly for the ebony wood (*Diospyros tesselaria*) and partly to open up

the land for agriculture. People also brought their pets, livestock and vermin to Mauritius, including crab-eating macaques (*Macaca fascicularis*) from Java. Much later, people introduced eucalyptus trees (*Eucalyptus* sp.) and pines (*Pinus* sp.) as plantation crops. The cutting down of the forest and the importation of new species changed the island's habitat. At least two dozen bird species have become extinct there in historic times, beginning with the dodo.

Heavy deforestation

Most of the island's 787 square miles (2,046 square kilometers) were originally forest—as much as 80 percent in the 1750s. About one percent of primary forest remained intact in 1984. This kestrel inhabits primary forests, which means that only one percent of the bird's habitat remains today, and this species has now adapted to living in secondary forest and scrub. Unlike its kestrel relatives, the Mauritius kestrel inhabits forests rather than open country. Instead of the long, pointed wings of most falcons, the Mauritius kestrel has shorter, rounder wings typical of forest birds. Its tail is longer than that of other falcons. The bird's upperparts are uniformly a warm, cinnamon brown with darker brown or black barring. The crown is streaked with brown, and the wings are nearly black. Its underparts are white with black spots.

In 1974 the Mauritius kestrel had the dubious honor of being the rarest bird in the world—only four specimens were known to exist at that time.

The Mauritius kestrel does not hunt in the same way that other kestrels do. It occasionally hovers while searching for food, and it will sit on an exposed perch so it can scan the area. However, it uses these techniques far less often than other kestrels. Most often, it directly pursues its prey. The Mauritius kestrel's favorite food is the small geckos (*Phelsuma* sp.) that sun themselves on tree branches. The kestrel will snatch these geckos, or hop from branch to branch in order to find geckos hidden beneath loose bark.

Cliff nesting

Most kestrel species nest in tree cavities, but the Mauritius kestrel uses large recesses in cliffs for nesting. This behavior may be an important adaptation in an area where cyclones can demolish trees. Nesting in cliffs cannot protect the kestrels from hungry macaques, however. Macaques readily eat any eggs and nestlings that they can find, including many bird species other than kestrels. Other exotic species also cause problems. Common mynas (*Acridotheres tristis*) and red-whiskered bulbuls (*Pycnonotus jocosus*) eat the same geckos that kestrels like to eat. Feral rock doves (*Columba livia*) compete for nesting spaces in the cliffs. The native white-tailed tropicbird (*Phaethon lepturus*) also uses cliff recesses for nesting. Some ornithologists believe the cliffs have so many holes that competition for a nesting site is not a significant problem. Other ornithologists believe that every setback creates a genuine problem for this species.

Exotic plants lessen the kestrel's habitat. Many are cultivated as crops, but sugarcane and tea are no substitute for primary forest. Plantations of pine and eucalyptus provide some forests or woodlands, but the kestrels have shown no willingness to use these plantations.

Altered habitat

Grazing animals such as Timor deer (*Cervus timorensis*), cattle (*Bos* sp.), and goats (*Capra* sp.) eat young native plants before they mature enough to produce seeds. This causes the loss of entire generations of forest trees. Indirect damage comes from ani-

By failing to preserve the original habitat, humans have doomed many native species on islands such as Mauritius.

mals distributing the seeds of exotic plants in their feces. Both events, grazing and spreading seeds, alter the composition of plant species in any given area.

As the plant community has changed in composition, the gecko population has declined because they have specific habitat requirements. A depressed prey population, with exotic as well as native species competing for it, means less food is available to the Mauritius kestrel.

As a result, the kestrel's habitat has shrunk. When the human population on Mauritius numbered only a few dozen Dutch colonists, people still managed to damage the land so severely that the dodo became extinct.

The human population on Mauritius is now in excess of one million, and so many people on such a small island creates an enormous demand for basic resources such as food, water,

and shelter. The Mauritius kestrel requires exactly the same basics for its own survival.

Legal protection

The Mauritius kestrel is protected by law; the last remaining areas of primary forest have been designated a reserve; and captive breeding helped boost the population to about 50 birds by 1990. Estimates from the early 1970s probably failed in their attempt to locate some of the nonbreeding birds. Even so, the population at this time must have been critically small.

The Mauritius kestrel will never be as familiar to people as are kestrels in other places. It will never become a common sight on telephone wires, as some kestrels are. Probably no more than 328 pairs—possibly 800 or so birds—ever lived on Mauritius. Sadly, too little habitat exists to accommodate that many kestrels today.

Kevin Cook

MAURITIUS KESTREL
Mauritius Island

KILLIFISHES

Class: Actinopterygii

Order: Atheriniformes

Killifishes can be found across the tropical and temperate latitudes of the world. They are capable of tolerating a range of environmental conditions, particularly in terms of salinity. They can be found in fresh water as well as in water that is more saline than sea water. Most killifishes prefer shallow water rich in aquatic vegetation; they use vegetation for cover and as a source of aquatic insects.

Killifishes are well known around the world to aquarium hobbyists and are prized for their diverse color patterning, relative tolerance of aquarium conditions, and the ease which which they spawn in captivity. In some cases this demand has been partially responsible for some killifishes becoming threatened or endangered. Additionally, because of their small size, many species are captured and used as bait fish.

All killifishes display a fairly uniform pattern of physical characteristics. They are less than 4 inches (10 centimeters) long, with an elongated, robust body, a plump belly, and a flattened tail. The rounded and fan-shaped fins are never large and lack spines for protection against predators. An upturned mouth, jutting lower jaw, and eyes set high on the head aid in the capture of insects at the surface.

CAPRIVI KILLIFISH
Africa

Caprivi Killifish

(Nothobranchius sp.*)*

IUCN: Endangered

Length: 1⅔ in. (4 cm)
Reproduction: Egg layer
Habitat: Shallow vegetated lakes or stream pools
Range: Caprivi Strip, Namibia

JUST NORTH OF the Okovango Swamp of northern Botswana in Africa is a narrow strip of land claimed by Namibia and called Caprivi. This land is the home of the Caprivi killifish, a beautiful fish of the Aplocheilidae family that must endure both natural and human-made hardships in order to survive in one of the most hostile environments in the world. These hardships include, on a seasonal basis, a complete lack of water in which to live. This species, and others of the genus *Nothobranchius,* are remarkable in their ability to survive in an environment that is intolerable to other fish. During the wet season, the Caprivi killifish spawns, depositing eggs in the bottom sediments. As the wet season passes and the dry season arrives, many areas that this fish occupies completely dry up.

The adult fish are not able to survive during this period, but the developing young within the eggs sense this lack of water and enter a phase of arrested development called diapause. Not until the rains return do the eggs continue to develop and hatch. As if this kind of hardship were not enough to endure, the Caprivi killifish, like other killifishes, is sought as an aquarium fish. This drain on the population, predation by birds and other animals, and the ongoing destruction by people living in the killifish habitat on the Caprivi Strip have brought this species to the brink of extinction. Given the growing demand for land and the potential for income to this developing nation, the future of this amazing fish is uncertain.

Easy breeder

The Caprivi killifish is like other killifish in body shape and size. With a total length of only 1⅔ inches (4 centimeters), bright coloration, and a propensity to breed in captivity, this warmwater species is an aquarist's dream. It has an upturned mouth and

To survive droughts, the eggs of this killifish enter a period of arrested development that lasts until the rain returns, when they develop and hatch.

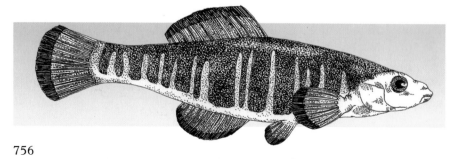

concave forehead for greater ease of feeding at the surface, and an overall shape that is fairly plump. The dorsal fin on the back, the anal fin and the tail fin are quite large and rounded; the dorsal fin is set far back along the body. In contrast, the paired pectoral fins just behind the gill covers and the pelvic fins on the belly are unusually small. The entire body, including the head and cheeks, is covered with a large number of scales. The skin is quite uniform in color but the scales are edged with a bold contrasting shade, creating a cross-hatch pattern. These colors continue into the fins—the dorsal fin has a spotty, blotchy appearance. The anal fin is striped at the base, and the tail fin is solidly pigmented.

This killifish is primarily an insect eater and has a voracious appetite for mosquitoes. It will consume other small aquatic animals when available.

Waccamaw Killifish

(Fundulus waccamensis)

IUCN: Vulnerable

Length: 3½ in. (9 cm)
Reproduction: Egg layer
Habitat: Shoal and inshore areas over clean sand
Range: Lakes Waccamaw and Phelps, North Carolina

THE COASTAL REGION of the United States stretching from Virginia to Georgia has long been an area of interest for both geologists and biologists. Within this particular region there is a series of lakes known as the Carolina Bays; most of these are concentrated in the southeastern region of North Carolina. Some scientists speculate that they were formed many thousands of years ago when a meteorite shower caused craters in the surface of the Earth along the mid- Atlantic coast. Over time the depressions filled up with water. Other experts theorize that underground artesian wells and wind and water forces eroded the basins over very many years.

Understanding evolution

Whatever the cause of the bays, the shallow Carolina Bays (Lake Waccamaw, in particular) have played an important role in our understanding of the evolutionary process. Studying the unique processes in Lake Waccamaw helps provide important clues that enable us to understand more about the different species that inhabit it.

Predatory fish in Lake Waccamaw depend on the Waccamaw killifish as a source of food. Likewise, local fishermen utilize this species, which has a tendency to school in shallow shoreline areas, as a reliable

Killifishes are some of the most spectacularly colored fish in the world. They display a variety of patterns and hues among individual fish and across species.

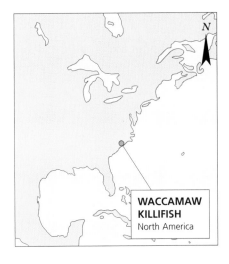
WACCAMAW KILLIFISH
North America

source of bait. Nonetheless, neither this fish's natural predators nor fishermen seeking bait (long-time traditional consumers of this fish) are responsible for the decline in the Waccamaw population. However, the presence of people does play an important role in this situation. As human development and agriculture encroach on areas surrounding the lake, the amount of sediment and nutrients that flow into Lake Waccamaw have increased. These materials smother eggs and food items and degrade the water quality for all Waccamaw fish.

As a result of concern for the survival of the Waccamaw killifish and other Waccamaw fishes, the lake is being offered protection. In addition, some protection against development of surrounding areas is also provided by Lake Waccamaw State Park.

William E. Manci

KINGFISHERS

Class: Aves

Order: Coraciiformes

Family: Alcedinidae

Subfamily: Daceloninae

Kingfishers are brightly colored birds that exhibit distinctive patterns of behavior. They also have a characteristic anatomy: their heads usually appear too large for their bodies, and their feet look too small. A few have shaggy crests. All kingfishers grow heavy, stout beaks, though not all eat fish. Some species prey on large and small invertebrates. The belted kingfishers of North America have been known to stake out bird feeders when winters turn especially harsh.

Many kingfishers are forest birds that eat large insects. Others are large enough to catch small lizards and birds. Australia's laughing kookaburra (*Dacelo gigas*) may be the most famous of all the kingfishers. Although many people besides bird enthusiasts have heard of it, few people realize that the kookaburra is a kingfisher. Traditionally, ornithologists recognized one family and three subfamilies of kingfishers. In 1990 a revised taxonomy was published, elevating each subfamily to family status, but this system has not yet been widely accepted. The single kingfisher family treatment recognizes 90 species.

Kingfishers as a species appear to be doing well. However, many kingfishers isolated on small islands appear to be in trouble. Islands often limit the population sizes of unique species. When human activities disturb the islands, those species can suffer quickly and dramatically.

Biak Paradise Kingfisher

(Tanysiptera riedelii)

IUCN: Lower risk

Length: 14 in. (35.6 cm)

Clutch size: Probably 5 eggs

Diet: Probably insects and earthworms

Habitat: Gallery forests

Range: Biak Island off the northern coast of New Guinea

THE COMMON PARADISE kingfisher (*Tanysiptera galatea*) inhabits humid lowland island forests in eastern Indonesia. These islands include the Moluccas and New Guinea. On one island the paradise kingfisher differs so much from other paradise kingfishers that some ornithologists see the group as a distinct species—the Biak kingfisher.

Biak lies off the coast of Irian Jaya, the western half of New Guinea. The island sprawls across the mouth of Geelvink Bay like a plug or barrier. Lying just a degree or two south of the equator, Biak can be very hot and humid. The Biak kingfisher thrives in such conditions.

The Biak kingfisher has a striking appearance. A rich, shiny blue colors its upperparts, except for a white rump. Its underparts are uniformly white. A bright red beak punctuates the bird's appearance. Its two central tail feathers grow much longer than its other feathers. From the tip of the tail outward the two feathers are just veinless shafts, but at their ends they flare out, giving the tail a racquetlike appearance.

The common paradise kingfisher nests in hollow branches, tree cavities, and chambers within termite nests. It often sits on a branch low to the ground, where it can watch for insects scuttling about the forest floor. The Biak kingfisher probably behaves in much the same way.

Many specific aspects of the Biak kingfisher's natural history remain unknown. Ornithologists have not determined whether the bird can adapt well enough to survive in secondary forest. At the rate primary forests are being cut down on Biak, the island's namesake kingfisher may become extinct before anyone learns much about it.

Blue-capped Wood Kingfisher

(Actenoides hombroni)

IUCN: Vulnerable

Habitat: Forest

Range: Mindanao, the Philippines

THE WESTERN PACIFIC Ocean is separated from the South China Sea by more than 7,000 loosely clustered islands stretching more than a thousand miles (1,600 kilometers) north to south. These are the Philippines, and of those 7,000 islands, the blue-capped wood kingfisher lives on just one.

This kingfisher inhabits the forests of Mindanao. A striking

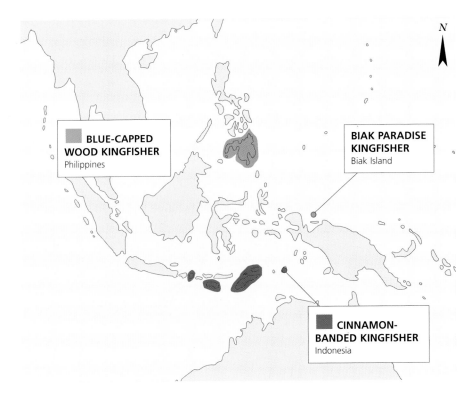

BLUE-CAPPED WOOD KINGFISHER
Philippines

BIAK PARADISE KINGFISHER
Biak Island

CINNAMON-BANDED KINGFISHER
Indonesia

bird, the male sports a blue crown and nape. A blue stripe separates the white chin and throat from the chestnut cheek. The upper back is also chestnut, but the lower back and rump are light blue. Its tail is dark blue, the wing a deep blue-green with rufous spots. The breast and belly are a pale rufous, with some scattered black spots. The female differs from the male: it has a greener crown and tail. Both the female and male have red beaks.

Rarely sighted
Ornithologists know little else about the blue-capped wood kingfisher. Its length, weight, clutch size, incubation, and diet are all unknown. This species was not documented by any ornithologist or skilled bird observer between 1939 and 1980. A specimen was collected one year at about 3,608 feet (1,100 meters) upon Mount Apo. Another bird was seen two years later on a different mountain. No other sightings have been recorded. Several explanations may account for such scant information about this rare kingfisher. First, the bird is naturally rare. Second, it lives in an area of the Philippines that is not well traveled by tourists. Many tourists are also bird watchers, and they often report rare or unusual birds they encounter. But tourists are just not likely to see the blue-capped wood kingfisher. Third, violent rebel groups fighting against the Philippine government have sometimes made traveling around the Philippines a dangerous prospect. Few people care to risk their lives just to measure and count rare birds. And fourth, the kingfisher may be declining due to an unclear set of factors related to habitat loss.

At 36,775 square miles (95,615 square kilometers), Mindanao is the second largest island in the Philippines, and holds many of the Philippines' 55 to 60 million people. Its forests have

been cut down both for lumber and for firewood. Lumber can be exported at a profit, and poor people need the firewood for cooking and heating. Whatever the motivation for cutting down the forests, the consequence is lost habitat for the blue-capped wood kingfisher.

Research needed
No estimates of this kingfisher's population have been offered. Without knowing how many blue-capped kingfishers exist, and because little is known about them, not much can be done on their behalf. Until research produces more data about the bird, only one action can help it. The Philippine government must regulate how much forest can be cut down, at what rate, and how much must be preserved.

Cinnamon-banded Kingfisher
(Todirhamphus australasia)

IUCN: Lower risk

Clutch size: Unknown, but 2 eggs common for genus
Diet: Probably insects and other invertebrates
Habitat: Wooded lowlands near water
Range: Lesser Sunda Islands of Indonesia

THE CINNAMON-BANDED kingfisher inhabits one of two main island groups situated in Indonesia. The Greater Sunda Islands include Borneo, Sumatra, and

Java. All three rank among the world's largest islands. The Lesser Sunda Islands trail off into the ocean east of Java. They include Bali, Lombok, Sumbawa, Wetar, Flores, Timor, and Tanimbar, plus many other much smaller islands. A few of them are home to the rare cinnamon-banded kingfisher.

Independent birds

This little-known kingfisher lives life its own way. Most of its relatives in the genus *Todirhamphus* spend their lives in forests. So does the cinnamon-banded kingfisher. If the feeding habits of this species are similar to those of its relatives, it preys largely on insects and other invertebrates. Other kingfishers capture their food by sitting on a perch and dropping to pluck prey from the forest floor. However, the cinnamon-banded kingfisher captures its food up in the treetops. It lives in the forest canopy and snatches food from the foliage of the trees. Little else is known of this bird's habits.

Ornithologists suspect this species is declining in some areas. Census work has not been conducted to provide any population estimates, but some insight into the bird's future can be gained by looking at other factors. Forests of the Lesser Sundas are being cut down, partly for their own value and partly to make way for more profitable crops. Primary forests are being cut down faster than secondary forests can regenerate the cut-over sites.

With less habitat, the cinnamon-banded kingfisher has already become scarce on Lombok, Sumba, and Timor.

Forest survival

Today, Indonesia's human population exceeds 160 million people. Some areas are desperately crowded. These people need space to live and farmland to produce food. However, it is important that the Indonesian people allow some tracts of primary forest to survive. In time, research may show how to manipulate secondary plant communities to support various wildlife species such as the cinnamon-banded kingfisher.

Guam Micronesian Kingfisher

(Todirhamphus cinnamomina cinnamomina)

ESA: Endangered

Length: 8–9½ in. (20–24 cm)
Weight: 2–2⅓ oz. (51–65 g)
Clutch size: 2 eggs (based on four nests)
Incubation: 21–23 days (in captivity)
Diet: Mostly insects, but also worms, skinks, small crabs
Habitat: Primary forest, coconut groves
Range: Guam, Marianas Islands

THE GUAM MICRONESIAN kingfisher has become one of the victims of the brown tree snake. As a full species, the Micronesian kingfisher occurs in the Ryukyu Islands between Japan and Taiwan, southward through the Marianas Islands, and into the Caroline Islands. Three unique subspecies of this kingfisher live on each of the islands of Pohnpei, Palau, and Guam. Whereas the Pohnpei and Palau subspecies are thriving, the endangered Guam Micronesian kingfisher now struggles to survive.

Appearance

The male Guam Micronesian kingfisher has a deep golden cinnamon head and underparts, contrasted by deep greenish blue wings, back, and tail. A narrow, dark, greenish blue band extends from eye to eye around the nape. The black beak is thick, long, and rather heavy looking.

The female resembles the male, except for a lighter chin and throat and an all white breast and belly. These kingfishers may grow up to 9½ inches (24 centimeters) in length.

A noisy forest bird, the Guam Micronesian kingfisher perches on exposed branches, from which it can watch the ground below. The kingfisher is insectivorous and, on spying an insect from its perch, will drop swiftly to the ground to seize it. The Guam Micronesian kingfisher also eats worms, small lizards, and small crabs. It does not eat fish, although its name would seem to imply otherwise.

Habitat loss

Human activity on Guam has eliminated much of the forest habitat that the kingfisher lived in. More than 100,000 people inhabit Guam's 209 square miles (543 square kilometers). The island's native plant communities have been largely cleared for livestock grazing, farming, and growing cities and towns. A crescent of primary forest survives along the limestone cliffs of the

The combination of human activity and the introduction of the brown tree snake on the island of Guam has severely depleted the population of the Guam Micronesian kingfisher.

northern coast, but the quality of the habitat has been severely compromised.

The fatal introduction

Sometime after World War II, the brown tree snake (*Boiga irregularis*) was moved to Guam. The island's bird life has yet to recover from its introduction.

The brown tree snake is native to Southeast Asia. Venomous and a good tree-climber, the snake specializes in eating birds, and it has harmed the kingfisher. It can catch adults as well as raid nests. Its skills and appetite make it extremely deadly to an island bird species that never had the opportunity to adapt to this predator.

When two animals, a predator and its prey, develop together over time, they each acquire a set of essential characteristics that help them survive. The prey develops a way to hide, and the predator develops a way to seek. The prey develops a way to flee, and the predator develops a way to chase. In natural circumstances, the predator never catches all of the prey, and the prey does not escape all the time. When a predator becomes established on an island full of birds that have no experience with surviving that predator, disaster usually follows. Because Guam had no native snakes, the island's birds did not develop protection against hungry, tree-climbing reptiles. Proper adaptation to predators would take time that Guam's birds do not have.

Nesting

The Guam Micronesian kingfisher nests in tree cavities that it painstakingly excavates itself. Lacking the specialized feet of the woodpecker, the kingfisher must hover while chiseling these cavities. The kingfishers are diurnal, but the brown tree snake is nocturnal. While the birds sleep in their cavities, the snake winds up the tree, finds the hole and attacks the occupants. What adults, nestlings, or eggs it does not consume one night, it can return for on subsequent nights. Moreover, brown tree snakes have had excellent reproductive success, so their population on Guam has grown enormously. This has delivered a critical blow to the island's native birds.

First these birds lost habitat to land development. Second, the island is now so populated with an exotic predator that the birds cannot survive in the remaining fragments of native habitat.

The Guam Micronesian kingfisher is not the only forest bird on Guam to suffer this problem. The solution for preserving one species would seem to be the solution for all. The brown tree snakes must be removed. Eradication may not be achieved, but a vigorous attempt may be adequate to save the birds of Guam from extinction.

The U.S. Fish and Wildlife Service has been studying the brown tree snake for many years. Researchers have now learned enough about this snake's natural history to be able to focus on finding a way of restricting the spread of this reptile.

Population decrease

Guam's population of Micronesian kingfishers dropped from an estimated 3,000 in the early 1980s to approximately seven birds in 1986. A captive-breeding program was initiated in the United States, with 29 birds captured before 1986. The Guam Micronesian Kingfisher is now being bred in zoos. There were 65 birds in captivity in 1991.

Marquesas Kingfisher

(Todirhampus godeffroyi)

IUCN: Endangered

Length: 6½ in. (16.5 cm)
Diet: Probably insects and other invertebrates
Habitat: Forest
Range: Marquesas Islands

ELEVEN SMALL HUMPS of land in the South Pacific make up the Marquesas Islands. Melanesian explorers discovered them in about C.E. 200. Many centuries later, the islands suffered a first encounter with modern civilization when Spanish explorers discovered them in 1595. The islanders were overpowered by the Spaniards' guns and swords.

Valuable crops
The French eventually won control of the islands and intended to cultivate the islands with crops that were valuable in international trade—coffee, tea, and other commodities. But Europeans imported more than their lifestyle and agriculture to the islands. They also brought diseases such as smallpox, tuberculosis, syphilis, and leprosy. The population of islanders dwindled from 100,000 at the beginning of the colonial era to a mere 3,000 by 1960. The islands' birds have also been affected by changing environmental conditions.

The Marquesas kingfisher once lived on at least two, and possibly five, of the islands in the chain. If it ever lived on the islands of Fatuiva, Mohotani, or Uapou, it has vanished from them completely. The kingfisher now survives only on Hivaoa, where about 100 birds were known to live in the late 1980s, and on Tahuata, where as many as 1,000 birds still live.

A forest bird, the Marquesas kingfisher probably feeds on insects, spiders, worms, and invertebrates in much the same way that other forest-dwelling kingfishers do. Ornithologists know that a bird cannot live without habitat, and on Hivaoa and Tahuata the kingfisher's habitat is disappearing. Native forests are still being cut down and the land replanted. Furthermore, great horned owls (*Bubo virginianus*) and common mynas (*Acridotheres tristis*) have been released on Hivaoa. Great-horned owls regularly eat birds the size of the Marquesas kingfisher. Common mynas nest in trees and have the potential to displace the cavity-nesting kingfisher.

A changed island
Just like the island peoples, the island birds have been displaced. The Marquesas kingfisher is a tiny bird on a tiny island. The bird was never abundant, so if it was to become extinct, its passing would not make headline news. Such an event would be unnecessary and avoidable. Habitat conservation, restraint on the introduction of non-native wildlife species to the kingfisher's habitat, and the replanting of forest communities are needed if the future of the Marquesas kingfisher is to be made more secure.

Kevin Cook

KITES

Class: Aves

Order: Falconiformes

Family: Accipitridae

Kites fly with a graceful style, though they are capable of neither the soaring ability of the great hawks nor the divebombing speed of the falcons. Their buoyancy in the air suits them for capturing large insects on the wing, and for picking other insects off the outer foliage of trees and shrubs. Some species of kites will even eat smaller birds as a regular part of their diet.

Many kite species nest in loose clusters. Their nests are spaced too far apart to qualify as colonies, but they are too close together to be treated merely as closely spaced mating pairs. They use the same breeding areas year after year.

Ornithologists have grouped kites differently over the years. Some have classified them into one or more subfamilies to distinguish them from other hawks. Osprey (*Pandion haliaetus*), fish-eagles, and sea-eagles appear more closely related to the kites than other hawks and eagles, but most ornithologists still do not place kites in a separate subfamily.

Wetland destruction is occurring on a worldwide scale today. Such devastation inevitably arises when vast tracts of land are needed for agriculture. Historically, many wetlands have been destroyed for reasons of public health: fewer wetlands means fewer disease-carrying mosquitos. Because so many kite species associate with one kind of wetland or another, many species have experienced decline.

Some kites, such as the red kite (*Milvus milvus*) in Europe, have been deliberately persecuted by humans. Most species recover quickly if the shooting and trapping can be controlled, but they always need habitat. Once habitat is destroyed, a species can only hope to recover to the extent that essential habitat is available.

Cuba Hook-billed Kite

(Chondrohierax uncinatus wilsonii)

ESA: Endangered

Length: 15–16 in (38–41 cm)

Weight: 12–14 oz. (340–397 g)

Clutch size: Probably 2–3 eggs

Diet: Mostly snails, but also insects, frogs, and salamanders

Range: Cuba

WHEN HOOK-BILLED kites cross the Rio Grande into Texas, word spreads like wildfire. Birdwatchers show up from all over the country in order to get a rare glimpse of this endangered bird in the United States.

Hook-billed kites range over all of Central America. They occupy all of northern South America and most of central South America east of the Andes. One small group of kites still lives in Cuba, and ornithologists have designated these birds as a separate subspecies. This group has declined over the years, and its survival is now in doubt.

Snail eater

The hook-billed kite is of average size for a hawk, although it has an unusual beak. This bird is appropriately named, because its oversized, heavy-looking beak curves down sharply at the tip. It uses its beak to open snails that it finds on trees.

Appearance

Typical of a forest bird, the hook-billed kite has a slightly shorter and broader wing than might be expected for a bird its size. This wing shape and proportion allows the bird to maneuver among the tangled limbs and twigs of forest trees. Like other forest birds, the hook-billed kite is also dark both above and below. The male sports a dark gray plumage, washed over with a faint brown hue. Its underparts are reddish brown, with white barring from the lower throat down across breast, belly, and side. Its tail is the same dark gray brown, but a white band sweeps across the middle. The female is browner and not so gray in color. The underparts are more orange and more rufous, with dingy buff separating the bars. These dark patterns probably help camouflage the bird.

Sugar threat

The population of Cuba hook-billed kites has been steadily dwindling for years. As the Cuban people drain swamps to develop more sugarcane plantations, the kite loses vital habitat. With more than ten million people, Cuba has both the size and population of Pennsylvania. Although the Cuban people raise various crops, including coffee, tobacco, bananas, and pineapples, sugarcane accounts for more of the island nation's farm exports than all the other crops combined. Sugarcane takes up space, and the best space in Cuba is south of the low mountains along the coastal plain. Swamps and drier forests once stretched across much of that area, and the Cuba hook-billed kite made its home in those forests.

An island dweller

No one knows for certain whether the numerous chemicals used to sustain the massive agricultural development have had any direct effect on the Cuba hook-billed kite. Useful population estimates are not available. However, comparing how much kite habitat used to exist on Cuba with how much of that habitat remains makes the problem and the solution clear: the only way to preserve the Cuban subspecies of the hook-billed kite is to preserve the bird's habitat. Commercial trade in Cuba hook-billed kites is prohibited by The Convention on International Trade in Endangered Species of Wild Fauna and Flora (CITES).

All species of kites appear to use the same breeding areas year after year. This arrangement leaves large areas of apparently suitable habitat unused.

Everglades Snail Kite

(Rostrhamus sociabilis plumbeus)

ESA: Endangered

Length: 17 in. (43 cm)
Weight: 13½ oz. (386 g)
Clutch size: 2–4 eggs
Incubation: 26–28 days
Diet: Snails
Habitat: Marshes
Range: The Everglades of southern Florida; Cuba, including the Isle of Pines

GLIDING OVER THE marsh, first flapping strongly then sailing lightly, then flapping again, the hawk scans for its prey. With no great drama of power and pursuit, the bird flares its wings and drops toward the water with feet and talons outstretched. Before hitting the water it flaps again, regaining flight just as its talons pluck a brown snail from the water. With steady wingbeats, it flies to a branch where it alights and quickly settles itself. Looking first left then right, it shows the profile of its specialized beak, the upper half of which curves sharply downward. The hawk bobs its head slightly, then turns its attention to the snail.

The male Everglades snail kite is sooty gray overall, with a two-tone tail. The base of the tail is white and the tip is slate gray. It is a long-winged bird, well built for a life of snatching snails from marshes. The Everglades snail kite eats apple snails (*Pomacea paludosa*) almost exclusively.

The snail defends itself from many would-be predators with an operculum, a tough, leathery plate that covers the shell opening. The kite overcomes this obstacle by inserting its needle-like upper beak between the operculum and shell. With a twist of its head it snaps the nerve that controls the muscles holding the operculum closed. Once the nerve is severed, the muscle goes limp, the obstacle is removed, and the kite scoops out the snail and proceeds to eat it.

The snail kite species ranges over nearly all of South America east of the Andes, portions of Central America, Cuba, and Florida. The Florida birds belong to a distinct subspecies. Originally, they inhabited much of the Everglades, a unique marshland sprawling over more than 13,000 square miles (33,800 square kilometers) of southernmost Florida. The vast open expanses of sawgrass (*Cladium jamaicense*) are the most distinctive feature of the region. Actually a sedge and not a grass, the sawgrass grows in the slowly moving water. Apple snails also live in that water. The apple snails must periodically come to the surface to breathe, and they leave the water to lay their eggs

on plant stems several inches above the water line.

In many places the sawgrass grows too tall and too dense for the Everglades snail kites to reach the snails. Some areas are more open than others, and it is in these open areas that the kites do most of their hunting. The Everglades is like a great puzzle of interlocking pieces, in which water, sawgrass apple snails, and kites all fit together. If something happens to one piece, there is a concomitant effect on all the other pieces. Much has happened in the Everglades to upset the balance of the environment, and the Everglades snail kite has suffered as a result.

During the early years of Florida's settlement, people largely disregarded the Everglades as too inhospitable to bother with. Various schemes to drain the Everglades were occasionally devised, but no single method succeeded. However, many unrelated activities affected the region. Working from the borderlands, people steadily drained small portions of the marshlands so they could build houses and plant crops. Agriculture meant using fertilizers and pesticides, both of which affected plant communities beyond farmers' fields. People dug peat from the marshes, built highways across the expanse of sawgrass, and redirected water flow.

In 1934 the land that was to become Everglades National Park was set aside. Much of the park's 2,186 square miles (5,684 square kilometers) includes portions of Florida Bay and coastal mangrove swamp. These areas, strictly speaking, are not portions of the true Everglades, although

Today enough people use the same recreation areas within the Everglades to cause major disturbance to nesting and feeding Everglades snail kites. Important nesting areas have subsequently been closed to public use.

they are intimately connected to it. Thus, the actual area of Everglades protected by the park is roughly 6 percent of the Everglades' original size. Everglades snail kites do seasonally use habitat inside the northern border of the park, but for the most part the surviving population resides outside the park. What happens to the Everglades beyond the park boundaries really determines what happens to the kite.

Historically, people have treated the Everglades as if it was expendable. Manipulation of water levels and chemical contamination from agricultural sources have combined to alter

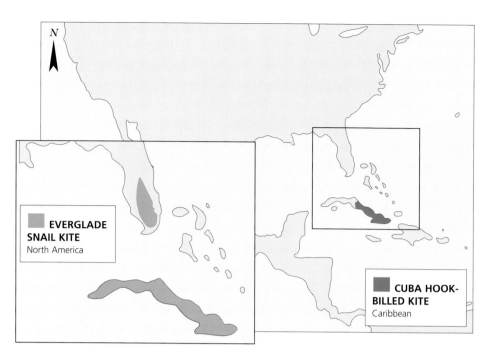

N

EVERGLADE
SNAIL KITE
North America

CUBA HOOK-
BILLED KITE
Caribbean

glades snail kite experiencing substantial loss of suitable habitat for nesting and hunting.

Everglades snail kites have frequented Loxahatchee National Wildlife Refuge and areas near Lake Okeechobee, as well as the Shark Valley area of Everglades National Park and the Miccosukee Indian Reservation (and some points in between).

Before 1970, the Everglades kite population was perhaps as low as 10. By the 1990s, surveys counted between 387 and 996 individuals. The population survived and rebuilt because wildlife specialists protected nesting sites from human disturbance. Preserving the Everglades snail kite depends on people's willingness to allow it to exist by protecting its habitat.

Kevin Cook

the natural landscape. These changes may have affected the apple snail population. Ordinarily, apple snails are so prolific that population changes would not

seriously affect the kites. However, artificial changes in the plant communities of the Everglades could affect the supply of snails to the kites, at least locally. This would result in the Ever-

Little Spotted Kiwi

(Apteryx owenii)

IUCN: Vulnerable

Class: Aves
Order: Apterygiformes
Family: Apterygidae
Length: 14–17¾ in. (35–45 cm)
Weight: 2½–3 lb. (1.1–1.4 kg)
Diet: Invertebrates, including earthworms and insects; fruits
Habitat: Evergreen forests with undergrowth; evergreen shrub land
Range: Kapiti Island, New Zealand

UNUSUALLY FOR A bird, the kiwi has a sense of smell. Its other distinctive features include shaggy,

hairlike feathers, weak wings with which it cannot fly, a long beak, large feet, and the lack of a tail.

Although the bird's appearance endears it to many people, it has been killed for its skin and its meat for centuries. As a result of its overexploitation, some species of kiwi have come very near to extinction.

The little spotted kiwi is one of three types of kiwi that live in the forests and dense shrub lands of New Zealand. The smallest of the trio, it has a gray-brown head and neck. The rounded body is largely a dull brown, textured by an off-white, giving the bird a vaguely barred or spotted look. The wings are tiny and usually hidden by the shaggy plumage. The feet and toes are powerfully built but are not used to scratch for food. The beak is long, slen-

der, and slightly decurved. The kiwi's face has many long, hairlike bristles that are thought to serve as whiskers.

Kiwi fossils go back 60 million years, making them the oldest bird group on the islands.

Divided land

New Zealand is composed of two large islands, North Island and South Island, and a third one called Stewart Island, in addition to many coastal isles and islets. The brown kiwi (*Apteryx australis*) formerly occurred over much of North Island, large tracts of South Island, and on Stewart Island. The great spotted kiwi (*Apteryx haastii*) inhabited only portions of South Island. The little spotted kiwi, smallest of the three, occupied much of North and South Islands, plus many small coastal isles. Although it is secretive and nocturnal, the little kiwi could not escape a hungry people. New Zealand had no large land mammals as a meat source, but it had many birds. The native Maoris hunted the birds and repeatedly burned the land. This eliminated the little spotted kiwi from one major island and several smaller ones. When the British colonized New Zealand in the mid-1800s, life became even more precarious for the little spotted kiwi.

Deadly predator

The British colonists imported various plants and animals and released them on the islands. They introduced elk (*Cervus elaphus*) and European rabbits (*Oryctolagus cuniculus*). Without natural controls in place to suppress their populations, the rabbit population exploded. The colonists had a solution: they

LITTLE
SPOTTED KIWI
New Zealand

imported a predator called a stoat, known in the United States as an ermine or short-tailed weasel (*Mustela erminea*), which they hoped would eat the rabbits. Unfortunately the stoat found various flightless ground birds to prey on instead, and the little spotted kiwi easily became one of their main targets.

Tunnel nests

Kiwis nest in long tunnels that they dig in embankments, especially among large, exposed tree roots. These tunnels may go back as much as 12 feet (3.5 meters) to the actual nesting chamber.

Flightless wings, a long beak, overgrown feet, shaggy feathers, and a lack of tail combine to create the unusual appearance of the kiwi.

The weasels, being long and skinny, had no trouble entering these burrows in search of nestlings. House cats (*Felis sylvestris*) also found their way into the New Zealand wilds, as did several rat species. All of these mammals preyed on the little spotted kiwis, but the presence of certain plants affected them, too. Many native forests on the islands of New Zealand were cut down and replaced by lodgepole pines (*Pinus contorta*) and Monterey pines (*Pinus radiata*). Pines are not native to the Southern Hemisphere, so vast acres of them on plantations are not recognizable or useful to native birds.

As New Zealand's population grew, sheep production for meat and wool became a major agricultural activity on the islands. The space needed for human pursuits left less space for the kiwis. Less habitat means fewer kiwis. As populations decline, hunting by exotic predators becomes a more serious threat.

New Zealand wildlife specialists have developed a strategy to save many of New Zealand's birds. They trap unwanted animals in order to remove them from the islands. Native birds are then moved to these islands and released into the wild. By 1995 the population of little spotted kiwis was estimated at 1,000 birds. Preserving the little spotted kiwi depends on guarding Kapiti Island against invasion by rats, cats, and weasels. Barring disasters, this species will probably survive, but the little spotted kiwi may have to adapt to an environment different from the one its ancestors knew.

Kevin Cook

Kiyi
(Coregonus kiyi)

IUCN: Vulnerable

Class: Actinopterygii
Order: Salmoniformes
Family: Salmonidae
Length: 10 in. (25 cm)
Reproduction: Egg layer
Habitat: Deep open water
Range: Lake Superior, possibly Lake Huron

THE KIYI IS A SPECIES of cisco and a member of a larger group commonly called whitefish that live mainly in the waters of northern latitudes and prefer large, pristine lakes. Some whitefish (such as *Coregonus artedi*) that live in the United States tolerate more fertile conditions and do well.

Centuries ago, Lake Superior, Lake Michigan, Lake Huron, Lake Ontario, and other nearby lakes were untouched by humans. Fish populations, including the ciscoes, flourished in clean water and were unthreatened by non-native fish. With the population explosion and industrial expansion came pollution, overfishing, and predators.

Ciscoes that were marketed under names such as lake herring, chub, tullibee, and bloater,

used to be considered delicacies in the United States before the 1950s. Fishers went out of their way to find new and better equipment to catch these prized fishes. By 1964 the kiyi was eliminated from Lake Ontario, and by the late 1960s and early 1970s there simply were not enough cisco left to justify a catch in any of the Great Lakes.

Pollution in the form of sewage and industrial waste, and predation by the sea lamprey on ciscoes and fish associated with ciscoes (such as lake trout, *Salvelinus namaycush*) added to the problem. Today in North America three species of cisco, including the kiyi, and three other whitefish are either threatened or are on the verge of extinction, and the kiyi is restricted to Lake Superior.

For the kiyi and other ciscoes to make a comeback in the Great Lakes, fishing must be controlled or halted until the fish recover. The decades of pollution in most of the lakes have left a legacy that will have future consequences. However, the Canadian and U. S. governments are at least beginning to curb the discharge of pollutants into the kiyi's only remaining home.

Ciscoes and other whitefish are related to species such as grayling, salmon, and trout,

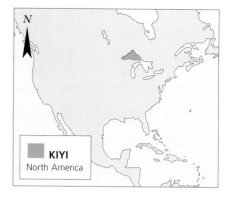

KIYI
North America

(*Salmonidae*), and controversy surrounds their classification and naming. There are 18 North American species of whitefish (including ciscoes) in the subfamily Coregoninae. Some argue that this group should be given family status. Others claim it is a subfamily under the family Salmonidae. There are valid arguments for both positions.

Even before the population crashes of the 1940s, 1950s and 1960s, fisheries people struggled with the appropriate naming of individual cisco species. A catastrophic result of the endangerment of some of these fishes has been their interbreeding with similar and more populous cisco species, creating a muddle of genes. If this process continues, the already fine lines between some of the 14 freshwater species in the genus *Coregonus* will disappear. Unfortunately, many other fish of this genus, including the houting (*Coregonus oxyrinchus*), kiyi (*Coregonus kiyi*), Atlantic whitefish (*Coregonus huntsmani*), Opeonga whitefish (*Coregonus* sp.) and Squanga whitefish (*Coregonus* sp.) are also threatened or endangered.

William E. Manci

Commercial fishing must be controlled if the many endangered fishes of the Great Lakes—including the kiyi—are to avoid extinction.

Western Klipspringer
(Oreotragus oreotragus porteousi)

IUCN: Endangered

Class: Mammalia
Order: Artiodactyla
Family: Bovidae
Subfamily: Bovinae
Tribe: Neotragini
Weight: 22–40 lb. (10–18 kg)
Shoulder height: 18–23 in. (45–60 cm)
Diet: Leaves, twigs, grasses
Gestation period: 210–220 days
Longevity: 12–15 years
Habitat: Rocky outcroppings and thick bush
Range: Nigeria

THE KLIPSPRINGER is a small antelope that dwells amid rock outcroppings and other rugged terrain; these outcroppings occur in the middle of vast plains. But the klipspringer is also found in other mountainous terrain and has been found at altitudes of up to 1,500 feet (400 meters).

Klipspringers tend to live alone or in pairs (a mother with a kid), and are most active at dusk, preferring the shade and shelter of the rocks by day. They will occasionally graze on grass, but they browse on whatever is available, including herbs, plants, and fruits. Klipspringers do not usually drink water, but instead absorb what liquid they need by eating succulent leaves or by licking up early morning dew.

The narrow hooves of the klipspringer seem too small to support its own weight. This antelope, however, is an excellent climber with superb balance.

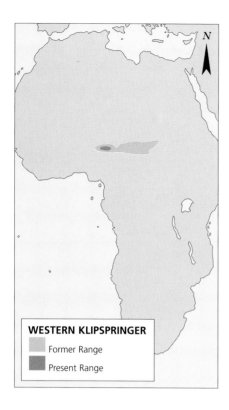

WESTERN KLIPSPRINGER

Former Range

Present Range

Cushioning coat

The klipspringer has a coarse, brittle blue-gray coat. This coat provides a thick cushion against bruises as the animal hops about in its rocky environment. The male has small, parallel horns that are about 6 inches (15.2 centimeters) long. One of its most distinguishing features is its manner of walking and climbing. A klipspringer stands on the tiptoes of its narrow cylindrical hooves, constantly seeming to be in danger of tipping over. Its sense of balance is very well-developed, however, and its excellent climbing ability is unequaled.

The klipspringer's habitat above surrounding plains allows it to observe and sense danger approaching. It makes a loud whistling noise to alert others. This animal also stands in one place for long periods to avoid detection, and its coloration is a camouflage, allowing it to blend into the background.

Klipspringers are strictly monogamous and are usually seen within a few feet of their mate. While one klipspringer eats, the other acts as a lookout. Males are strongly territorial over an area of five to ten acres.

Animal enemies

When klipspringers are frightened, they make roaring sounds with their mouths open. Their most common predator is the leopard, though they are occasionally pursued by a caracal or jackal. Even pythons will attack klipspringers; however, the animals are so agile it is difficult for a python to ambush them.

Klipspringers are found over much of southern and eastern Africa south of the Sahara, and

Although the klipspringer is generally classified as being at lower risk of extinction, the western klipspringer subspecies is classified as endangered.

they are still found in reasonable numbers over their entire range, with one exception. The western klipspringer, a subspecies, is found only in north-central Nigeria. Because of the encroachment in that country by humans, along with heavy hunting, political unrest, and civil wars, the western klipspringer (like much of the other Nigerian wildlife) has severely declined.

Management

Klipspringers do well in captivity; however, they do need careful management. There is now a small population in captivity.

Unfortunately, there is no group of western klipspringers available for captive breeding. A disaster in the wild could wipe out this subspecies. Population estimates of the species place it at less than 2,500 individuals.

Warren D. Thomas

Kokako

(Callaeas cinerea)

ESA: Endangered

IUCN: Endangered

Class: Aves
Order: Passeriformes
Family: Callaeidae
Length: 15 in. (38 cm)
Weight: 7–9½ oz. (195–270 g)
Clutch size: 2–3 eggs
Incubation: 25 days
Diet: Mostly leaves, berries, some insects
Habitat: Evergreen forests
Range: North, South, and Stewart Islands of New Zealand

ENDEMIC TO THE islands of New Zealand, the kokako is bluish gray, with darker wings and tail. It travels by hopping vigorously up a tree trunk, then gliding to another tree. During this process it loses height.

The kokako uses a variety of notes in its loud, pure song.

Recovery efforts

Of three wattle-bird species, the kokako, still exists, though its numbers have declined. There are two subspecies: the North Island kokako (*Callaeas cinerea wilsoni*) and the South Island kokako (*C. cinerea cinerea*).

When the first humans discovered New Zealand, the kokako inhabited many forests across North, South, and Stewart Islands. Polynesian explorers arrived about C.E. 950 and brought rats (*Rattus exulans*) and dogs (*Canis familiaris*) with them. Great Britain claimed the islands and established a settlement in 1840. For 30 years the British and the Maoris, descendants of the first Polynesian settlers, fought bitterly. The wars ended in 1870, but New Zealand had changed forever.

No terrestrial mammals made their home on New Zealand. British colonists established recreational hunting and fishing. Other groups and individuals imported wildlife. Their populations grew explosively, but their success came at the expense of native wildlife. Many New Zealand birds had lost their ability to fly because the absence of predatory mammals and reptiles made life on the ground much safer. When predators arrived, the birds were defenseless. Weasels (*Mustela erminea*) were imported to control rabbits. They were released in about 1890, and soon they preyed on many New Zealand birds, as well as rabbits.

The British cut the native forests partly for the lumber and partly to open the land for sheep grazing. Exotic plants, imported as crops or just for their appearance, escaped cultivation and became nuisance species responsible for degrading much New Zealand habitat. What the plants did not degrade, the exotic animals destroyed.

Within a century of British colonization, New Zealand had lost many of its unique life forms to extinction, and many other species became seriously threatened or endangered.

In the 1960s, New Zealand wildlife officials began a program of recovery. They trapped cats, rats, and weasels and successfully eliminated them from a few small coastal islands. They then captured seriously endangered birds

The future of the kokako is relatively positive. It is expected to survive, although in reduced numbers. Today wildlife specialists are working to preserve its habitat and control exotic predators.

and released them onto islands where exotic predators were not able to reach them.

Scattered population

The South Island kokako is believed to survive in remote areas of South Island and Stewart Island. Kokakos on North Island also still survive, but only in scattered pockets of native forest. Their absence in forests dominated by exotic plants testifies to the impact exotic plant species have on native birds. Kokakos have been transferred to Little Barrier Island and Kapiti Island.

The kokako will probably survive. Wildlife specialists are working to preserve its existing habitat, improve habitat quality, suppress or eradicate exotic predators, and educate people about this problem.

Kevin Cook

KOKAKO
New Zealand

Konye

(Konia eisentrauti)

IUCN: Critically endangered

Class: Actinopterygii
Order: Perciformes
Family: Cichlidae
Length: 3½ in. (9 cm)
Reproduction: Egg layer
Habitat: Open water
Range: Lake Barombi-Mbo, Cameroon

THE WEST AFRICAN crater lake called Barombi-Mbo, in the country of Cameroon, is the only stronghold of the cichlid species commonly called the konye. This small and relatively infertile but deep freshwater lake is only about 1½ miles in diameter (2.4 kilometers), yet is the primary source of food for the village of Barombi on its northern shore. Fishers jealously guard their right to fish the lake and, unfortunately, the konye and a total of ten other threatened and endangered cichlid fishes are sought by them as food.

Reducing threat

Because the konye can be found only in Lake Barombi-Mbo, clearly the species is vulnerable to natural or human-made problems or to prolonged overfishing.

However, the desire on the part of the Barombi villagers to maintain exclusive fishing rights on the lake may work to the advantage of the konye and other cichlids. Because the villagers have been able to maintain a workable balance between their required catch and the natural supply of fish and have resisted overfishing, government officials are hopeful that this balance can be continued.

Along with measures to prevent pollution in the lake, as well as the introduction of harmful non-native fishes such as the large and aggressively predatory Nile perch (*Lates niloticus*), conservationists would like to continue the ban on fishing by other villages and to educate the people of Barombi about the delicate balance of the ecosystem they currently exploit.

Despite their seemingly endless physical and behavioral differences, cichlids possess many similar physical characteristics. All cichlids have a fairly flattened appearance and are rounder than other streamlined and torpedo-like fish. Most of these fish have broad, hardened mouth parts used to scrape algae from surfaces or crush hard foods.

Digestion

As well as teeth located on the jaws, these fish also have hundreds of teeth situated on a platelike bone at the base of the mouth and throat to hold and process food items; these teeth found within the throat are known as pharyngeal teeth. Cichlids also have a long gut to further process and absorb nutrients from their food. The length of the gut is often more than two-and-a-half times the length of the fish, which grows up to 3½ inches (9 centimeters).

A distinctive characteristic of the konye, as well as of all other cichlids, is the long, spiny, protective dorsal fin on the back that can extend from just behind the head all the way to the tail section of the body. The dorsal fin segment near the tail is usually longer than the segment near the head. In many cichlids, the segment near the tail carries a dark blotch called a tilapia mark. The konye's dorsal fin does not carry a tilapia mark.

Appearance

The konye is different in appearance from other cichlids that live in Lake Barombi-Mbo. It has a sloping face and forehead and a horizontal mouth rather than one that is upturned. Body color patterning is very distinctive, with a row of large dark blotches down the back, a row of connected dark blotches on the sides from the cheeks to the base of the tail fin, and lighter patches below and behind the eye and on the snout. This patchwork of color covers a lighter background that is slightly darker on the back and lighter on the belly. The body and gill covers are well scaled. The cheeks have some scales but the rest of the head is bare.

The konye eats mayflies and various kinds of plant material. Using filtering devices on the gills, called gill rakers, the konye can remove floating algae from the water as it passes through the mouth cavity and then flows out past the gills. Other plants are scraped from rocks and parts are torn from the stem. Some konye are also known to eat fish eggs.

Ways of caring

The konye engages in a form of parental care called mouth brooding. After eggs are laid and fertilized, one or both of the parents picks up the eggs and protects them in the mouth cavity during the incubation period, which lasts from a week to ten days.

Parental care continues beyond hatching. Although the juvenile fish swim free, they keep close to the parent's mouth. At the first sign of danger, the parent opens its mouth and the newly hatched fish scurry inside, where they are protected from attack. This form of protection ensures maximum survival of the young. The konye produces relatively few young, only about 60 per female per cycle.

William E. Manci

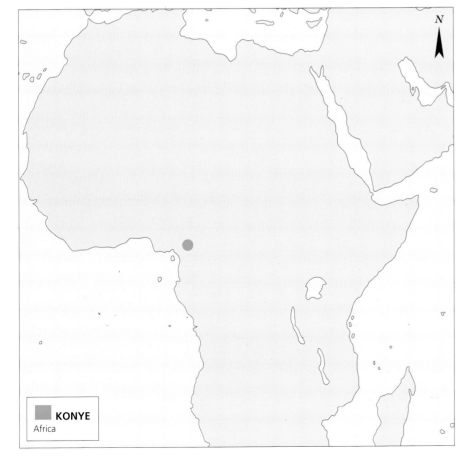

KONYE
Africa

Korrigum

(Damaliscus lunatus korrigum)

IUCN: Vulnerable

Class: Mammalia
Order: Artiodactyla
Family: Bovidae
Subfamily: Bovinae
Tribe: Alcelaphini
Weight: 330–375 lb.
(150–170 kg)
Shoulder height: 43–51 in.
(110–130 cm)
Diet: Grasses, leaves, and twigs
Gestation period: 225–240 days
Longevity: 12–15 years
Habitat: Scrub thornbush to
semi-arid grassland
Range: Senegal to
western Sudan

SINCE THE LATE 1960s, drought has been an almost constant reality for the people living in Senegal, Africa's westernmost nation. Despite this, wildlife thrives here, primarily because a wide range of vegetation is available. Senegal has large areas set aside to protect elephants, lions, and other animals, but poaching is still a problem. It is here that the korrigum can be found.

A hartebeest

Also known as the Senegal hartebeest, the korrigum is part of the genus *Damaliscus*, which is made up of smaller hartebeests with lyre-shaped horns. It has the typical brownish tawny coat, with black or dark flashings on the hip, shoulder, and face.

Both the male and female of the species are armed with horns, the male having much heavier horns than the female.

In its habits the korrigum is principally a grazer, found from open grasslands to scrub areas. It is occasionally found in ones and twos, but is most often seen in herds of between 15 and 20 individuals. Unfortunately, the korrigum is regarded as a nuisance by the people of Senegal and Sudan. Searching for food, it comes into the fields and grazing lands of farmers. These intrusions have multiplied during recent severe droughts. Naturally, the local human inhabitants do not take kindly to such intrusions by wild ungulates (even-toed, hoofed animals) such as the korrigum.

As with other hartebeests, korrigums rely on their ability to run away from danger in order to escape predation. Not only do these animals move particularly quickly but, like other hartebeests, they have a great deal of stamina and can outrun many predators. Korrigums will sometimes associate with other animals of the plain, such as local gazelles and even Cape buffalo.

Drought and poaching

The area of Africa in which the korrigum's habitat is found has been heavily used by people. Civil strife has disrupted the lands in the animal's range, and severe drought and poaching have combined to bring the korrigum population down to an alarmingly low level. For these reasons, the korrigum is considered to be a threatened animal. The species still exists in small pockets, although its range once ran from Senegal right through to western Sudan in an almost unbroken stretch. Its numbers now total less than 5,000, divided into six separate populations.

The korrigum and its relatives, the topis and the tsessebes (or sassabies), have been held in captivity, but only on a limited basis: they do only moderately well in a captive environment. At present, no captive population can support the wild korrigum population. With dwindling numbers and its habitat afflicted by drought and politics, the korrigum's future is looking dim.

Warren D. Thomas

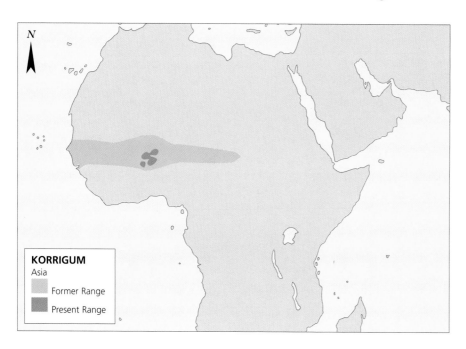

KORRIGUM
Asia

Former Range

Present Range

Kouprey
(Bos sauveli)

ESA: Endangered

IUCN: Critically endangered

Class: Mammalia
Order: Artiodactyla
Family: Bovidae
Subfamily: Bovinae
Tribe: Bovini
Weight: 1,543–1,985 lb.
(700–900 kg)
Shoulder height: 67–75 in.
(170–190 cm)
Diet: Grasses, leaves, twigs, and shoots
Habitat: Open forest
Range: Southeast Asia

The kouprey used to roam the open forest, grazing on land that boasted an abundance of the grasses, leaves, and twigs that made up its diet. Now these areas have been drastically changed by human beings.

THE KOUPREY, OR giant Cambodian forest ox, is a remarkable animal. It is one of the largest cattle forms found in Southeast Asia and is thought to range from Cambodia into Laos, Vietnam (although this is questionable today), and Thailand.

The kouprey has a distinctive appearance. It has a dewlap (a fold of skin that hangs from the nape of the neck) that is quite large. Bulls are dark in color, with white legs and yellowish horns. The horns have ribbed rings at the base and curve out, down, and then up again in a corkscrew fashion. The tips are frayed. Cows and offspring are lighter in color than the bulls, and the horns are more lyre-shaped.

Koupreys will inhabit any low rolling hill country if it is covered with patches of dense, deciduous forest, open forest, or monsoon forest, along with some open grassland. They are grazers and, when necessary, do some browsing among plants and trees as well. Koupreys are often found in the wild in the company of eld deer, sambar deer, or hog deer. They are also seen with herds of banteng. When they are not with other animals, koupreys are found in herds of 20 or more, usually consisting of one or two adult males; the rest are females and their young. The herd, as is common with wild cattle, tend to be led by an old female.

Solitary old bulls

Kouprey herds do not have a highly structured social organization. Instead, they split up and come back together again, which may be a reaction to the available food supply. All-male herds are found occasionally, but old bulls commonly appear to be solitary. The mating period occurs during April, with young being born in December and January. The female kouprey and her young usually remain by themselves. The female leaves the herd to give birth, and tends to stay by herself for a month or so before returning. This is quite different from the behavior of the gaur or banteng. In these species, the female with a newborn calf will remain with the herd.

Changed habitat

The local human population has burned the land in which the kouprey roams in order to clear fields for its own needs. However, these clearances generally take place at the time when the grass is young and tender shoots are abundant, so not only is the kouprey's range reduced, but its food source is destroyed as well. This has had a devastating effect on the animal.

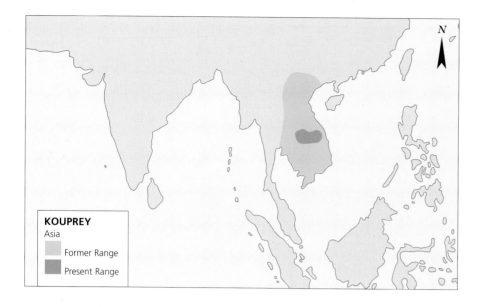

KOUPREY
Asia

Former Range

Present Range

Today, political conditions have produced civil unrest and warfare over the entire range of the kouprey. Experts doubt whether any pure-bred koupreys still exist in the wild at all. Crude estimates place the wild population at between 100 and 300 individuals. However, some animal experts question whether this is a genuine population, or one that is a hybrid resulting from crossbreeding with feral cattle, bantengs, gaur, or even zebus. In 1937 one live animal, a male, was obtained and taken to a zoo in Paris, where it lived for a number of years. However, a mate was never found, and no others were ever brought into captivity. There have been several expeditions to try to bring more animals out of the wild; however, these efforts have all failed.

Because the kouprey population was probably low to begin with, the constant hunting pressures and destruction of the kouprey's habitat have only made its situation worse. Since there are no captive animals, there is no population to fall back on to replenish the species. If pure captive populations could be obtained, it is possible that the kouprey could survive into the future. Otherwise, its future is by no means assured.

Warren D. Thomas

See also Banteng and Gaur.

Kululu

(Sarotherodon steinbachi)

IUCN: Critically endangered

Class: Actinopterygii
Order: Perciformes
Family: Cichlidae
Length: 5 in. (13 cm)
Reproduction: Egg layer
Habitat: Shallow inshore waters
Range: Lake Barombi-Mbo, Cameroon

THE CRATER LAKE called Barombi-Mbo in the West African country of Cameroon is the only home of the cichlid species known locally as the kululu. This modest and relatively sterile but deep freshwater lake is only about 1½ miles (2.4 kilometers) in diameter, yet is the principal source of food for the village of Barombi on its northern shore. Fishermen of this village protect their right to fish the lake and, unfortunately, the kululu and a total of ten other threatened cichlid fishes are sought by them as their best source of high-quality protein.

Because the kululu can be found only in Lake Barombi-Mbo, this species is considered vulnerable to both natural and artificial catastrophes as well as to sustained overfishing. However, the desire on the part of the Barombi villagers to maintain exclusive fishing rights on the lake may work to the benefit of the kululu and other cichlids. Because the villagers have been able to maintain a viable balance between their required catch and the natural supply of fish for many decades and have resisted over-fishing, Cameroon is hopeful that this balance can be maintained. Along with measures to alleviate pollution in the lake and prevent the invasion of non-native fish like the large and aggressively predatory Nile perch (*Lates niloticus*), conservationists look to continue the ban on fishing by other villages and to educate the people of Barombi about the fragile equilibrium of the ecosystem they are using.

A distinctive trait of the kululu as well as of all other cichlids is the long, spiny, defensive dorsal fin on the back that can extend from behind the head all the way to the tail section of the body. The dorsal fin portion near the tail is usually deeper than the segment near the head. In many cichlids the segment near the tail carries a dark blotch called a tilapia mark.

Well-shaped

Despite a multitude of distinct physical and behavioral variations, cichlids share many similar physical attributes. All cichlids present a fairly flattened and more round look (like a plate on its edge) than other more streamlined and torpedolike fish. The kululu has large eyes and is a visual feeder. Most have broad, hardened mouthparts that they use to scour algae from surfaces or crush hard food items. In addition to teeth on the jaws, these fish have hundreds of teeth on a platelike bone at the base of the mouth and throat to hold and prepare food items for digestion. These teeth within the throat are called pharyngeal teeth. Any nutrients in the food that cichlids swallow are processed and absorbed by their long alimentary canal, which may be over 2.5 times the length of the fish itself.

Other than the physical characteristics that it shares with other cichlids, the kululu has few distinctive features. The adult kululu has no markings on the body but does display a uniform pearly yellowish coloration, with shades of gray-blue on the back and cream on the belly. Growing up to 5 inches (13 centimeters) in length, the kululu is scaled except for the gill covers and portions of the face, chin, and throat.

Incubation

The kululu has been observed engaged in an activity called mouthbrooding. After eggs are

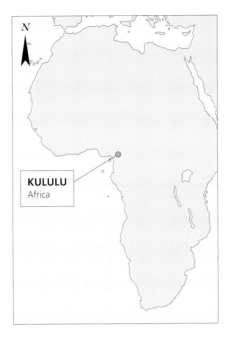

laid by a female and fertilized by a male, one or both of the parents (depending on the species) picks up the eggs with the mouth and guards them in a chamber in the mouth cavity where oxygenated water is pumped past them. The parent incubates the eggs until

Like the kululu, the cichlid *Sarotheradon mossambica* of Mozambique protects its eggs and offspring by keeping them in its mouth.

they hatch, after a period of one to two weeks. Even after the fish hatch, the free-swimming offspring continue to rely on the parent for protection. At the first sign of a predator or some other threat, the offspring race to their parent, where they immediately re-enter the parent's mouth. This protective behavior increases the chances that offspring will survive to adulthood.

The kululu eats a wide range of food items. Decaying organic matter, sponge spicules, floating algae called diatoms, plant hairs, and terrestrial insects have been found in the stomach of this fish.

Scientists have observed the kululu shoveling a mixture of sand and food into its mouth, removing items with its pharyngeal teeth, and spitting out the sand. However the pharyngeal teeth will eventually be worn down by this type of activity.

William E. Manci

See also Fissi, Konye, Myakamyaka, Leka keppe, Otjikota tilapia, and Unga.

LADIES' TRESSES

Order: Liliopsida

Family: Orchidaceae

Ladies' tresses (*Spiranthes*) belong to one of the largest families of flowering plants, the Orchidaceae. These are perennial herbs with complex and usually beautiful flowers. The *Spiranthes* form mutually beneficial relationships with soil microfungi called mycorrhizal associations. A lack of these fungi in the growing medium makes it difficult to cultivate the *Spiranthes*.

The name for the genus means "coiled flowers," which refers to the typical spiral arrangement of the flowers around the stem.

Canelo Hills Ladies' Tresses

(Spiranthes delitescens)

ESA: Endangered

IUCN: Endangered

Height: Up to 20 in. (51 cm) tall
Stems: Slender, erect
Leaves: 5–10 present, slender and grass like, occurring basally
Flowers: July when temperatures are 60–100° F (16–38° C). Twisted spikelike inflorescence contains up to 40 small white flowers
Pollination: By bees
Habitat: Wet meadow areas (ciénegas), mixed with grasses and sedges, usually at heights of around 5,000 ft. (1,500 m)
Range: Arizona

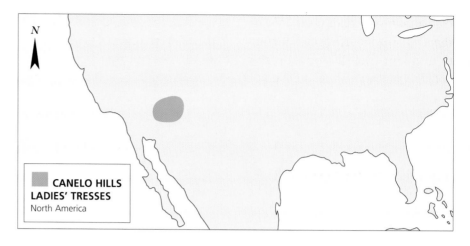

CANELO HILLS LADIES' TRESSES
North America

Spiranthes delitescens was originally thought to be a form of *Spiranthes graminea* and it was not until 1990 that the Canelo Hills (or Madrean) ladies' tresses was actually recognized as a distinct species of orchid. *Spiranthes diluvialis* is a more northerly version of a very similar species. *Spiranthes delitescens* differs from *Spiranthes graminea* in the chromosome number (74 as opposed to 44), and it also differs from both of the other two plants in floral morphology and several characters relating to the sepals. It is believed that Madrean ladies' tresses is a result of several hybridization events (hybridization to produce fertile offspring is very common within the orchid family) followed by genetic failures giving rise to multiple copies of chromosomes and finally geographic isolation. All these factors together will give rise to a new species. The original parental types are unknown. Once this species was officially recognized it was apparent that it was already critically low in numbers.

Currently there are four known sites for this species in Arizona, of which three are privately owned and grazed. The Nature Conservancy owns the fourth site. One of the privately owned sites shows a worrying trend. The orchid is very abundant, which at first seems good. However on further investigation it becomes clear that the orchid is abundant in only one area of the site. It is absent from other apparently suitable habitat adjacent to the site. So far, it is not known why the Madrean ladies' tresses is unable to colonize the remainder of this land.

Of the four sites where it is present, two are showing a decline in numbers. This species is very intolerant of competition, and one of the threats comes from competition posed by successional changes within the habitat. This plant benefits from the sporadic action of fires keeping competitors at bay. Other threats to the survival of this species arise from grazing. Cultivation has proven problematical because of the fungal symbiont that is present with all members of the orchid family. Without the fungus the plant will not grow, and the species of fungus in this partnership is still unknown. Some limited growth has taken place in the laboratory, but this has been to investigate how the plant develops. As yet there is no way to cultivate this orchid in sufficient numbers for transplantation exercises. While there is still insufficient information about the biology of this species, it will continue to be difficult to decide on the best course of action to ensure its survival.

Navasota Ladies' Tresses
(Spiranthes parksii)

ESA: Endangered

IUCN: Rare

Height: 8–12 in. (20–30 cm)
Stems: Simple and slender
Leaves: Linear—usually absent during flowering. Grasslike in appearance and basal
Flowers: Late October to early November (apparently not all plants flower annually). Cream-colored, spiraling loosely around stem, side petals have green central stripe and, directly below, the bracts have pointed white tips. Petals obovate with oval lip
Pollination: Self-fertilization or by bees
Habitat: Uplands of Post Oak Savanna in eroded drainage of the Navasota River Valley where elevation is in excess of 260 ft. (80 m)
Range: Texas

NAVASOTA LADIES' tresses is endemic to Texas. It was first described in 1947, but prior to that date it had been thought of as a minor variant of *Spiranthes gracilis*. The Navasota ladies' tresses orchid was not rediscovered in the wild until 1978. It is found in the Post Oak Savanna of east-central Texas. This habitat is found in old drainage systems, and the plant particularly favors open clearings within woods that are generally maintained by certain elements in the soil or by animal grazing. These sites have the characteristic features of mature woodland.

This plant is known from only 30 different populations with a total number of individuals of some 6,000. Many populations are believed to have been lost due to increased urbanization (particularly the recent increases in size of both Texas A&M University, and the towns of Bryan and College Station) and from damage caused by oil and lignite exploration. All currently known populations of the plant are on privately held land.

One of the main obstacles to the conservation of this species is lack of knowledge. Extensive studies and research are required, particularly into artificial cultivation. Wild plants do not survive transplantation and all attempts at growing plants from seed and cuttings have failed. This is probably partly due to the mycorrhizal nature of orchids, which means that orchids will grow only in association with the correct fungal partner. When this partner is absent the seeds will rapidly die from poor food reserves. Current conservation attempts are concentrating on attempting to buy up the land on which the known populations occur. This will allow the setting up of reserves that can be managed for the benefit of the orchid. If purchase attempts prove unsuccessful, then it is hoped that suitable management and conservation agreements can be arranged with the appropriate landowners.

Safe havens
Currently there is very little problem from plant collectors, however, as the rarity value of the plant increases, this will become more of an issue. Reserves are particularly sought in Brazos and Grimes Counties, as areas there hold the two largest populations.

It is felt that in the short term the establishment of two reserves that are safe from threat will be sufficient to hold the population at current levels until further work can be done to understand more fully the biology of this species. The main research currently being undertaken involves botanists from Texas A&M University, in College Station.

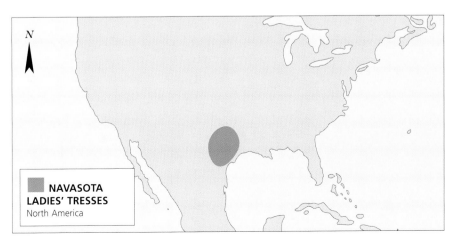

NAVASOTA LADIES' TRESSES
North America

Ute Ladies' Tresses

(Spiranthes diluvialis)

ESA: Threatened

IUCN: Vulnerable

Height: 8–20 in. (20–50 cm) tall

Stems: Single 8–20 in. (20–50 cm)

Leaves: ½ in. (1 cm) wide, up to 12 in. (30 cm) long, longest at base. Leaves persist during flowering

Flowers: August to early September. Inflorescence of few to many white or ivory flowers in a spike of three ranked spirals at top of stem. Sepals and petals ascending from or perpendicular to stem

Pollination: By bees

Habitat: Wet meadows fed by groundwater, and valley bottoms

Range: Colorado, Nevada, and Utah

UTE LADIES' TRESSES orchid was only recognized as a distinct species in 1984. The plant is found commonly in wet meadows that are fed by groundwater discharge, and it is also typically found in any damp alkaline con-

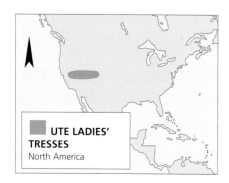

UTE LADIES' TRESSES
North America

ditions. The plant is often found with its stems emerging from shallow water. This species has been collected from only 10 sites, some of which have subcritical populations. In recent years three of these sites seem no longer to support this species. These three sites have suffered from an increase in urbanization, an increase in levels of grazing, and water inundation from Utah Lake. All three of these events have completely changed the respective habitats into areas that are no longer suitable for Ute ladies' tresses. Many areas of suitable habitat do exist, so if cultivation were ever successfully carried out, a reintroduction plan could be rapidly implemented.

Difficult to identify

It is possible that this species is underreported due to its similarities to other members of the *Spiranthes* genus, particularly *Spiranthes graminea* and *Spiranthes delitescens*. Fertile hybrids are also very common within this genus, and this makes identification more difficult still. The main difference between this and other *Spiranthes* species is in the floral characters. This plant shows intermediate characteristics between several different species, but due to its relatively widespread and separate distribution it was decided in 1984 to recognize it as a genuine species in its own right.

Since 1995 a recovery plan for this species has been in operation. This is mostly concerned with habitat preservation and trying to persuade private owners of sites to manage the areas for the benefit of the orchid, and to enter into conservation agreements.

Ute ladies' tresses prefers a damp environment and is occasionally found with its stems emerging from water.

There is an attempt to get adequate cultivation techniques in place so that sufficiently large numbers can be grown to reintroduce the species to the wild.

One area of conservation practice for this species is unusual. The orchid is pollinated by bees. To help recovery, an insecticide-free buffer zone is maintained around the plant's habitat during the flowering season. Nesting sites for bees are subject to conservation orders. However, there are many different suitable nesting sites.

With proper management and conservation over the short-term, Ute ladies' tresses should manage to recover from its threatened status.

Gordon Rutter

LANGURS

Class: Mammalia

Order: Primates

Family: Cercopithecidae

Subfamily: Colobinae

Langurs are part of the vast monkey family and are found in Asia. Monkeys are a complicated animal group to classify as there are so many categories into which they may be divided. Within the langurs, there is more than one species group and some 16 species exist overall.

Like other colobine monkeys (such as the colobuses of Madagascar), langurs have a highly specialized digestive tract that permits them to eat large quantities of leaves (explaining their other common name, leaf monkey). Leafy vegetation is hard to digest, so langurs have what is called a sacculated stomach. The stomach contains large quantities of bacteria that break down cellulose, the main nutrient in leaves. The langur's digestive system is similar to that of cows and other members of the cattle family.

When they are not eating, langurs spend much of their time resting in order to digest food.

Langurs are considered to be more primitive members of the primate family, such as New World monkeys and apes.

Black-shanked Douc Langur
(Pygathrix nemaeus nigripes)

IUCN: Endangered

Red-shanked Douc Langur
(Pygathrix nemaeus nemaeus)

ESA: Endangered

IUCN: Endangered

Weight: Approximately 15–22 lb. (7–10 kg)

Head/body length: 21–25 in. (53–72 cm)

Habitat: Tropical rain forest; gallery and monsoon forests

Range: Southeast Asia

DOUC LANGURS LIVE in the lush tropical rain forests of Laos and Vietnam. Reports that they have also been seen on Hainan Island, across the Gulf of Tonkin near China, have not yet been confirmed. Douc langurs are among the larger monkeys, with no size difference between the sexes. These distinctive primates are split into two subspecies: the red-shanked douc langur, which lives in central Vietnam and eastern Laos, and the southerly (and less common) black-shanked douc langur. Their fur follows a well-defined pattern that features a variety of hues: brown, yellow, orange, white, black, and gray.

Although the douc langur has a four-footed walking style on the ground, it is almost completely arboreal, transporting itself through the forest by frequent leaps. These leaps are as long as 15 to 18 feet (5 to 6 meters), with the arms stretched above the head and the hind limbs making initial contact with the landing point. These monkeys live in groups of three to eleven individuals, with a ratio of at least one male to two females. Females mature sexually at 4 years and males mature at 5 years of age.

Distinctive colorations

The red-shanked douc langur (also known as the Cochin China monkey) has a distinctive coat. It is white and black, with an orange band that occasionally

Monkeys, such as the red-shanked douc langur, were once used for target practice by soldiers in Southeast Asia. Conversion of forest to farmland and the ever-increasing human population continue to be problems for primates in this part of the world.

Douc langurs are among the larger monkeys. They are split between two subspecies: the black-shanked and the red-shanked douc langurs.

separates these colors between the throat and the chest. The face is also white, fringed with orange, and has a speckled gray crown. The black-shanked douc langur differs primarily from the red-shanked variety in its color; there is more black speckling on the gray forearm and black shank. Its facial skin is blue, with a reddish yellow tinge to the muzzle.

Conservation

Because of the political instability in the region, the status of these langurs in the wild is not well-known. The population of the red-shanked douc langur is thought to be larger than that of the black-shanked variety, although some biologists do not separate these two subspecies.

However, Vietnam now has a national conservation strategy with a few reserves to better protect these rare monkeys.

Years of warfare have taken their toll on both douc langur populations. Bombing and chemical defoliants (substances that kill vegetation) ruined large sections of langur habitat. The langurs that survive number less than 25,000, and continuing habitat destruction and hunting will keep them endangered unless action is taken.

Surveys needed

Red-shanked doucs have been captured and bred in the United States and Europe. In 1985 there were reportedly 58 of these animals; that number is undoubtedly much higher now, but more surveys are desperately needed, particularly in Laos, where the population size is not known.

Javan Langur

(Presbytis comata)

IUCN: Endangered

Weight: 13–19 lb. (6–8.6 kg)
Head-body length: 17–24 in. (43–60 cm)
Tail length: 22–33 in. (55–83 cm)
Diet: Leaves, fruit, buds, flowers, seeds, stems
Habitat: Tropical rain forest
Range: Java

THE JAVAN LANGUR, or Javan leaf monkey, also called the grizzled sureli, has black hands. The crown is black or brown, and the rest of the upper side of its body is gray, dotted with black or brown. The animal's underparts are white. This rare species is restricted to western Java, where it lives in remaining patches of evergreen tropical rain forest.

The Javan langur is known for its extraordinary leaping ability. Like other langurs, it dwells in small groups dominated by a single male. Since much of its range has been deforested it is, no doubt, endangered. The pressures of Java's increasing human population make it virtually impossible to create any new reserves for the protection of this monkey.

Reserves

The biggest populations of Javan langurs live on two reserves, one at Ujang Kulon/Gunung Honje, the other at Gunung Halimun. However, the protection currently offered needs upgrading. Extinction may occur unless the habitat is preserved.

Mentawai Langur

(Presbytis potenziani)

ESA: Threatened

IUCN: Vulnerable

Weight: 12–16 lb. (5.5–7 kg)
Head-body length: 17–23 in. (44–58 cm)
Habitat: Rain forests and mangrove forests
Range: Indonesia

THE MENTAWAI LANGUR, or Mentawai leaf monkey, has a small ridgelike crest on the crown of its head. Its upperparts and tail are black, the pubic region is yellowish white, and its brow, cheeks, chin, throat, upper chest, and sometimes the tip of the tail are whitish. The rest of its underparts and sometimes its collar are reddish orange, brown, or occasionally whitish orange.

Group living

This monkey is an important member of the unique primate fauna found on the Mentawai Islands. Most Mentawai langurs are found on Siberut island. Although little has been learned about the ecology of these

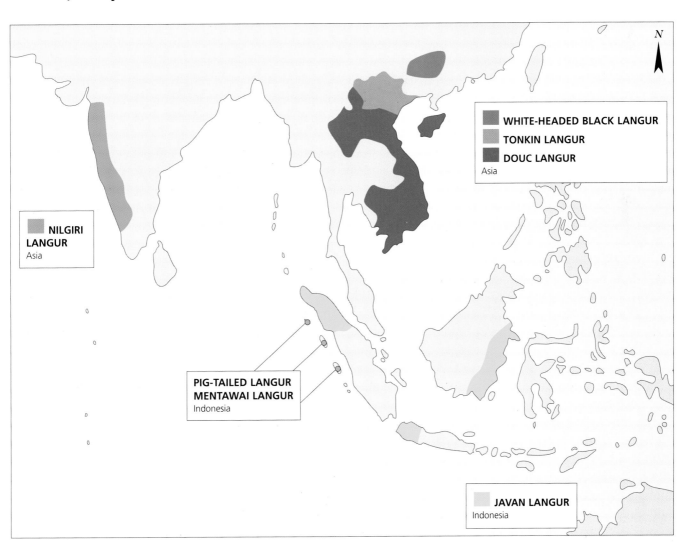

NILGIRI LANGUR
Asia

WHITE-HEADED BLACK LANGUR
TONKIN LANGUR
DOUC LANGUR
Asia

PIG-TAILED LANGUR
MENTAWAI LANGUR
Indonesia

JAVAN LANGUR
Indonesia

langurs, one research team in the 1970s documented that they form small monogamous groups in which one male and one female bond.

Deforestation and hunting are the chief reasons for the decline of the Mentawi langur, except on the island of Siberut. That entire island has now been designated a biosphere reserve by UNESCO. The langurs on the other islands are deliberately poisoned, as they are considered a pest by banana growers. In addition, logging and the harvesting of rattan are degrading what is left of this langur's habitat.

There are plans to expand the 25-square mile (65-square kilometer) Teitei Batti Game Sanctuary for a few species of primates. If successful, they may survive. The IUCN–The World Conservation Union has estimated that less than 25,000 Mentawai langurs remain.

Nilgiri Langur

(Trachypithecus johnii)

IUCN: Vulnerable

Weight: 21–30 lb. (9.5–13.6 kg)
Head/body length: 20–30 in. (51–76 cm)
Tail length: 28–38 in. (71–97 cm)
Diet: Mostly leaves
Habitat: Evergreen and riverine forest; deciduous woodland
Range: Southern India

THE NILGIRI LANGUR has blackish brown fur with a gray-speckled, short-haired rump. The gray color of the rump some-

times extends to the thighs and tail. It also has a purple face with white sideburns.

This langur has suffered at the hands of poachers for years and is now confined to isolated patches of the forest. It is almost entirely arboreal and is an excellent leaper. It appears to live in small, single-male groups.

Widespread deforestation has drastically reduced India's moist evergreen forest. Although logging is selective at present, other projects, such as hydroelectric plants, new roads, and railroads pose serious threats to the habitat of the Nilgiri langur.

Pig-tailed Langur

(Simias concolor)

ESA: Endangered

IUCN: Endangered

Weight: 15 lb. (6.8 kg)
Head/body length: 20 in. (51 cm)
Tail length: 6 in. (15 cm)
Diet: Leaves, fruits, and berries
Habitat: Rain forest, secondary forest, mangrove forest
Range: Mentawai Islands, Indonesia

THE PIG-TAILED LANGUR is also known as the simakobu. It is a medium-sized monkey with a stocky build and a short, almost hairless tail. This langur is unique among the leaf-eating monkeys because of its short, piglike tail. There is little difference in size between the sexes. Both males and females weigh around 15

pounds (6.8 kilograms) when adult. The blackish brown coat has some pale spots on the nape, shoulder, and upper back; the facial skin is black, bordered with whitish hairs, and one in four individuals are cream buff mixed with brown.

Groupings

The social organization of this langur is relatively simple, usually consisting of an adult pair with up to three young. In some areas, however, there are much larger groups with up to four adult females. While there is little information on reproduction, births have been observed during June and July. The family groups tend to be territorial, and when they encounter another group, the males start giving loud, but brief, calls to mark their borders. The pig-tailed langur is inconspicuous. It moves and feeds quietly and is heard only rarely. It is extensively hunted by the local Mentawai people, who have taken to hunting the simakobu on Saturday in order to provide ritual meat for their Sunday sabbath. Their modern hunting method is effective; air rifles loaded with poisoned pellets have replaced traditional bows and arrows. Although the use of air rifles is officially banned, the law is not enforced.

Defence

No protected reserve of any kind has been established for the pig-tailed langur. Its only defense is to conceal itself and remain quiet, or to make a speedy retreat along the ground.

This unique species is ranked by the IUCN's Action Plan for Asian Primate Conservation

The Nilgiri langur is also known as John's leaf monkey. Its habitat has been drastically reduced, partly because India's rain forests have been poorly studied and are not widely protected.

(1987–91) as one of the eight most highly endangered primates in Asia. Less than 10,000 individuals in the species remain, and no section of this population is safe from harm. It is the only member of its genus, making it even more irreplaceable. The pig-tailed langur is under great pressure, from hunting, from the commercial exploitation of the forests for logging, and from the conversion of land for agricultural use.

Tonkin Langur
(Trachypithecus francoisi)

ESA: Endangered

IUCN: Vulnerable

Weight: 13 lb. (6 kg)
Head-body length: 20–27 in. (51–68 cm)
Tail length: 32–36 in. (81–91 cm)
Diet: Mostly leaves
Habitat: Tropical monsoon forest
Range: Northern Vietnam and Laos, south-central China

ALSO KNOWN AS Francois' leaf monkey, there are six known subspecies of this langur that are all distinct from one another, and all endangered. In some areas these subspecies live together but do not interbreed, a behavior which may eventually reclassify them as separate species. Members of the genus *Trachypithecus* are called brow-ridged langurs. The most seriously endangered subspecies, *T. francoisi leucocephalus*, has been reduced to a mere 400 individuals in the Chinese province of Guangxi.

The Tonkin langur's coat is glossy black with white running from the corners of its mouth to its ears. It has a pointed crest and weighs around 13 pounds (6 kilograms) when adult. There is not a great deal of information available about these primates in Vietnam, although with forest cover reportedly reduced from 44 percent in 1943 to 21 percent at present, it is probable that this species is under threat.

Rapid increases in the local human population have made the situation for this langur much worse. Vietnam does have a National Conservation Strategy, but no primates are adequately protected under this program.

Sarah Dart and Gregory Lee

Ashy-headed Laughingthrush

(Garrulax cinereifrons)

IUCN: Vulnerable

Class: Aves
Order: Passeriformes
Family: Sylviidae
Subfamily: Garrulacinae
Clutch size: 3 eggs (single nest)
Diet: Insects
Habitat: Wet forests
Range: Sri Lanka

DARK BIRDS IN DARK forests can be hard to find. When those birds are also scarce it is possible to understand how 132 years could pass between discovering a bird and finding the first nest.

The ashy-headed laughingthrush was first described as a species in 1852. A plain-colored bird, it has dark, reddish brown upperparts and noticeably paler, grayer underparts. Its head is gray and its beak is black. Reliable size measurements have never been made, but the species was reported to be larger than the red-vented bulbul (*Pycnonotus cafer*) and smaller than a common myna (*Acridotheres tristis*), which is about 9 inches (23 centimeters) long. A denizen of forests in Sri Lanka's wet zone, the ashy-headed laughingthrush once occupied both lowland and montane forests up to about 5,000 feet (1,524 meters).

Until 1984 no one had seen and reported this bird's nest. That year, however, some observers discovered a single nest about 40 miles (64 kilometers) southwest of Colombo, Sri Lanka's capital city. The nest was in dense undergrowth beneath tall trees that grew on a steep hillside. There were three eggs inside. More than one bird gathered leaves and sticks, depositing them in a tree fork about 15 feet (4.6 meters) above ground. Rain interfered with access, so the discoverers could not follow the progress of the nest on a daily basis. All three eggs eventually disappeared and predation was suspected. Apart from discovering the first known nest of a species, however, this observation was important because it revealed helpers at the nest. At least three birds were seen to help build it. Nest helpers are known from other families such as jays and crows, but laughingthrushes are a different type of bird.

Through the years, ornithologists have classified babblers as both a discrete family and as a subfamily of the Old World flycatchers (*Muscicapidae*). A 1990 reclassification names the laughingthrushes as a subfamily of the Old World warblers (*Sylviidae*), but there is no agreement yet on the correct system of classification for these birds.

About 50 species make up the laughingthrush genus *Garrulax*. Some of these species are good singers and so are in demand in the cagebird market. This group, however, occurs only in Asia, with single species inhabiting India, China, Southeast Asia, or the East Indies. The ashy-headed laughingthrush is unique to the Sri Lankan wet zone.

Rain inhibits observation

Mountains in south-central Sri Lanka radically affect rainfall distribution on the island. As winds come ashore, they sweep up the mountains, which cool the air, and cause rain to fall. This part of Sri Lanka receives up to 200 inches (508 centimeters) of precipitation each year. The forests of the wet zone are dense with vegetation as a result.

Access can be severely hampered by bad weather, which further explains how this bird could remain unrecorded for more than a century.

The ashy-headed laughingthrush was first described in 1852, yet it was 132 years before the first nest was found. It took so long to locate these dark birds because they live in equally dark forests and are scarce to begin with.

The ashy-headed laughingthrush inhabits these forests of the wet zone, where it behaves in much the same way as other babblers. It moves close to the ground in small bands and stays in contact with other laughingthrushes by calling and making small chattering sounds. Sri Lanka's forests have grown quieter over the years as the numbers of ashy-headed laughingthrushes have declined.

Agriculture in the forest

Sri Lankan forests have been replaced by plantation crops and trees such as the eucalyptus, which the ashy-headed laughingthrush has shown no ability to accept. Some primary forest has been set aside, but protecting the forest has not been easy. Poor people desperate for cooking and heating fuel cut firewood in the reserve. Simple firewood cutting is severe enough to damage the primary forests. The cutting has degraded the primary forest and so threatens the ashy-headed laughingthrush. Preserving the laughingthrush depends on saving the forests of Sri Lanka. Preserving the forests may necessitate the introduction of an inexpensive fuel substitute to replace firewood.

Kevin Cook

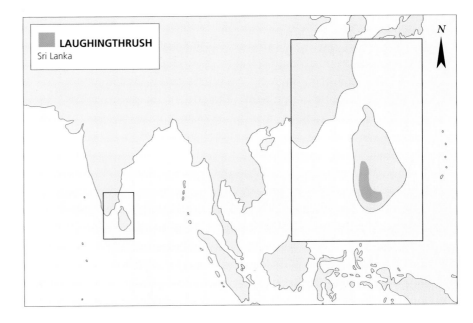

LAUGHINGTHRUSH
Sri Lanka

N

Lechwe

(Kobus leche)

ESA: Threatened

IUCN: Lower risk

Order: Artiodactyla
Family: Bovidae
Subfamily: Bovinae
Weight: 154–287 lb.
(70–130 kg)
Shoulder height: 36–43 in.
(90–110 cm)
Longevity: 15–18 years
Range: Southern Democratic
Republic of Congo, Northern
Botswana, Zambia, Namibia

THE LECHWE is accurately described as a water-loving antelope. It lives in swamps and open forest, and is rarely found more than a few miles away from a source of water. Its preferred habitat is a shallow, inundated flood plain next to a river and close to a swamp, particularly if there are high stands of papyrus reeds and semiaquatic grasses.

Three different subspecies of lechwe are considered here: the black lechwe (*Kobus leche smithemani*) from northern Zambia, the kafue lechwe (*K. leche rafuiensis*) from southern Zambia, and the red lechwe (*K. leche leche*), which ranges from southern Democratic Republic of Congo through Angola, Namibia, Botswana, and Zambia.

The lechwe uses water to escape predators, and it feeds on many of the water-loving plants. When seen on dry land, a lechwe has an awkward gait while running and, therefore, is not particularly quick on its feet. This is due to its long, narrow hooves, which are well adapted for running through marshy wetlands. Lechwes tend to be active before sunrise and in the early morning, and then again in the late afternoon. They are occasionally preyed on by lions and leopards, and in swampy areas they are sometimes eaten by crocodiles.

The lechwe is a fairly sociable animal and is usually found in small herds of 15 to 20, although these herds may merge into even larger groups. Like many other antelope species, the males are often found in bachelor groups.

The rutting season occurs in October, but only a few males defend territories and mate. Maintaining a territory against other males involves posturing,

The kafue lechwe (*Kobus leche rafuiensis*) is found in southern Zambia. All three subspecies of lechwe have a coat of long hair that ranges in color from bright chestnut to black with white underparts, depending upon the subspecies.

threats, and chasing rivals, with a fight breaking out occasionally. Females, however, move freely within the mating ground and mate with the dominant male.

Grass eaters

Lechwes eat semiaquatic grass almost exclusively, however, they will nibble on some types of leaves and twigs. The young may be born at any time during the year, but the predominant time for calving is usually between mid-July and mid-August. After a gestation period of between seven and eight months, the females give birth. They stay hidden with their young for the first

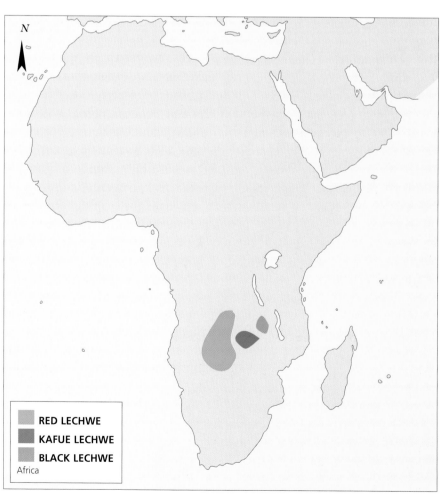

RED LECHWE
KAFUE LECHWE
BLACK LECHWE
Africa

two or three weeks. The females leave their young, go out and forage, and then come back and suckle in the early morning and late afternoon. It is then that calf mortality is at its highest, since they are unprotected and may be attacked by predators.

One of the major causes of this species' decline is hunting. Up until 1957 (when a law was passed to discontinue the practice) there were events known as lechwe drives, or chilas, held at the time of high flooding in the Kafue flats of Zambia. At these times, thousands of hunters gathered with their spears, dogs, and guns and hunted lechwes. It was not uncommon to see as many as 5,000 lechwes killed during a three-day period.

A significant proportion of females were killed during the hunt, and the population dwindled so rapidly that eventually this practice was banned.

Captive population

All of the three different types of lechwe, have succumbed to the same pressures: severe hunting, intrusion by people, and the subsequent destruction of lechwe habitat. The black lechwe in Zambia ranges in a restricted environment: there is only a single population of less than 40,000 individuals. This alone makes its wild status extremely vulnerable. A small captive population of black lechwes is currently breeding in Spain. There are reportedly about 40

individuals in this group, although it is too early to say whether the breeding program has proved successful.

Declining numbers

The kafue lechwe is also restricted to one population, which lives in Zambia. This population numbers only 25,000 or so, and the group is declining rapidly. There is a captive population of nearly 200 individuals.

The red lechwe is the only subspecies that occurs in more than one population over its wild range, but it is also declining. The

red lechwe population currently numbers an estimated 37,000 individuals and the total known captive population of red lechwe does not presently exceed 150 individuals.

Despite these very low numbers, the red lechwe appears to do reasonably well in a captive-breeding environment.

If these various breeding programs can be sustained, the lechwe may yet survive the environmental pressures of the early 21st century.

Warren D. Thomas

See also Antelopes.

The red lechwe (*Kobus leche leche*) ranges from southern Democratic Republic of Congo through Angola, Namibia, Botswana, and Zambia. It is the only subspecies that still occurs in more than one population.

Leka Keppe

(Sarotherodon lohbergeri)

> **IUCN:** Critically endangered

Class: Actinopterygii
Order: Perciformes
Family: Cichlidae
Length: 4¾ in. (12 cm)
Reproduction: Egg layer
Habitat: Inshore areas and river pools
Range: Lake Barombi-Mbo and Kumba River, Cameroon

As with several other threatened and endangered cichlids, the sole residence of the cichlid species called the leka keppe is the crater lake known as Barombi-Mbo in the African nation of Cameroon. A few individuals have been located in a small outlet stream called the Kumba River. The leka keppe is the only Lake Barombi-Mbo cichlid to escape to the Kumba River. This escape necessitated a demanding ride across a lake outlet sill, over a waterfall and into a gorge, then through some rapids to the river.

Lake Barombi-Mbo, a small, relatively infertile, deep freshwater lake, is about 1½ miles (2.4 kilometers) in diameter, yet is the primary source of food for the village of Barombi on its northern shore. Local fishers defend their right to fish the lake but, to the detriment of the leka keppe, this species and a total of ten other threatened and endangered cichlid fish are sought by the village inhabitants as food.

The leka keppe can be found only in Lake Barombi-Mbo and the adjacent river, and therefore it is vulnerable to natural or artificial catastrophes or to prolonged overfishing. However, the Barombi villagers' insistence on maintaining exclusive fishing rights on the lake may work to the advantage of the leka keppe and other cichlids. The villagers have been able to maintain a functional balance between their food needs and the natural supply of fish for many decades, and have resisted overfishing. If harmful non-native fish such as the destructive Nile perch (*Lates niloticus*) can be kept away from the lake, conservationists are hoping to continue the ban on fishing by other villages and to educate the people of Barombi about the delicate balance of the ecosystem on which they depend.

Similar features

Despite their many subtle physical and behavioral variations, cichlids exhibit many similar physical characteristics. All cichlids display a fairly flattened and rounder appearance than other streamlined and torpedolike fish. Many have broad and almost parrotlike mouthparts that they use to scrape algae from surfaces or to crush hard food items. In addition to having teeth on the jaws, these fish have numerous teeth on a platelike bone at the base of the mouth and throat to hold and process food items; these teeth within the throat are called pharyngeal teeth.

Spiny fin

One distinctive characteristic that the leka keppe has in common with all other cichlids is the long, spiny, protective dorsal fin on the back. This fin may extend from just behind the head all the way to the tail section of the body. The dark blotch in the dorsal fin segment near the tail of many cichlids is called a tilapia mark. However, the leka keppe's dorsal fin rarely carries this mark.

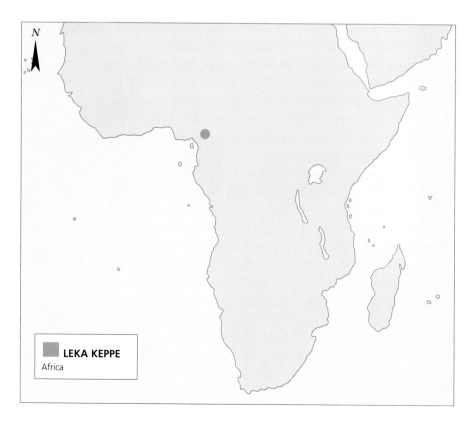

LEKA KEPPE
Africa

Visual feeder

This fish is silvery gray as an adult, with a prominent stripe from just behind the gill covers to just slightly forward of the base of the tail fin. A dusky spot is positioned slightly closer to the tail fin and follows the same line as the stripe. The lower jaw and face also have dark markings. The fins follow the coloration of the body with the exception of the anal fin, just behind the anus and genitals, which shows a hint of red and orange. The body is well scaled, but some portions of the head, chin, and throat are scaleless. The eyes are well developed for visual feeding, and teeth in the jaws are somewhat flexible to prevent them from breaking.

The leka keppe probably engages in an activity called mouthbrooding. No observations in the wild have been recorded, but aquarium specimens perform this behavior. After eggs are laid by a female and fertilized by a male, one or both of the parents (depending on the species) picks up the eggs with its mouth and guards them in a chamber in the mouth cavity where oxygenated water is pumped past them. The parent incubates the eggs until they hatch, after a period of one to two weeks. Even after the fish hatch, the freeswimming offspring continue to rely on the parent for protection. At the first sign of a predator, the offspring race to the parent and immediately re-enter its mouth. This protective behavior significantly increases the chances of offspring surviving to adulthood.

The leka keppe feeds on algae, sponge spicules, microscopic plankton in the water column, stems of rooted aquatic plants, and parts of terrestrial plants that fall into the lake.

Other cichlids

Some of the other cichlid fish that are listed in this series include the fissi (*Sarotherodon caroli*), kululu (*S. steinbachi*), unga (*S. linnellii*), myakamyaka (*Myaka myaka*), and Otjikota tilapia (*Tilapia guinasana*).

Westerners who are accustomed to plentifully stocked lakes all over North America may find it difficult to accept the fact that many species of these fish are in danger of extinction in other parts of the world.

William E. Manci

See also Fissi, Kululu, Myakamyada, Otjikota tilapia, and Unga.

LEMURS

Class: Mammalia

Order: Primates

Family:
Cheirogaleidae (*Dwarf Lemurs*)
Indriidae (*Indri, Woolly Lemurs*)
Lemuridae (*True Lemurs, Ruffed Lemurs and Gentle Lemurs*)
Lepilemuridae (*Sportive Lemurs*)

The island of Madagascar has been separated from the African mainland for more than 35 million years, creating a unique situation in which primates have evolved in a different environment from their neighbors, free from many of the predators and competitors present on the mainland. Madagascar is the world's fourth largest island, about 1,000 miles (1,600 kilometers) long and 360 miles (580 kilometers) wide.

Lemurs evolved in Madagascar and are found nowhere else in the world except for the tiny Comoro Islands.

The primate order is divided into two major groups: simians (consisting of the apes and monkeys) and prosimians (lemurs and a few smaller, nocturnal creatures from Africa and Asia). Prosimians are considered to be more primitive than monkeys, with smaller brains relative to their body size. Their faces are not as expressive as those of simians. Prosimians are also mostly nocturnal, relying primarily on their sense of smell.

Lemurs and monkeys also have different teeth: the front teeth on the lower jaw of the lemur project forward to form a dental comb that they use to groom fur and scrape gum off trees.

Lemurs are intelligent arboreal primates whose soft fur, long tails, distinctive snouts, large eyes, and nocturnal activity inspired their name (lemur is Latin for "spirit of the dead.") Lemurs diversified into more than 40 species. When people arrived on the island about 2,000 years ago, the habitat of these Malagasy primates changed. The introduction of cattle and goats, as well as hunting, caused the extinction of at least 14 species. Deforestation has also contributed to their demise. If deforestation on Madagascar continues at its present rate, all its forests could be gone in just 25 years. The human population has more than doubled in 30 years. Since the livelihood of many Malagasy people depends on agriculture, which requires forest clearance, the competition between humans and lemurs continues. But the Malagasy government is showing signs that it wants to preserve certain areas of the island for wildlife.

Coquerel's Dwarf Lemur

(Mirza coquereli)

IUCN: Vulnerable

Weight: 10½ oz. (300 g)
Head–body length: 8 in. (21 cm)
Tail length: 13 in. (33 cm)
Diet: Insects, fruit, flowers, small vertebrates, and the secretions from Homopteran larvae
Gestation period: 90 days
Longevity: 15 years
Habitat: Dry deciduous forest along rivers and ponds; rain forest in the Sambirano region
Range: West and northwestern Madagascar

DWARF LEMURS ARE found in both the tropical rain forests of eastern Madagascar and in the drier forests to the north, west, and southwest. The dwarf lemurs represent just one branch of the lemur family, with five species. Two are considered endangered or threatened.

One of these is the Coquerel's dwarf lemur, which possesses distinctive long, hairless, and membranous ears. The fur on its back is brown or gray brown, sometimes with rosy or yellowish tinges. On its front, the gray color of the downy hairs is visible beneath the yellowish or slightly russet tips. The tip of the tail is darker than the rest of its fur. Protruding eyes have developed to aid this nocturnal species.

This lemur is found in only three protected areas, distributed in isolated pockets along Madagascar's western coast. Population numbers are unknown, and there are wildly varying estimates of its density. It eats a wide variety of food such as insects, spiders, frogs, chameleons, small birds, fruit, flowers, buds, gums from trees, and insect secretions. In the dry season, cashew fruits are important sources of protein.

Nesting practice

The Coquerel's dwarf lemur spends the day in nests made from leaves, branches, and vines. It builds these nests in the forks of trees. The nests appear to be occupied by single males or by females with offspring.

In some areas adults defend the region close to their home range. Male lemurs tend to range farther than females into neighboring areas.

Mother dwarf lemurs carry their infants around in their mouths, in the same way that cats do, but for the first few weeks, infants remain in the nests. In one area of Madagascar called Ambanja, these lemurs have been seen to nest in "villages" that are created when several nests are clustered together in a small area. During the first part of the night, these lemurs forage and groom. In the second half of the night they engage in social activities such as play, mutual grooming, and vocalizing.

It is certain that the destruction of its habitat is a major threat to this animal's future. Farm animals reared in western Madagascar need to have grass to feed on, and this is acquired

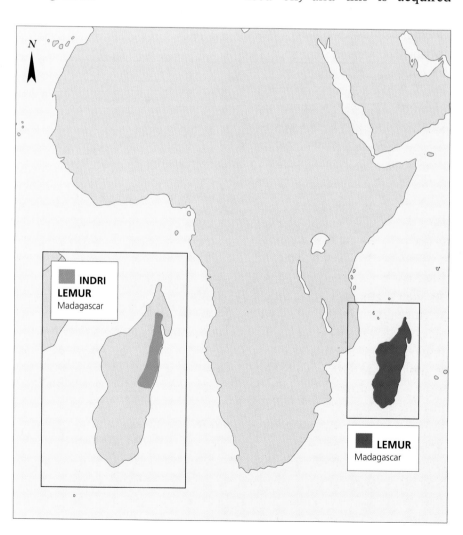

by slash-and-burn agricultural techniques that seriously jeopardize this lemur's habitat. The lemur does, however, breed well in captivity. There are some 75 individuals in zoos and primate research centers from San Francisco to Paris.

Hairy-eared Dwarf Lemur
(Allocebus trichotis)

IUCN: Critically endangered

Weight: 2⅔–3 oz. (75–85 g)
Head–body length: 5½ in. (14 cm)
Tail length: 6½ in. (16.5 cm)
Habitat: Lowland rain forest
Range: Northeastern Madagascar

A DWARF LEMUR IS small enough to fit in the palm of a hand. Its tail is longer than its entire body. Yet this tiny mammal, which is no bigger than a large mouse, belongs to the same scientific order as monkeys, chimpanzees, gorillas, and human beings.

Habits
The hairy-eared dwarf lemur is extremely rare, both in the wild and in captivity, and its population numbers in the wild are unknown. Until 1989 this lemur was known only from museum collections, and it was thought to be extinct. Experts consider it to be the rarest of all lemurs. Very little can be said about its habits. Local people have reported seeing several individual hairy-eared dwarf lemurs sleeping in the same tree hole. The locals call this species *tsidyala,* meaning "mouse lemur of the big forest."

The fur on the back of the hairy-eared dwarf lemur is pale brown, fading to a white or cream color underneath. Its ears are short but have pronounced tufts of long hair, which give the lemur its name. It also has a long tongue, which suggests it eats nectar from wild flowers. In captivity it has consumed insects, fruit, and honey.

Because lemurs, including the dwarf lemur, live only on the island of Madagascar, they have evolved differently from the primates of the African mainland. Lemurs are one of very few mammalian species on the island and are part of the primate group known as prosimians.

The hairy-eared dwarf lemur is nocturnal, sleeping in tree holes during the day and awakening at dusk. It has been noted to be a keen jumper. There is some evidence that it may hibernate (as some other dwarf lemurs do) during the dry season from June to September. In May lemurs develop a layer of fat all over their bodies, which may serve them well during hibernation.

Experts estimated that between 1950 and 1985 some 444 square miles (1,150 square kilometers) of rain forest had been cleared each year, and most of this has been lowland forest. If the felling of trees continues at this rate, extinction seems inevitable for this dwarf lemur.

Gentle Lemurs
(Hapalemur sp.)

ESA: Endangered

IUCN: Vulnerable to Critically endangered

Weight: 2–5 lb. (1–2.6 kg)
Head–body length: 11–16 in. (28–40 cm)
Tail length: 16 in. (40 cm)
Diet: Bamboo and reeds
Gestation period: 135–150 days
Longevity: 12 years in captivity
Habitat: Reed beds
Range: Madagascar

THREE SPECIES OF gentle lemur are generally recognized: the gray gentle lemur (*Hapalemur griseus*), the broad-nosed or greater bamboo lemur (*H. simus*), and the recently discovered golden bamboo lemur (*H. aureus*). All of the species mainly eat bamboo (the stalk, the leaves, and the shoots) or reeds. They appear to be active both day and night; however, in the midday sun they seclude themselves at the base of bamboo trunks. All species have fur ranging in varying shades of gray brown and they lack distinctive markings. They have powerful sex scent glands, differentiating them from true lemurs. These lemurs prefer to stay in small groups of between two to six individuals, and they communicate using a variety of high-pitched calls.

Gray gentle lemur

There are three subspecies of gray gentle lemurs, including the Alaotran (*H. griseus alaotrensis*), which is listed by the IUCN–The World Conservation Union as critically endangered, and the western (*H. griseus occidentalis*), which is listed as vulnerable. The Alaotran gentle lemur is so named because it ranges only amid the swampy reed beds around Lake Alaotra in eastern Madagascar. There is no bamboo near the lake, so this lemur feeds instead on reeds and on the buds and pith of papyrus.

The gray gentle lemur has a gray-brown coat. It has been reported that this arboreal creature never descends to the ground, yet it can swim quite well. Females with infants clinging to their backs have been seen crossing canals over 50 feet (15 meters) wide.

This lemur is most commonly seen in groups of three or four, but as many as 30 to 40 individuals have been seen together during the wet season (February). Females give birth in January and February, and the infants cling to their mother's back from birth until they become mature.

The annual burning of the reed beds around Lake Alaotra is a serious threat to the local lemurs, as is the local practice of catching the lemurs for food as they flee from the flames. People are steadily taking over this lemur's natural habitat without regard to the consequences of their actions. The lake is being drained to make way for rice plantations, and the local papyrus and reeds are cut for use in making mats and fencing. The Alaotran gray gentle lemur is not found in any protected area. There is presently a small captive population of about 35 individuals. Meanwhile, there are proposals to transform Lake Alaotra into a reserve to protect endangered lemurs and birds.

The western gentle lemur ranges in rain forest along the west coast of Madagascar near Lake Bemamba and Lake Sambirano. It occurs in two small populations, and is smaller and lighter-colored than the other gentle lemurs. It is active during the day, foraging on low-level vegetation in groups of from one to four individuals. The lemur's total population is unknown, but since its range is restricted, it cannot be numerous. There are about 10 western gentle lemurs in captivity. Deforestation by fires to make way for livestock in western Madagascar is contributing to the demise of this subspecies.

Golden bamboo gentle lemur

The golden bamboo gentle lemur *(H. aureus)* of southeastern Madagascar was only discovered in 1987 and, due to habitat destruction, is one of the most threatened primates there. Now listed by IUCN–The World Conservation Union as critically endangered, it lives in small patches of rain forest and eats only bamboo. It appears to tolerate the high level of toxins found in bamboo shoots that would be lethal to most mammals.

This lemur has a black face with golden eyebrows, cheeks, and throat; its underparts are yellow. There is gray-brown guard hair over pale orange fur on its back. Both sexes look similar. The golden bamboo gentle lemur lives in small family groups of adult pairs with immature offspring. It is reported to be active at dawn, dusk, and during the night. Around 200 to 400 individuals exist in total, and only four exist in captivity. Legislation prohibits trade in this lemur, but its natural habitat of bamboo has been so decimated that the species is unlikely to survive very far into the 21st century.

Greater bamboo gentle lemur

Also known as the broad-nosed gentle lemur, *(H. simus)*, this species' population is down to 200 to 400 individuals, probably even less numerous than the golden bamboo gentle lemur. This species is listed as critically endangered by the IUCN–The World Conservation Union. Slash-and-burn agriculture and the transformation of bamboo fields into rice paddies are the main threats to this lemur.

Little is known about this species, except that its coat is gray to gray brown, with lighter underparts and that it is larger and more heavily built than the other gentle lemurs. An area of 124,000 acres (50,000 hectares) around Ranomafana has been proposed as a national park. Perhaps this sanctuary will protect this lemur from extinction. There is a captive population of about 15 individuals.

Indri (Lemur)
(Indri indri)

IUCN: Endangered

Weight: 15½–22 lb. (7–10 kg)
Head-body length: 27–48 in. (70–120 cm)
Diet: Young leaves, shoots, fruit
Gestation period: 137 days
Habitat: Coastal rain forest
Range: East coast of Madagascar

THE INDRI IS THE largest member of the lemur family. Its name has an unusual origin. Indri means "There it is!" in Malagasy. An early zoologist misunderstood a local guide back in the 1700s, and the name stuck.

Habits
The indri has a thick, silky, black-and-white coat, making the animal difficult to see in the wild. There is, however, a great deal of variation in color among individuals. Occasionally, an indri may be almost totally black (or, more rarely, totally white). The indri's rump is almost always white, which is possibly useful in courtship displays, and its tail has been reduced to a stump. Its overall appearance is quite striking, and it is nicknamed the "ape of the prosimians."

Clinging and leaping
This lemur has powerful and flexible hindquarters that enable it to propel itself many feet when jumping from tree to tree. It performs these leaps vertically. This ability to make spectacular leaps is misleading since the animal spends most of its time foraging for food or resting.

The indri lives in family groups of up to five members consisting of a monogamous male and female and their offspring. Each group occupies a territory of 35 to 74 acres (14 to 30 hectares).

The family emits periodic doglike barks and mournful howling that intensifies when a territorial boundary is crossed by another animal. These vocalizations seem to be a peaceful substitute for real combat.

Mothers take great care of their infants. They give birth every two or three years after a gestation period of about 137 days, and carry the infant in front

The indri is also known as the *babakota*, which means "the father of man" or "the ancestor."

for the first four or five months. Thereafter, the infant rides on the mother's back and sleeps with her for the first year of its life. When adult the indri may reach up to 48 inches (120 centimeters) in length and weighs up to 22 pounds (10 kilograms).

Isolated populations
The population size of the indri is not known. It is found in four reserves in eastern Madagascar, but these areas are small and isolated from other blocks of forest.

The indri is severely threatened by the destruction of its habitat, which occurs even in areas where it is protected because of lax law enforcement. More funding is urgently needed to provide guards that can patrol these reserves.

It is thought to be taboo among local groups to hunt this species, but the population is still falling. This lemur has never been successfully kept in captivity, as it does not survive long when caged. The indri's notably slow rate of reproduction increases its vulnerability to extinction.

the black-and-white variety defending her group's territory. Ruffed lemurs appear to be active early in the morning and at dusk.

The black-and-white species is found on five reserves, but the black and red is not protected anywhere. There are no population estimates, but numbers are definitely declining and the species is threatened both by forest destruction and by hunting. There are, however, more than 700 of these lemurs in captivity, where they breed very well.

Ruffed Lemurs
(Varecia variegata)

ESA: Endangered
IUCN: Endangered

Weight: 7–10 lb. (3.3–4.5 kg)
Head–body length: 24 in. (61 cm)
Tail length: 24 in. (61 cm)
Diet: Fruit, leaves, nectar, and seeds
Gestation period: 90–112 days
Longevity: 19 years in captivity (one specimen)
Habitat: Rain forest
Range: Eastern coastal Madagascar

THE RUFFED LEMUR is the largest of the true lemurs, and is certainly one of the most striking. It has thick, beautifully colored fur, a prominent muzzle that is black and pointed, golden eyes, and tufted ears. This lemur moves on all fours, and its legs are longer than its arms.

There are two subspecies: the black and white ruffed lemur *(Varecia variegata variegata)* and

The striking ruffed lemur is the largest of the true lemurs. Like most of the wildlife on Madagascar, this primate's population has been reduced by forest destruction and hunting.

the black and red ruffed lemur *(V. variegata rubra)*. Both are endangered. The black-and-white variety shows a great deal of variation in its coat color and pattern, but individuals have a basic black-and-white patchwork look. They are found in the rain forests on the eastern side of Madagascar and on Nosy Mangabe Island. The black and red ruffed lemur is more uniform in color, with deep orange-red fur on its back and sides and black fur on its legs, tail, head, and underside. This species of lemur is restricted to the forest of the Masoala Peninsula.

Vocalization
Ruffed lemurs live in the upper parts of the forest, in families headed by a male and female pair. They give incredibly loud, raucous calls to coordinate group movements and define territory. There is one report of a female of

Sportive Lemurs
(Lepilemur sp.)

IUCN: Vulnerable

Weight: 18–28 oz. (500–800 g)
Head–body length: 10–11 in. (25–28 cm)
Tail length: 10–12 in. (25–30 cm)
Diet: Leaves and foliage, some fruit, and bark
Gestation period: 120–150 days
Longevity: 8–9 years in captivity
Range: Madagascar

THE SPORTIVE LEMUR was given its common name because when it is threatened it raises its hands like a boxer in order to punch its attacker. Zoologists have divided the sportive lemur into seven species, but they are all similar in coat color and overall anatomy. Sportive lemurs are found in all forested regions of Madagascar, from the evergreen forests of the east coast to the hot, dry forests of the southwest.

Nutrition

The sportive lemur is nocturnal. It does not eat insects, but lives entirely on plant foods. It eats tough foliage that is nutritionally quite poor, which means it must spend long periods of time in an inactive state so that it can digest this food and conserve energy.

These lemurs are also unique among primate species in that they will eat their own feces, much as rabbits do. This is a way of recycling material to maximize all available protein.

During the day a sportive lemur will sleep in a tree hollow, a forked branch, or in a tangle of vines, thus keeping out of the intense daytime heat. This lemur is medium-sized, slightly smaller than the typical lemur. Its preferred method of moving through the trees is by vertical clinging and leaping. When it is on the ground it hops like a rabbit.

Solitary creatures

Sportive lemurs appear to be especially solitary. The largest groups consist of females with immature offspring. Both males and females defend small territories, although the males' territories may overlap with the territories of two or three females. Personal space is guarded jealously and, as with gibbons, vocalizing is an important method of warding off strangers. Sportive lemurs keep watch over their space through visual surveillance, another unique behavior in primates in which lemurs will stare at one another for long periods of time.

The gray-backed sportive lemur (*Lepilemur dorsalis*) is also known as the Nosy Be sportive lemur, or apongy, among the local Malagasy people. It is one of the least widely distributed of the sportive lemurs. Its upperparts are medium to dark brown, and its underparts are a lighter brown. Its face is dark and its ears are small. It is found in only two areas: the Sambirano Region of northwestern Madagascar and the island of Nosy Be. Its total population is unknown. Few studies have been made of this lemur, but it is probably one of the rarest sportive lemurs. Its numbers are being reduced in tandem with forest clearing operations within its range.

There are no gray-backed sportive lemurs in captivity, but some are found in two reserves: Mamon Garivo on the mainland and Lokobe on Nosy Be. Neither of these reserves is safe from harm. On Nosy Be, not only are trees cut down to be later turned into canoes, but the land is also cleared for plantations.

Northern sportive lemur

Another variety, the northern lemur (*L. septentrionalis*) has gray upperparts that are darkest on the crown and become lighter toward its pale gray rump. There is a darker median stripe along its crown and back, and its underparts are gray.

The northern lemur is nocturnal, solitary, and leaf-eating. During the day, tree holes or bundles of foliage are used as resting places. These nests are generally 20 to 32 feet (6 to 8 meters) off the ground in live trees. At night adults roam solo, with only mothers and young associating with one another.

Malagasy law does protect sportive lemurs from hunting and unauthorized capture, but enforcement has proved almost impossible. Logging, burning, and overgrazing are still permitted on the only reserves for this species. No animals of this group exist in captivity, and captive breeding has never been successful. With no adequate protection, deforestation threatens to eliminate this animal forever.

True Lemurs

(Eulemur sp.)

ESA: Endangered

IUCN: Vulnerable to Critically endangered

Weight: 4½–8 lb. (2–3.5 kg)
Head–body length: 15–18 in. (38–45 cm)
Diet: Fruit, flowers, leaves, and bark

TRUE LEMURS ARE generally cat-sized, with a head and body length averaging 16½ inches (42 centimeters) and tails that are slightly longer than their body length. Their arms are shorter than their legs, and they usually move on all four limbs.

All lemurs are arboreal, but leaping ability varies across species, and some spend some more time on the ground than others. Lemurs are herbivorous, and eat fruit and seeds, flowers, leaves, and nectar. True lemurs inhabit moist and dry forest, but not open country.

This genus is the most widespread of all the lemurs. It comprises six species, all of which need to be conserved, mainly due to habitat loss.

Black lemur

The black lemur (*Eulemur macaco*) is found in evergreen forests of north and west Madagascar. It is primarily tree-dwelling, and it is awake during daylight hours and dusk, although some groups have been observed foraging at night. It forages in groups of 4 to 15 animals, and they gather together in the evenings.

The males are uniformly black, while the females are chestnut brown, with darker faces and heavy, white ear tufts. Both sexes are born black, but females change color at about six months of age. The differences between the sexes are more marked in this lemur than in any other. The black lemur is listed as vulnerable by IUCN–The World Conservation Union.

There are two black lemur subspecies: *E. macaco macaco* (vulnerable) and *E. macaco flavifrons* (critically endangered). Population numbers are at present unknown, but they may be declining due to destruction of the forest and slash-and-burn agriculture. The black lemur uses plantations and secondary forest,

and it is not dependent on undisturbed forest. This gives it a better chance of adapting to deforestation. However, when it is found raiding crops, it is chased and killed by farmers. Approximately 350 of these lemurs exist in captivity. The St. Louis Zoo and the Duke University Primate Center have the greatest numbers. A reserve on Nosy Komba Island is protected, but more areas need to be considered for development and conservation.

Brown lemur

There are a number of lemurs classified as brown lemurs (*Eulemur fulvus*). These lemurs have an interesting social system, nicknamed fission-fusion. This means that their society is similar to that of chimps or spider monkeys, where individuals travel in groups, but the groups constantly change in size and membership.

The population numbers and densities of the brown lemur subspecies, the collared lemur (*E. fulvus collaris*), are unknown. The males generally have a black neck, ears, face, and crown, while

these parts are gray in the female. Both sexes have pale orange cheeks that are bushy in the male. The upperparts are a dark brown or gray brown, with a darker stripe down the spine. The underparts are paler. Habitat destruction is the main threat facing this species.

This lemur is also widely hunted and is occasionally trapped to sell to the pet trade. A captive breeding program with over 100 individuals is underway. The collared lemur is listed as vulnerable by IUCN–The World Conservation Union.

Mayotte lemur

It is believed that the Mayotte lemur (*E. fulvus mayottensis*) was introduced to the island of Mayotte by people several hundred years ago. Its coloration is variable, and some zoologists have suggested that there is no distinction between this lemur and the brown lemur. Its upper parts and tail are grayish brown, its cheeks and beard are white, its muzzle and forehead are black, and its underparts are a creamy tan color. This subspecies is no longer evaluated by IUCN.

Mayotte is covered by large trees of secondary forest that support this animal even though lemurs usually only thrive in older, more established and undisturbed ecosystems. It is thought that deforestation of the island during the 1970s greatly reduced the population, maybe by as much as half, leaving as few as 25,000 lemurs. The continuing

The black lemur, like most lemurs, is a nocturnal animal that lives in evergreen forests. There are about 250 individuals in captivity.

construction of roads means there are no longer any remote, inaccessible areas providing sanctuary for these lemurs. There are no protected areas on the island, and without enforcement of conservation measures, this lemur's future is in serious jeopardy. At present, there are roughly 80 of these lemurs in captivity.

Sanford's lemur

Sanford's lemur (*E. fulvus sanfordi*) is another subspecies of the brown lemur that lives in a restricted range in the far north of Madagascar. Its population has not been estimated, but numbers are declining as forests are cleared. It is currently listed as vulnerable by the IUCN. The male and female of this species are easily distinguished: the male's upperparts are brownish gray and the underparts are a paler gray or cream. The crown of its head and its bushy cheeks are brown, while the muzzle is black. The male's ears are tufted with white hairs, and the forehead and areas around the eyes are white.

The female has gray, sometimes gray-brown, upperparts and paler underparts. She has a black muzzle, with the rest of the head a darkish gray. The female's ears are not tufted and she lacks bushy hair on the cheeks. Sanford's lemur has shown itself to be remarkably adaptable, often appearing to prefer life in a forest that has been tampered with by people. However, destruction of its habitat is still a problem, since it has such a tiny range. It lives only on the northern flanks of Mt. d'Ambre. Poaching is increasing, and bushfires and illegal tree felling are also a problem.

Between 10 and 20 animals are held in captivity, most of them at the Duke Primate Center, which is coordinating a captive-breeding program of brown lemurs.

White-collared lemur

Another subspecies of brown lemur is the white-collared lemur (*E. fulvus albocollaris*), which ranges between the Mananara and Faraony rivers. No studies have been made of this lemur, so population density is uncertain.

Brown lemurs have an uncommon social system: individuals travel in groups that constantly change in size and membership. This is much like the social systems of chimps and spider monkeys.

It is subject to the same threats as other lemurs: habitat destruction and local indifference to its importance. Some recommendations that would help the white-collared lemur are simple to implement, such as putting up more signs within the Manombo

The crowned lemur is a diurnal species, although it is also known to be active at night.

parts, whitish faces, a V-shaped orange marking above the forehead, and a black crown. The female underparts and head cap are lighter in color.

Some 80 to 90 individuals exist in captivity, both in the United States and in Europe. Most of these animals were born in captivity. Unfortunately, these lemurs are still poached in Montagne d'Ambre National Park, where illegal deforestation also continues, and bush fires threaten the edges of the park.

The species is considered to be vulnerable by the IUCN, The World Conservation Union, but further study of this lemur's ecology is needed.

Mongoose lemur

The mongoose lemur (*E. mongoz*) is one of only two lemur species found in both the Comoro Islands and mainland Madagascar. Despite this range, it has a limited distribution. More specific details about its total population are unknown. Its numbers are definitely diminishing due to habitat destruction, and it is found in only one protected area: Ankarafantsika. This reserve is not sufficiently well-managed to protect the lemurs within it. Some zoologists consider this one of the rarest of the true lemurs, and it is listed as vulnerable by the IUCN–The World Conservation Union.

This lemur is tree-dwelling and is active both day and night. It is usually seen in small family groups that consist of one adult pair and their offspring. The

Special Reserve to indicate the limits of the sole protected area for this lemur. Preserving this primate's habitat is also vital. There are just three white-collared lemurs in captivity, at the Strasbourg Zoo in France. This subspecies is listed as endangered by the IUCN.

Crowned lemur

The crowned lemur (*E. coronatus*) is found in the dry forests of extreme northern Madagascar.

The size of its population is unknown, and its small range is declining due to logging, burning, and cattle grazing within the forests. It is usually active during the day (and sometimes at night as well), and has been seen in groups of up to ten individuals. These groups consist of several adults of both sexes. It is most often seen in the trees, but it also travels frequently on the ground.

Males have medium-gray backs, lighter limbs and under-

males are gray with pale faces and have red cheeks and beards. The females have browner backs, dark faces, and white cheeks and beards. Groups rarely encounter one another, but when they do there is much threatening display and vocalization between them. There are currently about 100 mongoose lemurs held in captivity, but this species has a poor breeding record.

Red-bellied lemur

The red-bellied lemur (*E. rubriventer*) lives at medium-to-high altitudes in the rain forests of Madagascar's east coast. It is mostly diurnal, and exists in small groups. Its upperparts are chestnut brown; it has a dark face and a black tail. The underparts of the male are dark reddish brown, while those of the female are whitish. The lemur's fur is relatively long and dense, to keep it warm in the high mountains.

No accurate population numbers are available. However, it is clear that logging and agricultural encroachment continue to threaten the future of this lemur. This species is considered vulnerable by the IUCN–The World Conservation Union.

Ring-tailed lemur

The ring-tailed lemur *(Lemur catta)* is probably the best known of these diverse primates. There is little difference between the sexes, both having a characteristic and beautiful black-and-white ringed tail. The tail is not only used in visual recognition, but also acts as a kind of fan to waft pheromones for identification by scent. This lemur is found in the dry forests and bush of south and southwestern Madagascar. It

spends more time on the ground than any other species of lemur, and it is diurnal. The ring-tailed lemur's eyes, nose, and mouth are black, while the rest of its face and its ears are white. Its back fur is soft dove gray, and its limbs and belly are lighter, while the extremities are white.

The ring-tailed lemur lives in multiple male groups, ranging from 3 to 24 members. In ring-tailed lemur society, females are

dominant. Females remain in their birth groups all their lives, forming strong bonds, while males switch groups (sometimes several times) during a single life-time. Some males live solitarily between groups.

Ring-tailed lemurs interact socially while feeding and sun-

The mongoose lemur, *Eulemur mongoz*, is found both on Madagascar and the Comoro Islands.

offspring. At two and a half years, these lemurs are fully mature, and they can expect to live for 15 years in total.

Ring-tailed lemurs sometimes engage in territorial encounters. Females do most of the threatening, mainly by running at each other and vocalizing. These lemurs have a complex means of chemical communication. Both males and females mark ranges with genital secretions during aggressive moments. Males also have what are called stink fights, secreting a strong-smelling chemical from special glands on the chest. The males rub their tails across these glands, then get down on all fours and wave their tails at their opponent. This behaviour is most common during breeding.

Satellite pictures have been used to monitor the destruction of Madagascan forest, and these show that acreage is declining at an alarming rate. Local farmers set fire to the forest in order to promote the growth of grass. They graze cattle on the land and fell trees for charcoal production. In addition, they use dogs to hunt down ring-tailed lemurs.

Several steps are being taken to reduce the hunting problem. There are a few protected areas within the lemur's range, and better management plans are under way to protect the lemurs from extinction. All of these steps, however, are very difficult

bathing. Sunbathing occurs during the early hours of the morning before feeding. The lemurs sit upright, their front legs resting on their hind legs, exposing their stomachs to the sun

The mating season (March to April) is brief, lasting two weeks at the most. The female is ready to mate when a slight swelling and flushing of the genitalia occurs. She is only fertile for one day a year, resulting in all newborns arriving at the same time,

120 to 135 days later. Females usually have their first offspring at the age of three years and continue to produce offspring annually. The mortality rate of infants during their first year of life is 30 to 50 percent.

The infant ring-tailed lemur is about 4 inches (10 centimeters) in length and is a miniature replica of its parents. After three days it is actively scrambling over its mother's body. Groups of mothers will groom each others'

for the authorities to enforce. Meanwhile, the ring-tailed lemur breeds well in captivity, and there are estimated to be over 1,200 individuals in zoos and other institutions.

Woolly Lemur (avahi)
(Avahi laniger)

ESA: Endangered

Weight: 1½ lb. (0.68 kg)
Head-body length: 12 in. (30 cm)
Diet: Leaves and buds
Gestation period: 120–150 days
Habitat: Rain forest and dry, deciduous forest
Range: Eastern Madagascar

THE WOOLLY LEMUR is the smallest and only nocturnal member of the Indriidae family. It has soft, light brown fur, with a white band above the eyes. It lives in family groups of two or three individuals, with a single offspring born in August or September. The animal sleeps during the day, usually lying in a forked tree branch.

The woolly lemur appears to be a monogamous animal, living only within small territories.

There are two subspecies of woolly lemur. The eastern woolly lemur (*A. laniger laniger*) lives in the moist rain forest. *A. laniger occidentalis* prefers the drier forest of Ankarafantsika. Both of these lemurs are threatened.

Like the indris, woolly lemurs are skillful vertical leapers. This is even more noteworthy consider-

ing that the woolly lemurs prefer to carry out this activity in the darkness of night.

The eastern woolly lemur is found in six protected areas of Madagascar, while *A. laniger occidentalis* is found in only two. There are no population numbers for either group, but they are presumed to be declining due to the destruction of their limited habitat. There are no woolly lemurs in captivity, and those that have been in captivity were unable to survive and reproduce.

Sarah Dart, Thaya du Bois, Gregory Lee

See also: Aye-aye, Zanzibar Bushbaby, Pygmy Loris, Sifakas.

The ring-tailed lemur looks a little like a raccoon. It is probably the best-known member of the lemur family and breeds well in captivity.

LEOPARDS

Class: Mammalia

Order: Carnivora

Family: Felidae

The leopard (*Panthera pardus*) is a large, powerful, spotted cat found in Asia and Africa. The name leopard has also been used to describe two other quite different cat species, the clouded leopard and the snow leopard. These cats differ in many ways from the ordinary leopard, particularly the clouded leopard, which is such a unique cat that it is the single member of its genus. The clouded leopard and the snow leopard have one important thing in common: populations of both cats are declining.

Clouded Leopard

(Neofelis nebulosa)

ESA: Endangered

IUCN: Vulnerable

Size: 24–40 in. (60–100 cm)

Shoulder height: 16–20 in. (40–50 cm)

Tail length: 21–35 in. (53–90 cm)

Weight: 35⅓–50¾ lb. (16–23 kg)

Gestation period: 86–93 days

Litter size: 1–5, normally 2

Diet: Birds, various mammals

Habitat: Forests in elevations to 9,800 ft. (3,000 m)

Range: From Nepal to south-eastern China and the Malay Peninsula; also in Taiwan, Hainan, Sumatra, and Borneo

MOST AUTHORITIES consider the clouded leopard a distinct genus with only one species. The coat of this unusual animal is grayish or yellowish. It features large gray markings that look a little like clouds, and this is where the animal gets its common name. The markings, which have dark circles around them, cover the forehead, legs, and the base of the tail; the remainder of the tail is banded. Occasionally melanistic, or all black, individuals have been observed. This leopard has a long tail that makes up about half of its total length, and short, stout legs with wide paws. The upper canine teeth are longer than those of any other cat, helping it bite into its prey.

The clouded leopard is unusual because it combines characteristics of both the great and the small cats. The structure of its skull and its teeth are like those of the leopard (*panthera pardus*), but it purrs like a small cat and has a pattern similar to that of the marbled cat. The two species are often confused, although the clouded leopard is much bigger. In terms of its behavior, this cat is much more like larger felids. For example, it does not groom itself as much as small cats do, concentrating primarily on the nose and paws. In addition, its eating habits are those of a big cat: grabbing meat with the incisors and canines and

The clouded leopard will eat birds as well as various small mammals, from monkeys to cattle. It will even eat porcupines. Its special teeth enable it to strike its prey without using its forelegs, helping it maintain balance should it choose to hunt birds or other arboreal creatures.

tearing it off the prey by jerking its head upward.

This cat lives in various kinds of forests, preferring mountainous regions. It is found at elevations up to 9,800 feet (3,000 meters) above sea level. Many scientists believe it to be arboreal, hunting in trees and springing on grounded prey from overhanging branches. If this is true, the tactic is unique to the species. Other scientists consider it to be a more terrestrial animal, using trees only as resting sites where it builds nests by breaking up branches. The species is most active in cool morning or late-afternoon hours.

Easy to tame

The clouded leopard is easily tamed and establishes a close relationship with its caretakers. Zoos began to have success breeding the animal in captivity in the 1960s. Reproductive habits are known only from captive breeding efforts, where births have occurred from March through August. The gestation period appears to be 86 to 93 days. Young weigh about 5 to 6 ounces (140 to 170 grams) at birth and are fed by the mother until the age of five months. However, they do show interest in solid food after six weeks. By the age of just three months they have been observed killing live chickens using their large teeth.

The clouded leopard has a relatively large range, but destruction of its habitat has played a major role in the animal's decline, particularly in Thailand and Malaysia. It has also been hunted for its beautiful skin. International trade for its pelt has only recently been restricted. The clouded leopard is protected over most of its range and is present in numerous parks and reserves.

Fortunately, the clouded leopard is kept in most larger zoos and is known to breed fairly regularly in captivity. Together with strict protection of those individuals in the wild, the strong captive population can probably help sustain this unusual member of the cat family.

Snow Leopard
(Uncia uncia)

ESA: Endangered

IUCN: Endangered

Size: 40–50 in. (100–130 cm)
Shoulder height: 23½ in. (60 cm)
Weight: 55–165 lb. (25–75 kg)
Gestation period: 90–103 days
Litter size: 1–5, usually 2–3
Diet: Various mammals
Habitat: Woodlands, true forest
Range: High altitudes of the Soviet Union, China, Mongolia, India, Nepal, Pakistan, and Afghanistan

THE SNOW LEOPARD, also called the irbis or the ounce, shares the genus *Panthera* with the other big cats. This genus includes other leopards (except for the unusual clouded leopard, which is the single species of its genus), tigers, jaguars, and lions. The nomenclature of cats is almost always a problem for scientists, and the use of the term *Panthera* is no exception. Some scientists prefer to place large cats in the generic genus *Leo*, while others simply do not consider these animals to be distinct from the genus *Felis*, which includes most of the smaller cats.

There are two ways in which members of the genus *Panthera* differ from those of the genus *Felis*. The larger cats have an

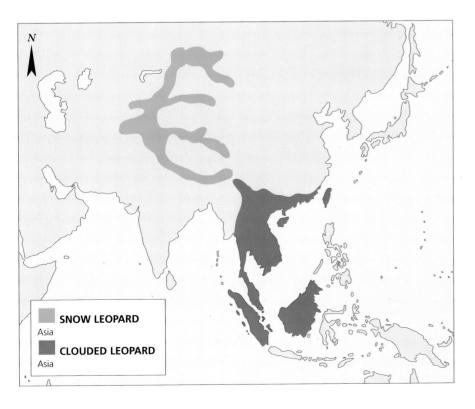

SNOW LEOPARD
Asia

CLOUDED LEOPARD
Asia

many ways as well. For example, the shape of the skull is quite distinct. The snow leopard's eyes are set high on the head, allowing it to peer over rocks while remaining unseen as it hunts for prey. The color pattern and thick, long-haired coat of this cat are quite different from those of the common leopard and are probably an adaptation for living in cold climates.

The background color of the snow leopard varies from a pale gray to a creamy, smoky gray, and the upperparts are whitish. The coat is exceptionally thick and long.

Asian cat

This striking cat lives in the high-altitude regions of Central Asia, from eastern Turkestan to Kashmir and Sikkim in India, from the Altai and Pamir Mountains of China to southeast Tibet. There is some question regarding the species' former range, as it may have occurred from northern Iran and Turkestan east and northward to more of China, Mongolia, and parts of Russia. Normally the snow leopard prefers to live and hunt in regions at a height between 5,900 and 9,800 feet (1,800 and 3,000 meters). It lives between the tree line and permanent snow, descending into upper valley bottoms in the cold winter months. In the hot season the snow leopard will move to mountain regions as high as 19,600 feet (5,970 meters).

The snow leopard has been observed using caves and rock crevices for refuge or breeding. It is often active during the day, especially in the early morning and late afternoon hours. This

elastic ligament in the throat near the base of the tongue that allows them to roar but limits purring to times of exhaling. While the snow leopard possesses this ligament, it apparently does not roar. Smaller cats do not roar, in general, although certain species, such as the black-footed cat (*F. nigripes*), produce a full roar that is not as fierce as that of a lion or tiger simply because of the size difference between the animals. The purr of a small cat is not interrupted when it inhales; rather it is

The head, neck, and lower limbs of the snow leopard display solid spots, while the back, sides, and tail have large rings or rosettes that often enclose smaller spots.

capable of purring when both inhaling and exhaling. The other difference between *Panthera* and *Felis* is that members of *Panthera* have hair that extends to the front of the nose.

The snow leopard shares similar characteristics with its relative, the common leopard (*P. pardus*), but it is different in

distinctive animal has been reported to leap as far as 16½ yards (15 meters). It captures its prey by either stalking or ambushing it.

One study in Nepal found five to ten snow leopards in a region of approximately 100 square miles (260 square kilometers). The snow leopards in this group had home ranges of approximately 12 to 40 square miles (30 to 100 square kilometers). These ranges would overlap among individuals, although the animals kept well apart from each other. It is possible that a pair of snow leopards will share a single range. It seems that this cat is primarily solitary, but not unsociable.

Although the snow leopard does not roar, it does possess several vocalizations, including a loud moaning that is associated with mating. Births occur from April to June, both in the wild and in captivity. The young, in litters of from one to five, are born in rocky shelters lined with the mother's fur. The cubs weigh about 16 ounces (450 grams) at birth, and eat solid food at two months. By three months of age they begin to follow their mother, and are hunting with her by their first winter. Sexual maturity occurs at about two years.

Illegal hunting

Because of the remoteness of this leopard's range, habitat destruction has not played a major role in its decline, although many of its prey species have been affected by changes to the environment. This has created a problem in some parts of this leopard's range, particularly in Nepal where there is an increased use of alpine land for pasture. Nonetheless, the primary cause of this animal's decline is that its pelt has long been a favorite of fur trappers. The animal is protected in most of its range, but illegal hunting and trapping continue. As recently as 1985 furs were still being trapped and hunted for commerce. In China the snow leopard continues to be hunted and is sold on the open market. Another cause of decline is that the animal is considered a pest because it preys on livestock. There are 3,000 to 10,000 snow leopards in the wild and another 400 in captivity. Fortunately, captive specimens breed regularly. The creation of captive-bred reserves could ensure the future of the species in the wild.

Elizabeth Sirimarc

Malheur Wire-lettuce
(Stephanomeria malheurensis)

ESA: Endangered

IUCN: Endangered

Class: Dicot
Order: Asterales
Family: Asteraceae (Compositae)
Leaves: Smooth, hairless leaves, long and thin; widest near the tip, to about 3 in. (8 cm) long
Flowers: Straplike ray flowers
Height: Up to 24 in. (60 cm),
Habitat: Desertlike sagebrush steppe
Range: A single, hilltop locality near Harney Lake, southeast Oregon

MALHEUR WIRE-LETTUCE is an obligately inbreeding annual herbaceous plant. This means that a seed develops into a nonwoody flowering plant within a single growing season, pollinates itself, and then dies. Seeds germinate in late winter to early spring (April–May). They then form a rosette of leaves that fan out on the ground in a circle. The plant produces a central flowering stem, usually in June. This may reach a height of 24 inches (60 centimeters), and the stem bears many lateral branches. Each branch produces numerous flowering heads, and the flowers look rather like those of the common dandelion (*Taraxacum* spp.). Although the species appears to have very little genetic diversity, flower color ranges from white to dark pink.

Known only from a single hilltop site, and never exceeding more than about a thousand plants in any year, this intensively studied annual plant apparently became extinct in the wild in the mid-1980s. Fortunately, the botanist who discovered, described, and studied the malheur wire-lettuce, Dr. Leslie Gottlieb, had been saving seeds from the plant for 20 years. It is only because seeds were saved that it was possible to reintroduce this species to its original habitat after it became extinct in the wild.

Malheur wire-lettuce is native to the high, wind-swept, desertlike sagebrush steppe of eastern Oregon, in the rain shadow of the Cascade Mountains. Its ideal habitat appears to have been in the bare, sandy areas between scattered clumps of shrubs such as big sage, *Artemisia tridentata*, and rabbitbrush, *Chrysothamnus vicidiflorous*, and a native bunch-grass, Great Basin Wildrye, *Elymus cinereus*. Unfortunately, high quality habitat may no longer exist. The strongly competitive, non-native cheat grass, *Bromus tectorum*, invaded the site after a fire swept through the area in 1972. It has remained dominant in this area, and competition with it is one of the chief threats to the malheur wire-lettuce.

Abundant relative

The malheur wire-lettuce population shares its hilltop habitat with the much more abundant *Stephanomeria exigua coronaria*, from which it is thought to have evolved. The malheur wire-lettuce exists very near the northern limit of *S. exigua coronaria's* range, which extends through the Sierra Nevada to southern California. As far as science has been able to determine, the malheur wire-lettuce contains a subset of the genetic diversity found in the more widespread *S. exigua coronaria*, and at the molecular level it appears to have no unique properties. There are, however, a few biological differences that may be critical. One is that the malheur wire-lettuce plants pollinate themselves, while *S. exigua coronaria* plants cannot. While self-pollination guarantees viable seeds, it severely restricts the creation of new combinations of genes, and thus does not enable the plants to readily adapt to

Buena Vista Lake in Malheur Wildlife Refuge, southeast Oregon. The malheur wire-lettuce is found on only a single hilltop near Harney Lake in this nature reserve.

environmental change. Another important difference is that the malheur wire-lettuce lacks the seed dormancy found in *S. exigua coronaria*. As a result the malheur wire-lettuce seeds sometimes germinate in the fall, only to perish in the harsh winter. More important, perhaps, without dormancy, the malheur wire-lettuce does not seem to be able to sustain a long-term soil seed bank. A soil seed bank allows an annual plant species to survive through a succession of unfavorable growing seasons, and it will increase in numbers rapidly when more favorable conditions occur.

Human responsibility

European peoples brought with them, intentionally or not, a highly aggressive annual grass from Eurasia.

Humans were also the cause of the 1972 fire that devastated the wire-lettuce's habitat and created conditions suitable for the growth of cheat grass. The existence of a much more abundant ancestral species in the same location as an endangered species allows scientists a rare opportunity to separate what is happening to the endangered species at a specific site from the effects of more widespread conditions. The few years leading up

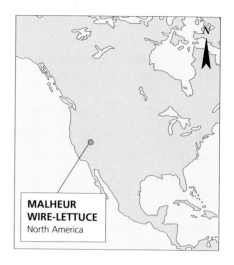

MALHEUR WIRE-LETTUCE
North America

to the extinction of the wild malheur wire-lettuce were wetter than the long-term average. The more common species' populations also dropped from tens of thousands to a mere handful during this period, suggesting that some problems faced by this wire-lettuce affected other species as well.

Conservation

Using seeds that Gottlieb had collected and maintained in his laboratory for almost 20 years, the Berry Botanic Garden in Portland, Oregon, produced about 1,000 seedlings in 1987 that were planted in its original habitat by the Bureau of Land Management.

However, the reintroduced population is still struggling and success is not assured. During this same period of time, the Berry Botanic Garden has been able to increase, to tens of thousands, the numbers of seeds in storage by propagating this species at the Garden.

Even though this species is still endangered, there will be hope for it as long as there is sufficient stored seed to reintroduce it.

Edward O. Guerrant, Jr.

Florida Perforate Cladonia

(Cladonia perforata)

ESA: Endangered

Height: Up to 2½ in. (6 cm) tall
Diameter: Up to 3 in. (8 cm)
Reproduction: Vegetative fragmentation
Habitat: Small hills of drained sand
Range: Florida

Florida perforate cladonia (*Cladonia perforata*) is a lichen that prefers a sandy environment.

FLORIDA PERFORATE cladonia is a lichen, which is a complex plant made up of a fungus and an alga. These plants do not produce flowers, nor do they look like conventional plants. The Florida perforate cladonia is quite conspicuous—it forms dense tufts that can be up to 2½ inches (6 centimeters) tall. The diameter of these tufts is variable depending on the age of the plant. When looked at closely it becomes clear that the plant is actually made up of a number of discrete plants. Each of these is up to 2½ inches (6 centimeters) tall, but they have a maximum diameter of up to 6 millimeters. The whole structure has a branching formation, which means that this lichen is a member of the class of lichens known as the fruticose lichens. Normally the visible part of the lichen (the fruit body) is a growth occurring from the vegetative body of the fungus. This lichen does not behave in the normal manner. There is no vegetative growth apparent; instead the lichen that can be seen has arisen from the spore-producing structures (the reproductive parts of the lichen). This growth gives rise to the lichen's pale yellow-gray tufts. This method of growth is unusual and is only seen in a very small number of lichen types. This species is quite variable in size, and examples of up 3 inches (8 centimeters) in diameter and several inches in height have been found. Because of lack of knowledge of this species, the growth rate is currently unknown. As far as has been observed, the Florida perforate cladonia does not reproduce in a sexual manner, instead relying on vegetative fragmentation, when small pieces break off the main body of the plant and continue to grow in new areas.

This lichen is endemic to Florida, and it is currently known from only 27 different sites within the state. It is estimated that there are some 26,000 individuals represented at these 27 sites. About 85 percent are on private land. A survey was carried out in 1991 to search for the Florida perforate cladonia, and only 12 sites were identified at that time. The remaining 15 known sites have been located in subsequent smaller searches. The historic range of this lichen is completely unknown and as such it is unknown whether the current distribution is the whole range or if it is a relic of a much larger distribution. As of 1992 only 15 percent of the historic range of Florida scrubland was still extant.

At a small number of known sites, this lichen is the dominant bare ground cover, with densely crowded and overlapping plants. In its natural habitat it can be found growing with Florida rosemary and reindeer lichens (also known, incorrectly, as reindeer moss). Due to the coverage by other species, it is probable that there are other sites within Florida that are not yet known. In common with many other species, one of the greatest threats to the continued survival of the Florida perforate cladonia is habitat loss and destruction. This is mainly brought about by residential development.

Because it grows among well-drained sand dunes, this species also suffers from trampling by people using adjacent beach sites. In recent years the use of off-road vehicles has also presented a problem. Hurricane washover and improper land management have been increasing threats to this sort of habitat. In 1995 Hurricane Opal damaged 50 percent of the potential sites for Florida perforate cladonia on Santa Rosa Island. Large areas of land were swept clean and then were inundated with salt water.

Conservation of this species can be best brought about by habitat management and preservation. In those areas where trampling occurs, the provision of clear artificial walkways will reduce this.

In private locations the habitat ideally should be maintained with an occasional thinning. If thinning does not take place, the

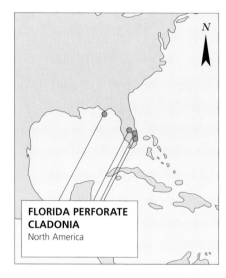

FLORIDA PERFORATE CLADONIA
North America

areas may become overgrown, which will shade out the lichens, leading to their eventual loss.

Bush fires

One problem associated with rosemary is that it is very prone to bush fires. These fires can potentially wipe out a whole population of the delicate lichens in one event. Where fires are carried out as part of land management, complete burn should be avoided to allow suitable habitat to persist from which recolonization can take place. Each site of Florida perforate cladonia is unique, and because of this there is no single conservation solution. Exclusion of damaging activities is a practical start, and future management at each site will depend upon the prevailing problems at that area.

Gordon Rutter

Western Lily

(Lilium occidentale Purdy)

ESA: Endangered

IUCN: Endangered

Class: Monocot
Order: Liliales
Family: Liliaceae
Height: Up to 8 ft. (2.5 m)
Leaves: 1½–7½ in.
(4–19 cm) long
Flowers: 1–3 brilliant crimson flowers with a golden star at the center
Habitat: Bogs or coastal scrub communities on poorly drained soils
Range: California-Oregon border, on the edge of the Pacific Ocean

THE WESTERN LILY, also called the bog lily, is an herbaceous perennial plant that dies back to the ground each year, overwintering as a dormant, bulblike, scaly rhizome. Young plants produce a single aboveground leaf, while larger plants have a single unbranched stem bearing leaves produced singly or in whorls along the shoot. Flowers face downward and are pollinated by hummingbirds.

Lilium, the genus of lilies, is broadly distributed across the Northern Hemisphere in North America, Europe, and Asia. The western lily is restricted to a narrow strip of land along the Pacific Ocean, about 200 miles (320 kilometers) long, straddling the California-Oregon border. The climate is characterized by cool wet winters and warm dry summers. Fog is common in summer, and moisture dripping off trees may increase annual rainfall by as much as 25 percent. Of the 60 or so populations so far discovered, almost half have been destroyed, mostly due to habitat conversion to agricultural or other uses. Another serious and certainly more insidious threat, because it is invisible to the casual observer, is competitive exclusion by shrubs and trees. The aggressive suppression of fires that remove old trees and shrubbery, thereby allowing the western lily access to light, and to pollinators, has characterized land management this last century. It has resulted in considerable loss of the Western lily's habitat.

The Western lily seems to require a habitat that maintains a precarious balance between hav-

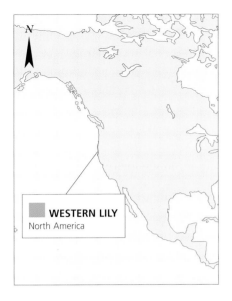

WESTERN LILY
North America

ing some surrounding shrubbery, perhaps for mechanical support, but not so much that the plant will be shaded out. Flowers often just poke their heads above the surrounding shrubbery where they are exposed to direct sunlight, and are also available to their hummingbird pollinators,

Fires regularly set by Native Americans to encourage bulbous foods and other useful plants to grow (and to make it more difficult for enemies to approach their villages unseen) probably served to keep shrubby vegetation in a size range suitable for lily growth.

Natural habitat?

Determining what this lily's pristine or natural habitat might have looked like is difficult. This is partly because remnant populations are found in a wide variety of habitats, and because many of the best sites, especially in the northern part of its range, coincide with the discovery of archaeological evidence of Native American communities. Even the meaning of the term *pristine habitat* is problematic. If the best sites are not forested because Native

Americans regularly burned fires there for thousands of years, are these sites pristine?

Monitored population

The Western lily typically occurs in bogs or coastal scrub communities on poorly drained soils. The species appears to either require or at least tolerate some sporadic disturbance, such as fire, to burn back excessive growth of competing plants.

For more than a decade, a population in northern California along the edge of a forest was carefully monitored. Plants near the edge, that received some direct sun, grew larger and flowered occasionally. The plants in the shady forest interior remained small and usually single-leaved.

It is possible they could survive for many years, even decades, in this condition. When

The brilliant crimson flowers of the western lily, or bog lily, have a golden star at the center. Many of the populations of this herbaceous perennial plant have been destroyed due to loss of habitat.

a few trees and lower limbs were experimentally removed, many of the small plants died.

After a few years, however, the surviving plants had grown and constituted the main concentration of flowering individuals in the larger population.

Conservation

Efforts to conserve the western lily have inspired the creation of a spontaneous, cooperative, public–private partnership. The U.S.F.W.S. is legally in charge of this species' recovery.

However, well before the species was listed as endangered, the states of Oregon and California, a host of private groups (e.g., the Nature Conservancy, the Berry Botanic Garden, and the native plant societies in both states), and many private individuals had assembled a loosely coordinated effort to recover the western lily.

Recovery plan

The recovery plan has three primary components. The first, and most important is to secure and manage a sufficient number of wild populations distributed across the western lily's range to allow it to recover.

Second, there is an effort to gather genetically representative seed samples and store them in a seed bank. This will help prevent the irretrievable loss of valuable genetic information and provide a means to replace the population if it does get destroyed.

Third, there is a public component of recovery designed to make society aware of the value of the Western lily and of the necessity to conserve the species.

Edward O. Guerrant, Jr.

Asiatic Lion

(Panthera leo persica)

ESA: Endangered

IUCN: Endangered

Class: Mammalia
Order: Carnivora
Family: Felidae
Weight: Male, 330–551 lb.
(150–250 kg); female,
265–400 lb. (120–182 kg)
Head–body length: Male,
67–98 in. (170–250 cm); female,
55–69 in. (140–175 cm)
Tail length: Male, 35–41 in.
(90–105 cm); female, 28–39 in.
(70–100 cm)
Shoulder height: Male, 48 in.
(123 cm); female, 42 in.
(107 cm)
Gestation period: 100–119 days
Diet: Various animals
Habitat: Tropical forest
Range: Formerly western Iran
to eastern India; today in the
Gir Animal Reserve, India,
and vicinity

IN SIZE AND general appearance, the Asian and African lions are very similar. Coloration can vary widely from a light buff and silvery gray to yellowish red and golden brown. The male has a distinctive mane that apparently protects the neck when lions fight one another. The mane darkens as the cat grows older, sometimes becoming black. The Asiatic lion is said to have a scantier mane than its African counterpart, as well as a thicker coat, a longer tail tassel, and a more pronounced belly fringe. Some scientists do not think that these differences warrant full differentiation between the two lion species, especially because of the wide variation among African lions in their general coloration, length of mane, and other distinctions that also occur between the Asian and African species.

Lions prefer grassy plains, savannas, open woodland, and scrub country. Sometimes they are observed in semidesert and forest, and they have been found at elevations of up to 16,500 feet (5,000 meters).

The lion can run for short distances at 30–40 miles per hour (48–64 kilometers per hour), but normally walks at about three miles per hour (4.8 kilometers per hour). Although this cat is not a skilled climber, it can readily enter trees by jumping. Leaps of up to 39 feet (12 meters) have been recorded. The lion can be active around-the-clock, particularly in places where it is safe from human harassment, but it appears to prefer twilight and nighttime. On average, the lion is inactive for more than 20 hours a day. Lions live in groups, known as prides, that range in size from 4 to 37 animals.

Normally, the lion hunts by a slow stalk, creeping and freezing, and using the landscape for cover. It then leaps upon its prey. Because the lion only runs for short distances, if the prey is not captured within 150 to 300 feet (50 to 100 meters), it will usually give up. Small prey can be killed by a blow from the lion's massive paw, while larger victims are seized by the throat and strangled. Sometimes the lion will suffocate an animal by clamping its jaws over the mouth and nostrils. Two lions, or even an entire pride, may ambush prey. Because

ASIATIC LION
Asia

the majority of hunts end in failure, hunting as a group increases the chances of catching prey. A lion will eat anything it can catch, as well as eating carrion.

Social organization

Prides are generally made up of a group of related females and their young, and are closed to strange females. There is a ranking system among the females of a group, and a female is the leader of the pride, even when males are present. Nonetheless, males always dominate with respect to feeding. Females do almost all of the hunting. There is often competition for food after a kill, and the pride can be seen quarreling among themselves over a catch.

Lions breed throughout the year in India, but in any pride all females appear to give birth at approximately the same time. Cubs follow the mother after about three months and are weaned by six or seven months. At 11 months they will begin to take part in kills, but are probably not capable of surviving on their own until they are at least 30 months old. Sexual maturity occurs at about three or four years, but growth continues until about the age of six.

Shrinking range

Lions have the greatest distribution of any animal except for people and their domestic animals. About 10,000 years ago the lion occurred in most of Africa, Eurasia, North America, and northern South America. It is thought to have disappeared from Europe as a result of the development of dense forests; it probably vanished from the west-

ern hemisphere as a result of growing human population, which took its toll on prey animals.

Today, the lion has continued to decline as a result of continued human expansion. The lion came into direct competition with human interests primarily because it preyed upon domestic livestock, but in part because it presented a potential threat to human life. As weapons improved, the threat to the great cat became severe. Up to the mid-19th century, the Asiatic lion was still common from Asia Minor to central India. By 1940, however, it had been eliminated throughout these regions, with the exception of the Gir Forest of western India. Through vigorous conservation efforts, the population in that region has managed to survive. An estimated 180 cats are said to live there today.

The Gir Forest covers about 309,000 acres, having shrunk

A single male lion or a group of males will join a pride of females for an indefinite period of time to defend it against the approach of outside males. Eventually, usually within three years, the males are driven off by a new group of males that takes over the position within the pride.

from 786,000 since the 1880s. Each year, the nearby Gir Thar Desert advances into the forest by about ½ mile (0.8 kilometers). The Gir forest is the only large forested area remaining in the region, and it has been increasingly used and cultivated by people in the 20th century. Although the area is a sanctuary, with legal protection given to animal populations within its boundaries, the rules are difficult to enforce. The fundamental problem in the Gir Forest is that the human population, and with it the livestock population, has grown significantly. As humans and domestic animals use ever-increasing portions of the forest, there is less territory available for wild animal populations. All wildlife in the area is affected by the abuse of the land.

Water seems to be available in the forest for the greater part of the year, and there is probably little competition for it. Unfortunately, natural prey species in the forest are decreasing as humans make greater use of other resources in the region, such as vegetation and natural cover. The lions have therefore been forced to eat domestic animals; in turn, humans kill the lions because they threaten the livestock. During the dry part of the year there is little cover for the lions, which also hinders them in their search for food.

Relocating people

Even if human and livestock populations in the area do not continue to grow, the present levels of land degradation will eventually destroy the Gir Forest. Overstocking is the primary source of the problem in the forest, and the answer lies in greatly reducing the numbers of domestic animals in the area. Since the 1970s the Indian government has begun relocating families and farms that once lived in the area. With strict protection of the Gir Forest, the Asiatic lion population, as well as other endangered species in the protected forest, may stabilize. The survival of the Asiatic lion is linked to the survival of the Gir Forest; without the forest, this endangered lion will disappear forever.

Elizabeth Sirimarco

As young male lions approach maturity, they set out on their own. Several adult males may group together, or they may remain solitary.

LIZARDS

Class: Reptilia

Order: Squamata

Suborder: Sauria

Scientists use the name lizard to refer to any of a large group of scaly reptiles that are related to snakes. They are the most abundant of all reptiles and are found throughout the world in tropical and temperate areas. They occur as far north as the Arctic Circle in Europe and as far south as Tierra del Fuego in South America, but are much more common in warmer areas. There are some 3,000 living species of lizards, usually classified into 19 different families.

There is a great deal of variety among the forms of lizards. Some are long and slender, some are stumpy and short-bodied, and some have no limbs of any kind, much like a snake. External ear openings and eyelids are two major characteristics that distinguish most kinds of lizards from snakes. The body of these reptiles is covered with layers of scales that are separated from each other by thin, flexible skin. Scales also differ greatly among different species of lizards. Some are rough while others are smooth and glossy with an enamel-like texture, such as those found on skinks.

The tail is perhaps the most interesting feature of the lizard. It is useful to this reptile as a limb and helps to balance the body. Some species are able to run on their hind legs with the help of their tail. In some forms the tail is prehensile, meaning it is able to grasp or hook on to twigs as the lizard climbs. Some lizards have the ability to break off the tail if necessary. Usually the break occurs at a fracture plane where a lizard has been attacked by a predator, and as the severed tail continues to move, the predator is often distracted and the lizard is able to escape. The lizard will regenerate a new tail, although it is generally shorter than the old one, but that can also be used for escape. Hungry lizards have been known to deliberately break off their own tail to eat it.

Most lizards are active during the day, although some are nocturnal in warm regions. Because these reptiles are ectotherms, or cold-blooded animals, they must use their environments to regulate their body temperature. For example, diurnal species will bask in the sun to get warm, then move to a shady spot when they get too hot. Lizards can also raise their temperature with slight muscle movements. In colder habitats, lizards hibernate during winter.

Coachella Valley Fringe-toed Lizard

(Uma inornata)

ESA: Threatened

IUCN: Endangered

Length: 6–9½ in. (150–240 mm) total length

Clutch size: 1–5 eggs

Diet: Primarily insects, but will take plant material

Habitat: Desert areas and vegetation that maintains insect populations

THE COACHELLA Valley fringe-toed lizard (*Uma inornata*) lives only in sandy habitats on the floor of California's Coachella Valley. This is a particularly harsh environment, and the lizard seems to have a number of adaptations that allow it to survive there. Its critical habitat, or the range that possesses the physical and biological features essential for the conservation of the species, is made up of just 18.6 square miles (48 square kilometers) of private land and 1.08 square miles (2.8 square kilometers) of federally-owned land.

U. inornata was first described in 1895, and there has been much confusion about the species since this time. For many years this lizard was thought to be synonymous with the Colorado Desert fringe-toed lizard, *U. notata*, or the Mojave fringe-toed lizard, *U. scoparia*. It was not until 1963 that the *U. inornata* was permanently granted species status, but even as recently as 1980, certain researchers have still maintained that all three lizards are subspecies of *U. notata*. Today, however, most biologists familiar with the genus consider the Coachella Valley lizard to be a distinct species.

The Coachella Valley fringe-toed lizard is different from its close relatives in color. It is whitish to pale gray on the back, with patterns that resemble eyes formed by dark markings. The stomach is white, with one or several black dots on each side of the abdomen. There are grayish lines on the throat.

Scales

The scales of all lizards from the *Uma* genus are smooth and overlap evenly, giving the skin a soft, velvety texture. They are called "fringe-toed" because of a lateral row of long scales on the edge of

The Coachella Valley fringe-toed lizard has a number of adaptations that help it to survive in a harsh desert environment where ground temperatures are known to reach 160 degrees Fahrenheit (71 degrees Centigrade).

the toes. These scales help the lizard live in its sandy habitat by increasing the surface area of the foot, helping the lizard to move along and beneath the sand.

Other adaptations include the lizard's ability to run across the sand at relatively high speeds and literally dive into it. Once underneath the sand, it may move short distances, a movement known as sand swimming, until it is completely buried. Its smooth scales reduce friction when it moves through the sand. The light, constantly wind-blown sand is an aid to the reptile, as packed sand would be impossible to penetrate. Numerous adaptations help the lizard to keep sand out of its body openings and limit abrasion. *U. inornata* can partially close its nostrils to keep sand out, and if some does get in, it is trapped in a U-shaped nasal passage and blown out by a burst of air. The snout is shovel-shaped

and blunt, spreading the sand as the lizard dives. The upper jaw is longer than the lower, keeping sand out of the mouth. Fringed eyelids with a double seal and a loose flap that covers the ears are two other adaptations that protect this sand-diving lizard.

Cool underground

Sand swimming protects the Coachella Valley fringe-toed lizard from predators, but it also helps the lizard reach cooler underground areas in its harsh environment, where ground temperatures can exceed 160 degrees Fahrenheit (71 degrees Centigrade). The activity of the *U. inornata* is limited by temperatures. It is most active when ground surface temperatures are between 97 and 138 degrees Fahrenheit (36 and 59 degrees Centigrade). As the seasons change, the difference in the behavior of the lizard reflects its preference for this temperature range. The *U. inornata* may be active as early as February, but when temperatures are extremely hot—from May through September—the lizard is seldom active during midday. At that time it

will move underground, where temperatures are much cooler.

The mating season begins in late April and extends to mid-August. The location and timing of egg-laying in the wild is not known, but more than one clutch may be laid in one year. Hatchlings have been observed from late August through the fall.

Habitat loss

The primary reason for the decline in *U. inornata* populations has been loss of habitat from urban and agricultural development and off-road vehicles. Until recently this lizard existed with little interference from humans. Since the 1940s, however, the Coachella Valley has undergone dramatic development. In 1940 some 12,000 people lived in the area; by 1980 the permanent and part-time populations were estimated at more than 220,000. As the human population continues to grow, this lizard's habitat will become smaller and smaller.

In addition, humans have cultivated certain plants locally to act as windbreaks. However, *U. inornata* needs the wind to keep the sand soft enough to burrow in. As windbreaks are built, more and more of the lizard's habitat becomes untenable.

Major highways in the area may also act as barriers between distinct populations of the Coachella Valley fringe-toed lizard, and at some point in time this may lead to weakened gene pools due to the isolation of localized populations.

Advisory committee

Serious efforts to help *U. inornata* began in 1977 with a meeting of an advisory committee composed of scientists and resource managers dedicated to saving the species from extinction. This committee provided essential data which contributed to the lizard's official (U.S. Fish and Wildlife Service) threatened status. Since that time, efforts have been made to acquire a reserve that will provide critical habitat to house the *U. inornata*. The Nature Conservancy environmental organization has worked to acquire land for a reserve and has negotiated to purchase 1,900 acres (769 hectares) at a cost of $2 million. Further acreage may be added at a later date.

Survival

Management plans will be established to ensure the survival of the species. Because so many people are dedicated to the conservation of the Coachella Valley fringe-toed lizard, its chances of survival are good.

Island Night Lizard

(Xantusia riveriana)

ESA: Threatened

IUCN: Vulnerable

Length: 2½–4⅓ in. (65–109 mm) snout-to-vent length
Clutch size: 3–4
Diet: Primarily insects, but will take plant material
Habitat: Areas in which rocks, dense vegetation, or other objects provide cover
Range: Channel Islands off the coast of California

THE ISLAND NIGHT lizard is a moderate-sized reptile, although it is considered large for its genus. It is quite different from some of its relatives, which inhabit California's mainland.

Fossils indicate that this particular species was extinct on the mainland as long as one million years ago, leaving relic populations on three of the Channel Islands: San Clemente, San Nicholas, and Santa Barbara. Little obvious variation exists between the lizard inhabitants of each island, although there are slight differences in the scales, color, pattern, body size, and clutch size among populations.

Like other members of the family Xantusidae, the island night lizard is very secretive and requires shelter. Rocks, cacti, or dense undergrowth are optimal, but these lizards will also hide beneath boards or debris if they are available. Cover protects lizards from predators and also allows them to regulate their body temperature. This species requires lower temperatures than most lizard species and cannot tolerate temperatures much in

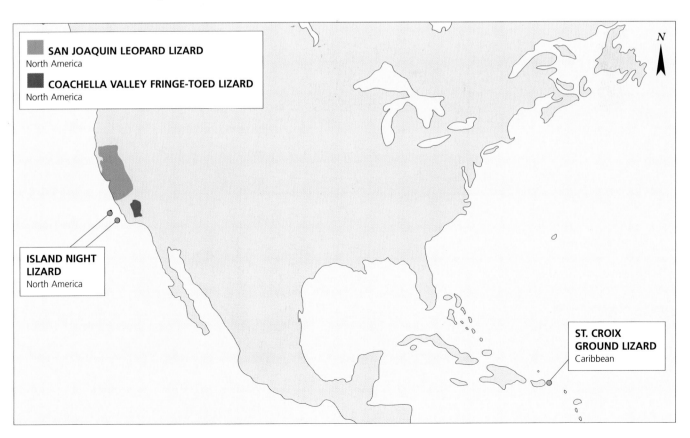

excess of 100 degrees Fahrenheit (38 degrees Centigrade). These lizards must be able to retreat from extreme surface temperatures, and the best cover for this is provided by thick vegetation.

The island night lizard begins mating in March, and gestation proceeds through the summer, with the young appearing in September. Only about half of the adult female population is reproductively active in a given year. The mean brood size is 3.8, which leaves a potential of 1.9 young produced per female in the entire population. This is low when compared to other lizards. In addition, the species does not reach sexual maturity until the third or fourth year of life, which

The island night lizard requires lower temperatures than most lizards. Its habitat must supply cover such as rocks or vegetation so that the lizard may retreat from the sun on hot days.

is quite late for a lizard of this size. The result is a low reproductive capacity. For this reason, the island night lizard cannot withstand high rates of predation.

A variety of mammals and birds may prey on this lizard. Among these are the common raven, the burrowing owl, foxes, feral cats, and possibly rats. The lizard itself is omnivorous, feeding on a wide variety of insects and plant material. As captives, these lizards will cannibalize other small lizards, including other species of the family Xantusidae, indicating that in the wild they may cannibalize juveniles of their own species.

Special habitat

The Channel Islands provide a special habitat for this lizard. Predator densities are relatively low, and climactic conditions are relatively stable. This may be the

reason why the reptile has survived on the islands, but not on the mainland. The island night lizard has evolved a low reproductive potential and a long life span, but this pattern is sensitive to any disturbances caused by habitat destruction or by the introduction of non-native species to the environment.

The largest population of the island night lizard is located in maritime desert scrub on the northwest coast of San Clemente Island. No data exists on the status of the island night lizard prior to ranching activities and the introduction of animals such as feral cats on San Clemente Island. However, it is possible to deduce the effects of such things on the lizard. Grazing and soil erosion have replaced shrub and vegetation with grassland, cactus, and bare ground, reducing the protective cover that is needed by

the lizards. Rocky areas are now exposed to direct sun due to the loss of original vegetation.

The effect of cats on the island night lizard population is uncertain. Although cats frequently feed on lizards, the lizard population does not appear to be adversely affected by cat predation in areas of optimal habitat, where lizards can still find cover. Cats also may not be sufficiently numerous to have a severe impact on the lizard.

Military operations on San Clemente have had a small effect on lizards because of development in parts of the lizards' range. This affects only a small area. Goats and sheep that were released on San Nicholas island in the 19th century caused great habitat modification by grazing. Although the animals were removed after World War II, the habitat has not fully recovered.

Habitat restoration

The largest populations of the lizard occur in specific sites on San Clemente, so the island has been designated a critical habitat. Smaller areas on San Nicholas and Santa Barbara have also been cited as essential to lizard survival. The main objective of the species' recovery plan is to restore and protect habitat that can support the populations. Extra data about the natural history and ecology of the lizard must be obtained to facilitate recovery. Removal of exotic animals and plants, control of unnatural erosion and revegetation with indigenous plants are important. Once threats to the lizard have been removed, the animals must be managed to assure their continued survival.

San Joaquin Leopard Lizard
(Gambelia silus)

ESA: Endangered

IUCN: Endangered

Length: 9–15 in. (23–38 cm)
Diet: Primarily insects
Habitat: Sparsely vegetated plains, alkali flats, grasslands, low foothills, canyon floors, large washes
Range: Scattered localities in San Joaquin Valley, California

THE SAN JOAQUIN leopard lizard resembles the common leopard lizard but has a blunter snout, which is why it is also known as the blunt-nosed leopard lizard. It has a spotted throat rather than the streaked throat typical of its relative. It has a slender, large body with a rounded tail and is generally gray or brown. The markings of the lizard consist of a series of light crossbars and dark spots. A female carrying eggs may have slightly different coloration or patterns on the sides of

Development continues at a fast pace in California, and the environment is changing rapidly. This has left wildlife, such as the San Joaquin leopard lizard, in a vulnerable position.

its body. Like other leopard lizards, the San Joaquin lizard is swift and agile, moving fairly quickly from one bush to another in search of insects. It will also prey upon smaller lizards. In order to catch them, it will lie quietly in dark areas and then ambush them. The San Joaquin leopard lizard will stay absolutely still when danger approaches and then run for cover if threatened.

Bush lover

This lizard can be found in various places in California's San Joaquin Valley, including the Sierran foothills, eastern parts of the Coast Range foothills, and on the Carrizo Plain. It prefers to inhabit areas with scattered bushes or low vegetation.

The primary cause for decline of this species is habitat destruction resulting from a great amount of development throughout its relatively small range. Agriculture and water control measures have also contributed to the vulnerability of this reptile. There is little hope for the survival of the natural flora and fauna of this arid region unless reserves are established.

The San Joaquin leopard lizard is protected by state law in California, prohibiting the capture, possession, or sale of the species. The state is trying to provide protection for remnants of the habitat that exist on public lands and to preserve critical habitat on private lands through acquisition or agreements with owners. The species is also fully protected by the United States Endangered Species Act.

St. Croix Ground Lizard

(Ameiva polops)

ESA: Endangered

IUCN: Critically endangered

Length: 1½–3 in. (3.5–8 cm)
Diet: Small crustaceans, insects
Habitat: Beach areas and upland forests
Range: St. Croix, U.S. Virgin Islands; offshore islands and cays

THE ST. CROIX GROUND lizard is a small species of the genus *Ameiva*. It has a light brown stripe in the middle of its back continuing down the tail, bordered by wide, dark brown or black stripes; below these are narrow stripes of brown, black, and white. The tail has alternating rings of blue and black. The top of the head is a uniform brown. The chin, throat, chest, sides of the snout, and undersides of the forelegs are deep pinkish red. The belly is light gray with lateral bluish markings.

Vegetation
The St. Croix ground lizard appears to prefer beach areas and upland forests, with the predominant plant species being the *Hippomane, Mancinella, Tabebuia heterophylla*, and *Exostema caribaeum*. Optimal sites appear to be those with both exposed and canopied areas, leaf or tidal debris, loose substrate, and crab burrows. Smaller lizards exist in more exposed habitat, while larger ones prefer canopied sites.

This species will actively prowl, root, and dig for prey. They appear to eat amphipods, a group of small crustaceans that are abundant along the beach. These lizards have also been observed taking small white moths from under forest litter and are known to forage out of sight beneath litter or in shallow holes that they have dug. Foraging is the major activity observed in the St. Croix ground lizards, with heat regulation being their next most frequently recorded characteristic.

Distribution
Before land development in the Virgin Islands, this species was probably restricted to St. Croix and its offshore islands and cays. Early in the 20th century the St. Croix ground lizard was thought to be extinct, although it was reported to exist as late as the 1920s. By 1937 it was found in St. Croix's Christiansted Harbor and on Green and Protestant Cays, which are situated off the north shore of St. Croix. In 1967, it was estimated that 200 lizards lived on Protestant Cay and approximately 300 on Green Cay; since 1968, the species has not been recorded on St. Croix. As of 1983, the two cays are the only sites where the species exists. Population estimates in the 1980s suggested that there were between 360 and 43,000 individuals on Green Cay; the population on Protestant Cay is about 50 individuals.

Although figures indicate an increase in population, biologists believe it is probably the result of improved census-taking rather than an actual population increase. It appears, however, that the two cay populations are stable and will remain so if no significant changes occur at either site.

Protection
The decline of the species may coincide with the arrival of the small Indian mongoose (*Herpestes auropunctatus*) in 1884. The mongoose is responsible for reducing the numbers of various terrestrial animals on the Virgin Islands. Extensive real estate development of coastal areas may have also contributed to the decline of the ground lizard.

The St. Croix ground lizard has been listed as an endangered species since 1977.

A refuge on Green Cay was purchased that year and provides protection for 14 of the 18 acres of critical habitat. The remaining four acres on Protestant Cay are at present leased for private use. With the protection of the Green Cay refuge, this ground lizard has a good chance of recovery.

Elizabeth Sirimarco

Spotted Loach
(Lepidocephalichthys jonklaasi)

IUCN: Endangered

Class: Actinopterygii
Order: Cypriniformes
Family: Cobitidae
Reproduction: Egg layer
Habitat: Mountain streams and ponds.
Range: Sri Lanka

THE SPOTTED LOACH is a most unusual fish and is highly adaptable to changing environmental conditions. As a member of the genus *Lepidocephalichthys*, the spotted loach is capable of very unusual behavior. During times of drought, this species can survive in streambeds or basins that hold no water. As the spotted loach rests quietly in moist sand or mud, it can survive by swallowing air and forcing it through its digestive tract. Its intestine is highly veined with small blood vessels, much like a lung, and the spotted loach uses its intestine to absorb life-sustaining oxygen from the air it holds. After the oxygen is used up and replaced with the by-product, carbon dioxide, the gas is expelled and more air is swallowed. This process can continue for long periods of time, until the drought period has passed.

Despite its extremely adaptable nature, the spotted loach is under severe threat of extinction within its home range on Sri Lanka. The main threat to this species is sedimentation that is brought about by deforestation.

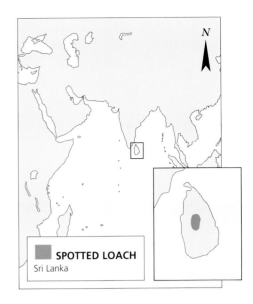

SPOTTED LOACH
Sri Lanka

Sedimentation has a particularly devastating effect on water life because of the fouling of feeding and breeding sites and other profound changes that the process causes in otherwise pristine aquatic environments.

William E. Manci

LOGPERCHES

Class: Actinopterygii

Order: Perciformes

Family: Percidae

Despite a difference in the common name, logperches are classified in the same genus, *Percina*, as several of the darters and should be included in this larger group. Logperches and darters share many common physical and behavioral characteristics. Only three genera are used to name all darters and logperches: *Ammocrypta*, *Etheostoma*, and *Percina*. The genus *Etheostoma* encompasses most of these brightly colored fish. This highly diverse group of freshwater fish contains a total of about 150 species, of which 24 darter species are considered vulnerable or endangered, and two logperches that are so considered. Their diversity in North America is second only to the family Cyprinidae, a group that includes minnows and chubs. Dispersed across the Mississippi River system and rivers of the Great Lakes, Hudson Bay, Atlantic Coast, and Gulf of Mexico regions, and some rare occurrences on the Pacific Coast of Mexico, darters and logperches have achieved a broad continental distribution.

As a group, darters and logperches are distinctive in shape and size and are small relative to more commonly known fish such as trout or bass. They reach a maximum total length of only 2 to 8 inches (5 to 20 centimeters). Their long, torpedolike bodies include two prominent dorsal fins on the back as well as pronounced pectoral fins on the sides for steering and maneuvering. The first, or spiny, dorsal fin contains spines for protection against predators. The second, or soft, dorsal fin has no spines. Darters and logperches are generally brightly colored.

The preferred environments of these fish are the fast-moving, shallow, "rapids" areas of streams. Stream riffles generally hold abundant supplies of food organisms, such as insects, that are poorly utilized by other fish until these organisms move downstream to pool areas.

Despite the advantages of river life, darters and logperches comprise the largest group of vulnerable and endangered fish in the world. Darters and logperches cannot compete with the destructive power of reservoirs and flood control projects, pollution, stream bank and watershed deforestation that causes siltation, and other human activities that lead to the death of fish populations.

Conasauga Logperch
(Percina jenkinsi)

ESA: Endangered

IUCN: Vulnerable

Length: 6 in. (15 cm)
Reproduction: Egg layer
Habitat: Stream riffles and pools over sand and gravel
Range: Upper Conasauga River, Tennessee and Georgia

RESTRICTED TO AN 11-mile (16-kilometer) stretch of the Conasauga River in southern Tennessee and northern Georgia, the Conasauga logperch is considered highly threatened. A member of the same genus as many of the darters, the Conasauga logperch relies on high-quality flowing water and a silt-free river bottom for its continued existence.

Shape and size

The Conasauga logperch is a large darter that measures almost 6 inches (15 centimeters) in total length. Despite its length, this fish is not as stout and robust as other darter fish and is, instead, very long and slender. This difference is accented by a very pointed, almost needlelike snout.

Its coloration pattern is very distinct, with alternating dark vertical bars and spots on the sides decorating and covering a yellow background.

The fins are primarily clear but are lightly spotted in patterns that suggest bands.

Breeding and feeding

Little is known about the Conasauga logperch's breeding and feeding habits. However, based on observations of the condition of the eggs in collected specimens, this logperch is most likely to lay its eggs in the spring in gravel stream riffles and in shallow rapids.

Direct observations indicate that this darter species favors aquatic invertebrates, such as insects, as its principal source of

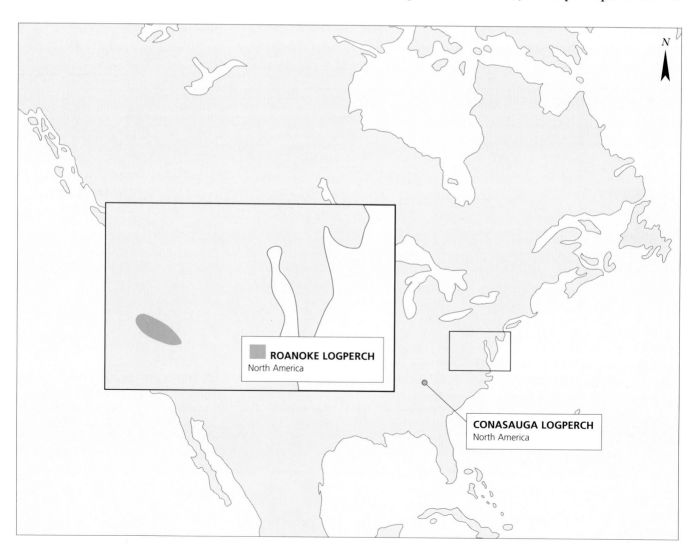

ROANOKE LOGPERCH
North America

CONASAUGA LOGPERCH
North America

The Roanoke logperch lives in the Upper Roanoke River Basin of Virginia, a biologically diverse river system that is home to a number of other species.

food. This logperch uses its pointed snout to help it overturn stones as it seeks out its prey.

Threat

The primary threats to the fish are agricultural and urban development in the Conasauga River Basin and the pollution associated with this. State and federal officials fear that a single event such as a chemical spill could destroy all the remaining individuals of this species.

Additionally, a dam construction project slated for the lower Conasauga River could affect the logperch and other upstream fishes. Often, after dam construction and reservoir development is complete, fish such as the common carp (*Cyprinus carpio*) tend to dominate the reservoir fishery.

If destructive fish such as the common carp move upstream to the upper Conasauga River, the Conasauga logperch could suffer from the alteration of habitat caused by the common carp.

Protected habitat

The U. S. Fish and Wildlife Service has designated the 11-mile stretch of the Conasauga River currently occupied by the Conasauga logperch as habitat that is critical to its survival. Hopefully this status, plus the protection that is afforded by the Chattahoochee and Cherokee National Forests that surround upper sections of the Conasauga River, will be adequate until some individuals can be relocated elsewhere.

Roanoke Logperch
(*Percina rex*)

ESA: Endangered

IUCN: Vulnerable

Length: 5 in. (13 cm)
Reproduction: Egg layer
Habitat: Riffles in moderate to large streams
Range: Upper Roanoke River Basin, Virginia

A RESIDENT OF THE most biologically diverse river system on the eastern seaboard of the United States, the Roanoke logperch inhabits the Roanoke River Basin in southern Virginia. This fish, along with several other species, is found only in the Roanoke River system. Sharing all or part of the river with nearly 200 other fish species, it most often lives in close association with the orangefin madtom, a small catfish. Before cities such as Roanoke and Salem began to spring up along the river, the Roanoke logperch could be found from the river's headwaters all the way to Albemarle Sound in North Carolina, where the river empties into the Atlantic Ocean. Human over-exploitation of natural systems has slowly put a stranglehold on the river's finite resources, however, and forced this fish farther and farther upstream. Urbanization and deforestation have released tons of silt into the river. Sewage has robbed the water of oxygen and choked the river with vegetation. Toxic chemicals have rendered any remaining marginal habitat uninhabitable, and stream channeling to minimize flooding has turned sections of the river that are critical to spawning and feeding into worthless canals.

Visual feeder

The presence of the Roanoke logperch is an excellent indicator of good water quality. This fish is a visual feeder that relies on hunting between small spaces and under pebbles to find its food and is therefore intolerant of silt, thick vegetation, and other impediments to the hunting process. If the Roanoke logperch is to survive in the wild, much greater care must be given to preserving high water quality in the Roanoke River and its tributaries. Given that the Roanoke River is used as a water supply for thousands of people who inhabit its banks, maintaining good water quality is important to people as well as to native Roanoke River fish such as this logperch.

Typical darter

This fish possesses typical darter characteristics. Growing to 5 inches (13 centimeters) long, its sleek torpedolike body reduces drag in swift water, while large pectoral fins just behind the gills make maneuvering an easy task.

The blunt snout is used to overturn stones and rocks in search for food. The Roanoke logperch has two dorsal fins on the back: a forward, spiny-rayed fin for protection against predators followed by a somewhat longer, soft-rayed fin for additional stability. Overall coloration is olive green with several dark saddlelike blotches on the back, dark vertical bars on the sides, a dark vertical slash across each eye, and a uniformly lighter colored belly. The spiny dorsal fin is dark green with the exception of a prominent red band. The soft dorsal fin, tail fin, and pectoral fins are spotted with dark green over a light green background that suggests bands or stripes. The anal fin behind the anus and the pelvic fins just below the pectorals are a solid light green.

The Roanoke logperch spawns in April by depositing fertilized eggs directly into sand or small gravel; the parents rely on well-oxygenated, silt-free water to prevent their offspring from being smothered in the nest. For this reason, spawning efforts are frequently unsuccessful.

Favorite foods of this fish include aquatic insects such as midges, blackflies, and caddis. Small crawfish and other invertebrates will also be consumed when the opportunity arises.

Degraded habitat

Increasing isolation in degraded habitat is the gravest problem for the Roanoke logperch. Not only does an inferior environment interfere with this fish's breeding habits, but it also affects the quality of the food that the fish needs to survive. Many species face this same danger.

William E. Manci

LORIKEETS

Class: Aves

Order: Psittaciformes

Family: Loriidae

Lorikeets look like many other parrots, but they have one major difference. Lorikeets have brushlike tongues that other parrots do not have. This unique tongue allows them to feed extensively on pollen and nectar. Many ornithologists claim this specialization is sufficient reason to recognize the lorikeets as a separate family from the parrots.

There are 55 lorikeet species. Lorikeets probably originated in New Guinea. At least two species are severely threatened, and might be considered endangered if more was known about them.

Blue Lorikeet

(Vini peruviana)

IUCN: Vulnerable

Length: 5½ in. (14 cm)
Weight: 1–1¼ oz. (31–34 g)
Clutch size: 1–2 eggs
Incubation: 25 days
Diet: Nectar, pollen, small fruits
Habitat: Coastal and lowland forests and woodlands
Range: Cook Islands, Society Islands, and westernmost Tuamotu Islands

BLUE LORIKEETS gather in small flocks and wander nomadically, searching for trees in bloom. They grow only as long as an average ballpoint pen, but have a distinctive appearance.

Blue lorikeets are uniformly purplish blue above, and feature white across the cheek, chin, throat, and breast, so they appear as if they are wearing a bib. A bright orange beak and yellow-orange foot and toe add a little contrasting color. Sadly, this uniquely colored bird is slipping into the realm of extinction.

Blue lorikeets once inhabited at least two dozen islands in eastern Polynesia. Ornithologists cannot determine which islands they originally inhabited, and to which islands they were later introduced. One early observer wrote that blue lorikeets are weak fliers, but their distribution across so many islands separated by ocean seems to suggest otherwise. These birds have now vanished from most of the islands where they were known to occur.

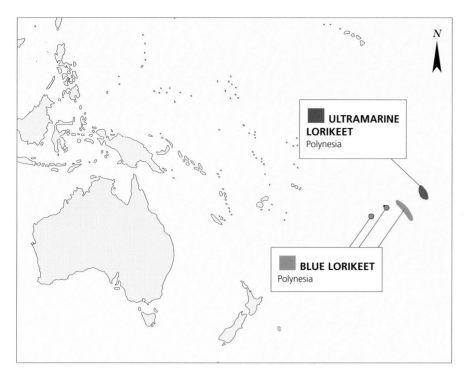

As of 1990, blue lorikeets were found only on Aitutaki, Apataki, Arutua, Bellinghausen, Rangiroa, Scilly, and Tikehau. Many islands have not been surveyed recently, but in 1993 birds were seen on Rangiroa, and it is thought that several hundred birds could be living on this atoll. Since many small islands and atolls are not inhabited by people and are seldom visited, they could be harboring blue lorikeets.

Completely arboreal, blue lorikeets even drink water that collects on tree leaves. Some lorikeets bathe in ground pools and streams, and others bathe in rain or rainwater gathered on palm fronds. Because they eat the pollen of tree flowers, they must move around for fresh supplies. In the tropics where lorikeets live, flowers do not bloom seasonally as they do in temperate climates. Instead, they bloom year-round. However, the flowers are usually not very abundant in any one place, so the birds must constantly move to find food.

Although pairs nest individually, after the breeding season blue lorikeets flock in small groups. Many birds moving together can spread out to search a broader area. When one or more birds finds a new tree in bloom, their feeding activity attracts the attention of other birds in the flock.

Deforestation

Because blue lorikeets are so arboreal, they do not feed on ground-blooming flowers. People on the islands where blue lorikeets live have been cutting down native forests for centuries. Since the colonial era of the 1700s and 1800s, lumber, grazing, and tourism have become important. Tourism requires airports, hotels, and other facilities, all of which demand space once covered by forest. The consequence has been less habitat for the blue lorikeet.

The habitat that remains has been degraded by the spread of rats. Both Polynesian rats (*Rattus exulans*) and black rats (*R. rattus*)

climb trees, and both readily eat birds' eggs and nestlings. Other species may be affecting blue lorikeets as well. The swamp harrier (*Circus approximans*) has been extending its range through Polynesia and the great horned owl (*Bubo virginianus*) of North America has been introduced to at least one island in the Marquesas, possibly to control rats. Whether the great horned owl has survived or even spread to other islands has not been documented. Both harrier and owl, however, do eat birds.

Habitat has not been the only issue. As members of the parrot order, blue lorikeets are of value to collectors. Although never abundant in captivity, blue lorikeets were trapped and their nests raided. Small populations on small islands can be easily damaged by collecting. Ironically, lorikeets make bad pets.

All lorikeets, including *Vini peruviana*, are covered by the Convention on International Trade in Endangered Species of Wild Fauna and Flora (CITES). More than 140 nations have joined the Convention, which regulates the international trade in species listed in any of its three appendices. The blue lorikeet is listed in Appendix II, so trade in this species is strictly controlled.

The blue lorikeet's population was estimated at 680 pairs, or from 1,400 to 1,500 individuals (counting nonbreeding birds), in the late 1980s. These were optimistic figures, and the total number may be much lower. However, with so many unsurveyed islands a realistic total is unknown. The way to preserve lorikeets is to preserve the quantity and quality of their habitat.

Ultramarine Lorikeet

(Vini ultramarina)

IUCN: Endangered

Length: 7 in. (18 cm)
Clutch size: 2 eggs (known from one nest in captivity)
Diet: Pollen, nectar, small fruits
Habitat: Forests from coast to highest mountain ridges
Range: Fatuhiva, Nukuhiva, Uapou, and Uahuka of the Marquesas Islands

THE ULTRAMARINE lorikeet is aptly named for its blue shades. The bird's shoulder, back, rump, and tail are colored somewhere between turquoise and lapis lazuli. A dark purplish blue covers the crown and nape, but the forehead is azure. The cheek, chin, and throat are basically white, but the feathers have dark blue bases with white tips, so the throat and breast look spotted. A dark purplish blue band across the lower breast highlights the whitish belly. A small but bright red beak is the only other accent to this bird's blue coloration.

Arboreal birds

Pollen and nectar comprise most of the ultramarine lorikeet's diet. An arboreal species, it specializes in tree flowers but also eats small fruits. Insects found in the crops of birds collected as specimens are believed to have been swallowed as the lorikeets lapped up pollen and were probably not hunted intentionally.

Several ultramarine lorikeets may band together outside the breeding season to travel in search of pollen. Unlike the blue lorikeet, which stays at lower elevations, the ultramarine lorikeet wanders as high up the mountains as the pollen and nectar can be found. Perhaps some flexibility of diet or a lack of competing species explains why it ranges so much higher than the blue lorikeet. Specific details about the ultramarine lorikeet, however, are not known.

Habitat destruction on Nukuhiva threatens the survival of many birds unique to that and other Marquesas Islands and it is possible that the ultramarine lorikeet is extinct on Nukahiva. The destruction of island habitat may have accelerated in recent decades, but it is nothing new. Island conquest and modification are deeply rooted in global history. The French originally fought for many South Pacific islands in order to start plantations growing coffee, cocoa, tea, tobacco, spices, and tropical fruits. These crops were grown

Lorikeets are in a different family than parakeets, but they share a similar appearance.

on islands where native islanders or indentured laborers were used as a cheap labor force. These colonial ambitions had two unforseen consequences.

The Europeans carried diseases that devastated the populations of native islanders, while the conversion of island landscapes from native plant communities to agriculture endangered many species.

Plummeting population

On Uapou an estimated population of 500 to 600 ultramarine lorikeets in 1975 plummeted to no more than 240 birds in 1990. Only 70 of these lorikeets were found on Nukuhiva in 1990. An introduced population on Uahuka was found to be steady at 400 to 500 birds at the same date. Introduced predators such as rats and feral cats may pose some hazard to the lorikeet; the great horned owl (*Bubo virginianus*) was introduced to Hivaoa to eat birds. Introduced avian malaria may also be affecting native birds. In 1992 and 1993 a total of 14 birds were translocated to Fatuhiva Island, which was free of rats. Since then more birds have been translocated, bringing the total to 29 birds by the end of 1995.

The birds of the Marquesas Islands need to be thoroughly studied. More information would help ornithologists learn how ultramarine lorikeets and other island birds might be able to coexist with humans with only slight modifications in human activities. The only way to guarantee ultramarine lorikeets any future is to plan to preserve their habitat while there is still time.

Kevin Cook

Pygmy Loris

(Nycticebus pygmaeus)

ESA: Threatened

IUCN: Vulnerable

Class: Mammalia
Order: Primates
Family: Lorisidae
Weight: Average 33 oz. (935 g)
Head-body length: 7–8 in. (18–21 cm)
Tail length: Vestigial
Diet: Mainly fruit, plus insects, leaves, seeds, lizards, birds eggs
Gestation period: 193 days
Longevity: Probably 12–14 years
Habitat: Tropical forest, secondary forest, and shrub
Range: Vietnam

IN THE JUNGLES of Vietnam lives a small creature that is one of the most unusual primates in the world: the pygmy loris. It has thick brown, reddish brown, or gray fur, with a reddish-brown stripe between its eyes from muzzle to forehead. This stripe continues and becomes brownish-black as it extends toward the crown and between the ears.

Lorises are nocturnal, spending their day sleeping, wound in tight balls, hidden in dense foliage. Zoologists suspect that they are solitary. Pygmy lorises use urine to mark their territory. These animals never leap, and this gives rise to their other common name, "slow loris."

Although its status is unclear, the pygmy loris has suffered from warfare and habitat destruction that has been inflicted upon its native country. The greatest threat to its population growth is the clearing of more forest for agriculture. Although not often used for food, the pygmy loris is sometimes kept as a pet and can be seen for sale in markets in Hanoi, the capital city.

Thaya du Bois

Spanish Lynx

(Lynx pardina)

ESA: Endangered

IUCN: Endangered

Class: Mammalia
Order: Carnivora
Family: Felidae
Weight: To 40 lb. (18 kg)
Head-body length: 2½–3½ ft. (85–110 cm)
Shoulder height: 18–28 in. (60–70 cm)
Gestation period: 63–73 days
Range: Southwest Iberian peninsula

THE SPANISH LYNX is yellowish red above and white below. There are round black spots on the

SPANISH LYNX
Europe

The lynx is a hardy cat, managing to withstand trapping, starvation, and habitat decline all over the Northern Hemisphere. In Siberia, where this lynx comes from, the maximum population density is five individuals per 38.5 square miles (100 square kilometers).

body, tail, and limbs, and the triangular ears have pronounced tufts. The face has especially long whiskers. The fur tends to be long and thick, especially on the lower cheeks. This gives it a bearded appearance, particularly in winter. Its tail is relatively short. It can grow up to 3½ feet (110 centimeters) in length and weigh up to 40 pounds (18 kilograms). In general, lynx are nocturnal animals, and the Spanish lynx shares this characteristic.

It tends to remain in one area, but it will migrate if conditions require it to. Lynx are excellent climbers, swimmers, and hunters. This particular species prefers open forests and thickets, and the diameter of its home range is between 2½ and 6 miles (4 and 10 kilometers).

Stalker

Usually a lynx will stalk its prey to within a few bounds, or alternatively it might wait in ambush. Generally, its diet consists of rabbits, but it will eat other small mammals and birds.

The Spanish lynx is generally treated as a full species separate from other lynx. It is the most endangered of all lynx, with a population estimate at just 1,000 to 1,500 individuals.

While the species has occasionally been the victim of fur trappers and hunted as a predator of domestic animals, these are not the most ominous threats. Most damaging to its populations has been the steady decline of its prey species. For example, the Spanish lynx population was significantly diminished in the 1950s and 1960s when a disease called myxomatosis struck the rabbit population. As suitable habitat diminishes, both the lynx and the rabbit populations have continued to decline.

Hybridization

The lynx has been known to breed in captivity and has a gestation period of between 63 and 73 days. There is, however, concern that hybridization has occurred among different subspecies of lynx.

The Spanish lynx occurs in presumably growing populations at the Coto Doñana reserve. A study in 1983 marked 12 animals; just five years later, another study marked 25.

Elizabeth Sirimarco

See also Cats.

MACAQUES

Class: Mammalia

Order: Primates

Family: Cercopithecidae

Subfamily: Cercopithecinae

Macaques are heavily built monkeys with tails that vary in size. Some have no tails at all, while others have tails that are longer than their body length. The male is larger than the female, often a great deal larger. They live in Southeast Asia, Japan, Gibraltar, and North Africa in a highly developed social system. Macaques have rigid dominance hierarchies, and those at the bottom of the system often lead stressful, unpleasant lives with less access to food.

There is some disagreement over the classification of macaques, with the number of separate species varying between 13 and 19. One problem is the identification of species on the Indonesian island of Sulawesi (formerly Celebes).

Everyday existence for the macaque is fraught with such hazards as disease, stress, starvation, and almost constant fighting, and nearly 90 percent of the members of certain species die before they reach adulthood. Humans, however, have greatly increased the suffering of macaques.

During the 1950s, up to 200,000 rhesus macaques were exported each year from India to the West. They were used for scientific research, particularly for the testing of vaccines. When this exportation ceased in 1977, Southeast Asia filled the gap in the market, starting up their own monkey trading, which brought in great financial rewards. These factors, along with habitat destruction and hunting, have greatly reduced the abundance of macaques throughout their range.

The macaque's coat is generally a dullish brown but its facial skin and rump may be bright red. Ischial callosities, the pads on the rump, are prominent. The macaque has well-developed cheek pouches for temporary food storage. The ears are bare, pointed, and protrude from the head.

Some species exhibit swelling of the sexual organs in the mating season. Mostly macaques are seasonal breeders. They mate in the fall, and give birth in the spring, with an approximate 5½-month gestation period. Females mature sexually at 3½ years, and males at 4½ years. However it takes 6 years for females, and 10 years for males, to become fully grown.

Macaques live in groups that often include several adult males. Females generally spend their entire lives with their original family, but males leave at adolescence and then live either alone or in small groups of males as they attempt to work their way into established groups containing females.

Communication is very intricate. Macaques use body language, vocalization, and facial expressions to communicate with each other.

The macaque seems to be able to adapt to virtually any ecological situation, from tropical rain forest to artificial habitats to snow-covered winter landscapes. In general they are omnivorous, eating vegetables, insects, meat, and various marine animals.

There is a famous colony of macaques that lives on the Rock of Gibraltar in the Mediterranean Sea. The colony was fed by the British Army, and legend had it that if the macaques left the Rock, the British would lose Gibraltar.

Barbary Macaque

(Macaca sylvanus)

IUCN: Vulnerable

Weight: 24–33 lb. (11–15 kg)

Head-body length: 20–24 in. (50–60 cm)

Tail length: Absent

Diet: Fruit, young leaves, bark, roots; sometimes invertebrates

Gestation period: Average 166 days

Longevity: 25 years in captivity

Habitat: Mid- to high-altitude forest, scrub, and cliffs

Range: North Algeria, Morocco, Gibraltar

THE BARBARY macaque, also known as the Barbary ape or rock ape, is the only species of macaque living in Africa.

Once widespread throughout North Africa, this macaque is now restricted to patches of scrub and forest in Northern Algeria and Morocco; there is also a small population in Gibraltar. Seventy-five percent of the wild population lives in the Middle Atlas, Morocco. Estimates of this macaque's population vary between 9,000 and 24,000. They breed very successfully in captive colonies, where over 900 exist. However, they are under increasing threat from a variety of factors, including capture for use as pets and being shot as agricultural pests. Human encroachment has brought habitat destruction, and they have to compete for herbaceous foods with goats, sheep, and cattle. Macaques are still used for medical research, but most of the animals taken for this purpose are not from the wild, but are either from Gibraltar or are taken from captivity.

Lion-tailed Macaque

(Macaca silenus)

ESA: Endangered

IUCN: Endangered

Weight: 15 lb. (7 kg)
Head-body length: 18–24 in. (46–61 cm)
Tail length: 10–15 in. (25–38 cm)
Diet: Omnivorous
Gestation period: 166 days
Longevity: 25 years in captivity
Habitat: Moist evergreen forest
Range: Southern India

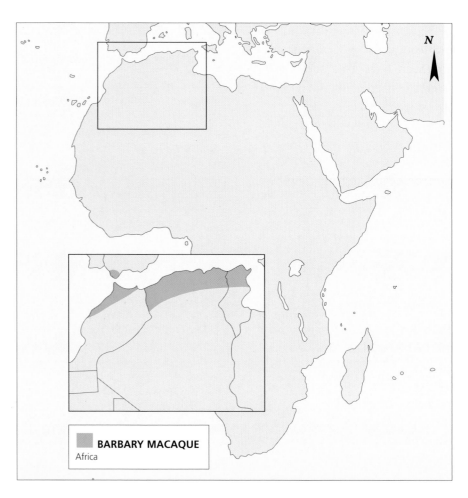

BARBARY MACAQUE
Africa

THE LION-TAILED macaque is a spectacular-looking monkey with a black coat and a gray ruff around its face. Its tail has a slight tuft at the tip. The ruff, as well as the macaque's stance, lends it the appearance of a lion. It is a shy animal that inhabits dense forests on the west coast of southern India. Although it occasionally descends to the ground to play or to splash about in water, it is an arboreal monkey. It moves through the trees in groups of between 10 and 20, with a dominant male acting as a scout. This male carefully maneuvers through the forest canopy some distance ahead of the group, leading the way.

Because they have no tail, Barbary macaques have been referred to as apes, although they are not apes at all.

Extensive deforestation has reduced moist evergreen forest of southern India to a series of isolated patches. This is one of the world's least-studied rainforests. Presently, logging has declined, but the most serious threats are development projects such as hydroelectric dams, railroads, and roads—not to mention human resettlements in the forest. More research on this macaque, and better protection of its habitat are needed.

The lion-tailed macaque is rated at six in the IUCN's Action Plan for Asian Primate Conservation, which means that it is highly endangered. Less than 10,000 individuals remain, and no large section of its population is really secure. The most recent estimate places the species' numbers at around 3,000.

Yakushima Macaque

(Macaca fuscata yakui)

ESA: Threatened

Weight: 18–33 lb. (8–15 kg)
Head-body length: 19–24 in. (47–60 cm)
Tail length: 3–5 in. (7–12 cm)
Diet: Fruit, insects, young leaves, crops, small animals
Habitat: Forest
Range: Yaku Island, Japan archipelago

THE YAKUSHIMA macaque is a subspecies of the Japanese macaque, or snow monkey. It is found only on Yaku Island, 37 miles (60 kilometers) south of Kyushu in Japan. It can be found

snuggled together in groups of four or five, trying to keep warm in the high mountains. It also has the northernmost range of any monkey, and its coat has adapted well to dealing with the harsh realities of life in a cold climate. Its fur is very thick, and it is pale in color. Its face and rump skin are naked and red in the adult. It is not uncommon for snow to gather on its head but, thanks to its fur, this macaque is able to survive the winter. Some lucky

Lion-tailed macaques are being successfully bred at the San Diego Zoo. Some of the zoo's monkeys were received several years ago from the private zoo of Prince Rainier of Monaco.

members of this species have learned that crouching in hot springs makes a welcome natural sauna on a freezing day. They take turns wading, single file, through the snow, searching for meager morsels of food such as seeds and pieces of bark.

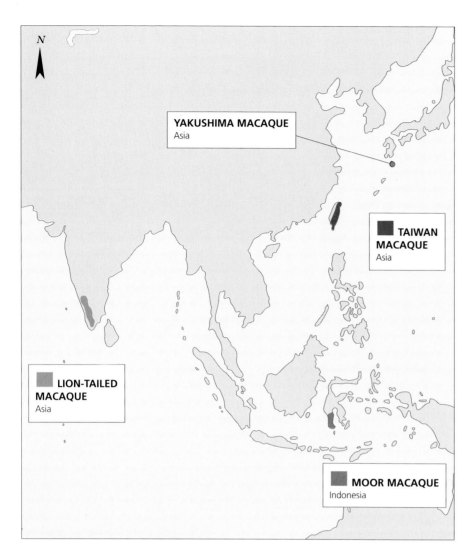

YAKUSHIMA MACAQUE
Asia

TAIWAN
MACAQUE
Asia

LION-TAILED
MACAQUE
Asia

MOOR MACAQUE
Indonesia

The Moor macaque (*Macaca maura*) is another species that is classified as endangered. It makes its home on the Indonesian island of Sulawesi.

In the summer months there is a lush supply of vegetation, and the Yakushima macaque spends the summer lazing around, grooming the other members of its group. The grooming ritual is important, both to eliminate parasites and as a way of maintaining friendly bonds. Males partake much less readily than females in the grooming ceremony and are content to lie around waiting for the attentions of a subordinate male.

The young are born after a five- to seven-month pregnancy, the birth coinciding with the melting of the harsh winter snows. The plentiful food supply in springtime allows the youngster to grow rapidly. However, it will be another year before it will leave its mother and take its first steps on its own.

Uncertain future

Population estimates for the Yakushima macaque suggest that they number 3,000 individuals.

A national park has been established on Yaku Island, containing about 450 monkeys. The future of the rest of these monkeys remains uncertain. They are regarded as pests because of their raids on orange plantations, and are trapped in large numbers.

Their natural forest habitat has been turned into conifer plantations, thus denying them their regular diet. If the present pattern of trapping continues, numbers will dwindle to a few hundred in several years.

Steps that could be taken to alleviate the problem include surveying the population on the island in depth, and possibly declaring the Yakushima macaque a National Treasure, which would automatically enhance its status.

Sarah Dart

Three other species of macaque are considered threatened or endangered:

Mentawai Macaque
(*Macaca pagensis*)
IUCN: Critically endangered
Range: Mentawai Island

Moor Macaque
(*Macaca maura*)
IUCN: Endangered
Range: Sulawesi

Taiwan Macaque
(*Macaca cyclopis*)
ESA: Threatened
IUCN: Vulnerable
Range: Taiwan

MACAWS

Class: Aves

Order: Psittaciformes

Family: Psittacidae

Macaws fly above the tropical forests of the New World. Their large size, bright colors, and long tails give them a stately appearance shared by few other birds. There are about 19 species in this group. Some species have enormous ranges that cover most of northern South America, but other species inhabit only single islands of the West Indies.

Macaws have been extremely popular as pets since Europeans first began settling the Americas. Their popularity has not waned, although their habitat has. Many people find them more appealing as they become more rare. The illegal trade in macaws, with some specimens going for thousands of dollars, only increases their value. Many of the macaws are listed as protected species in the Convention on the International Trade in Endangered Species of Wild Fauna and Flora (CITES), but quite often the damage has already been done by the time law enforcement officials intervene. Several macaws have experienced at least slight population declines. Two species are now severely endangered, and one of them may already be extinct.

Lear's Macaw

(Anodorhynchus leari)

ESA: Endangered

IUCN: Critically endangered

Length: 29½ in. (75 cm)

Weight (captive birds): Female 1⅔ lb. (750 g), Male 2 lb. (900 g)

Clutch size: 1–3 eggs

Incubation: 28–32 days

Diet: Fruits of licuri palm and probably other fruits

Habitat: Dry shrub land

Range: Northeast Bahia, Brazil

EVERYONE LOVES a good mystery, but the mystery surrounding an endangered species may carry greater significance than the usual tales of fiction. Nearly everything about Lear's macaw involves some mystery. It begins with the bird's identity and ends with its future.

Lear's macaw belongs to the same genus (*Anodorhynchus*) as the hyacinth macaw (*A. hyacinthinus*) and the glaucous macaw (*A. glaucus*). Largest of all the world's parrots, the hyacinth macaw probably has been popular in captivity since people first settled in South America. Even the ancient peoples of that continent liked to keep pet birds. When Europeans discovered the continent and began colonizing it, they sent hyacinth macaws back across the Atlantic Ocean. The great blue birds became immensely popular in zoos and private collections. The glaucous macaw closely resembles the hyacinth macaw but is 10 to 12 inches (25.5 to 30.5 centimeters) shorter. The last known sighting of a live glaucous macaw was in 1915. Ornithologists believe the bird to be extinct, but this is an unresolved mystery.

The Lear's macaw grows only slightly larger than the glaucous macaw. One theory says that the Lear's macaw is a hybrid between the hyacinth and glaucous macaw, but this theory has little credibility. One fact that argues against the hybrid theory is the range of Lear's macaw. It inhabits a dry plateau in eastern Brazil. The glaucous macaw lived much farther south, where Paraguay, Brazil, and Argentina converge. If hyacinth and glaucous macaws were interbreeding, then all their offspring were flying a thousand miles northeast and relocating in the same area.

Rich coloration

A rich cobalt blue above and a greener blue below, the Lear's macaw sports a yellow ring of bare skin around the eye and a patch of bare yellow skin at the base of the beak. The glaucous and hyacinth macaws appear much the same. A powerful beak suggests the bird eats large seeds and fruits, which it cracks open.

Virtually nothing about the natural history of Lear's macaw was known before 1978. Although the bird was described as a species in 1856, ornithologists knew only that the Lear's macaw occasionally turned up in shipments of the larger hyacinth macaws. They did not even know which country it inhabited. Then, in 1978, ornithologists found a small population of about 60 Lear's macaws living near cliffs in Bahia, Brazil. They reported that the Lear's macaw eats palm fruits and roosts at night in crevices and hollows on the cliffs.

Habitat loss through human activities is a contributing factor in this bird's population decline, but heavy collecting for the pet trade is undoubtedly the leading cause of this species' disappearance. The species has declined through hunting for meat, and the bird's dependence on the fruits of the licuri palm. The habitat of the licuri palm has gradually been lost to agriculture and grazing, and its fruits are used for livestock feed. Educational programs have eliminated hunting in most of its range.

The mystery of the Lear's macaw ends with questions. Can enough habitat be preserved and protected quickly enough to help the Lear's macaw survive? Can the illegal marketing of parrots be curtailed and enforced to keep the last few Lear's macaws in the wild? Can the Lear's macaw survive with such a low population even if habitat is preserved and illegal trapping is stopped? Extinction would finally answer these questions.

Spix's (little blue) Macaw
(Cyanopsitta spixii)

ESA: Endangered

IUCN: Critically endangered

Length: 22 in. (56 cm)
Weight: ¾ lb. (345 g)
Clutch size: 1–4 eggs
Habitat: Caraiba gallery woodland
Range: Bahia, Brazil

ENTIRELY BLUE, Spix's macaw looks like any other blue macaw until a second look reveals more detail. The back, wing, and tail shine with some purple color. The breast and belly carry a hint

of green washed across the blue. A little pale gray lightens the cheek. The beak, foot, and toe are all black. Only the bright yellow eye adds any contrasting color. The uniform coloring lends the bird a different kind of beauty than the splashy yellows, greens, and reds of other parrots. This subtle beauty has long attracted people who admire parrots.

No one has specifically studied wild Spix's macaws. They have been popular pets since their discovery in 1832, but their natural history remains almost completely unknown. Their population has diminished drastically. In the early 1980s only three birds remained in the wild. These birds were thought to be captured for the illegal trade between 1987 and 1988. The species was believed extinct in the wild, but one bird was seen in 1990. A captive female was introduced to this single male in 1995.

Too much attention
Many birds suffer because people do not consider their needs while planning plantations, airports, housing developments, and other commercial activities. These types of activities can either destroy or degrade habitat for many bird species. The Spix's macaw has disappeared because people paid too much attention to it. For centuries before Europeans colonized South America, people hunted and trapped the bird, both for food and as a pet. Europeans expanded the market for attractive tropical birds, even

The known population of Lear's macaws now occupies an ecological reserve originally established for other species, so further habitat loss is less likely to occur.

though the supply once seemed limitless. The Spix's macaw is now critically endangered and faces extinction because trapping continued without any restraint for far too long. Prior to 1970 the main threat to the species was habitat loss. After 1970 illegal trade became the main threat.

Key to future

During the 1970s, observers reported that the habitat of Spix's macaw appeared to be safe from destruction. The species' habitat is scattered across patches of woodland in Bahia, Brazil. Some birds may yet survive in this remaining habitat.

The captive breeding program is considered to be particularly vital to the future survival of Spix's macaw.

Kevin Cook

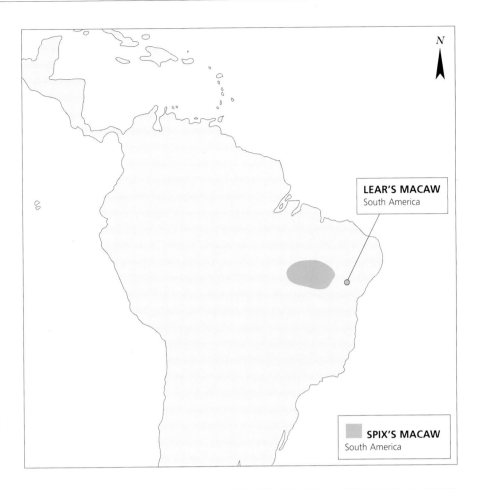

N

LEAR'S MACAW
South America

SPIX'S MACAW
South America

MADTOMS

Class: Actinopterygii

Order: Siluriformes

Family: Ictaluridae

Members of the family Ictaluridae (catfish), the madtoms play an important role in the overall ecology and balance of many aquatic systems. A fairly specialized group of fish, they fill a vital niche as they scour the bottom zones of streams. They were given the name *madtom* because their habit of swimming erratically in search of food is one characteristic that sets them apart from other catfish.

The name *catfish* conjures up an immediate image in the minds of most people. The most distinguishing features of this ancient group of fish are the catlike barbels, or whiskers, that all catfish exhibit. Barbels are not hairs, they are sensitive organs containing taste buds and other sensors that collect chemical cues from their surroundings. Catfish have been successful in adapting to a wide range of environments.

Catfish are not only diverse in their distribution but also in their various forms, and are categorized under several scientific genera. They generally occupy warmwater environments and can tolerate high temperatures and low levels of oxygen. The madtoms are somewhat different in this respect. Catfish occur in streams and lakes, caves and springs, and at both deep and shallow depths. They easily adapt to new environments. The exotic walking catfish, *Clarias batrachus*, of Florida is a perfect example of a species that has supremely adapted to a totally new environment. Native to Asia, the walking catfish was introduced to Florida and has displaced some of the less aggressive native fishes. When state officials tried to poison some of the walking catfish in their new living quarters, the fish simply swam to the surface and walked on land while breathing air and moved to untreated waters, leaving the native fish to die.

Some catfish and madtoms are in danger of extinction from human destruction of their habitat and pollution of their water.

Catfish share some common characteristics. The skin is scaleless, they have an adipose (fatty) fin on the back, some fins have spines for protection, and the anal fin just behind the anus and genitals is unusually long and wide. This feature helps keep the thin, wide mouth in contact with the bottom as the fish swims in search of food.

Caddo Madtom

(Noturus taylori)

IUCN: Vulnerable

Length: 2½ in. (6 cm)
Reproduction: Egg layer
Habitat: Shallow river areas over small rocks
Range: Ouachita River Basin, Arkansas

As THE COMMON name partially suggests, the Caddo madtom occupies the upper reaches of the Caddo River, Little Missouri River, and Ouachita River in southwestern Arkansas. The Caddo River and Little Missouri River are tributaries of the much larger Ouachita River. All three of these rivers have been subjected over the past several decades to massive dam construction projects designed to control flooding and supply water to nearby communities. Lake Ouachita, the reservoir formed by the construction of a dam on the main stem of the Ouachita River near the city of Hot Springs, has been particularly destructive to habitat preferred by the Caddo madtom. A river fish, the Caddo madtom requires shallow, flowing water over small rocks to flourish.

Flooding

The Lake Ouachita Project inundated many miles of this fish's prime habitat. Likewise, dams on the Caddo and Little Missouri Rivers have flooded habitat, restricted movement by the Caddo madtom up and down the river channels, and dramatically affected water quality below the dams by disrupting seasonal

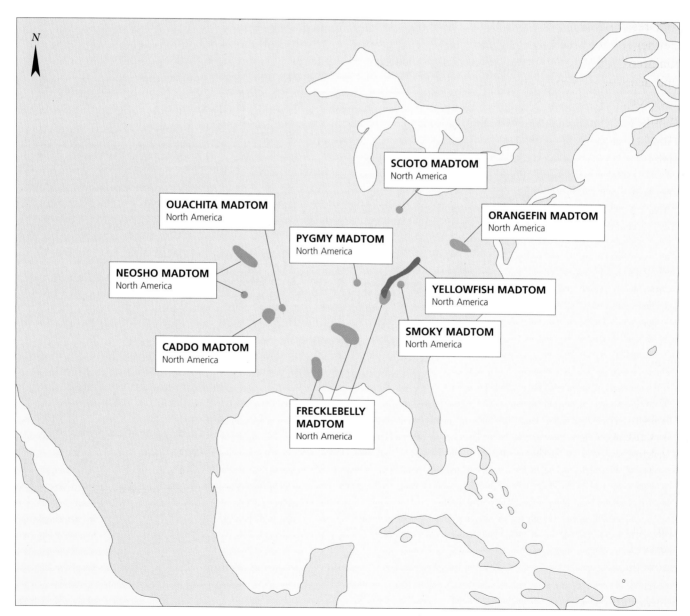

The frecklebelly madtom averages just over 3 inches (7.5 centimeters) in length and conforms closely to the typical madtom physique.

water flow and temperature patterns. While removal of the dams and restoration of these areas is neither realistic nor practical, the maintenance of remaining prime and acceptable river stretches for the conservation of the Caddo madtom will be necessary to ensure the continued survival of this threatened species.

Appearance

This small, unassuming fish presents a typical madtom profile with barbels on the face, a compressed and shallowly sloped head, a long keel-like adipose fin on the back between the dorsal fin and tail fin, and a long and wide anal fin just behind the anus. This is used to lift the tail and maintain contact with the bottom during swimming and feeding. Growing up to 2½ inches (6 centimeters) in length, the Caddo madtom is dark brown on the back and speckled brown on the sides, with a creamy color on the belly. All fins are mainly light and creamy in color, but the dorsal fins, anal fins, and tail fins show dark banding at the edges.

Little is known about the reproductive or feeding habits of the Caddo madtom, but it probably spawns its adhesive eggs in the spring in crevices or other covered areas in flowing water. Most likely, a parent provides protection until the offspring hatch. It is safe to assume that the Caddo madtom consumes riverbottom insects and other invertebrate animals.

Frecklebelly Madtom

(Noturus munitus)

IUCN: Lower risk

Length: 3 in. (7.5 cm)
Reproduction: Egg layer
Habitat: Riffle and rapids of large rivers
Range: Eastern Louisiana to eastern Tennessee

THROUGHOUT ITS range in the southeastern states of the United States, the frecklebelly madtom is under severe ecological pressure. As appropriate habitat is wiped out by human development, this small fish is forced to survive in higher densities; otherwise entire populations are eliminated. Flood control and water supply projects are a high priority in the states of Louisiana, Mississippi, Alabama, Georgia, and Tennessee. Most of these projects involve the construction of dams and the modification of stream channels to stabilize seasonal water flow rates and reduce resistance to flow in the channel.

Damming

The impacts of these activities on stream fish such as the frecklebelly madtom are devastating. Dams create reservoirs that flood stream channels and produce habitat that is unhealthy for these fish. Also, much of this work, in addition to deforestation of the surrounding watershed and pollution from agricultural, domestic, and commercial sources, causes and promotes erosion and siltation in the rivers and further degrades vital living space and water quality. This madtom relies on clean flowing water that is free of pollution, silt, and debris in order to find food, successfully reproduce, and thrive.

Principal river systems that support the frecklebelly madtom include the Pearl, the upper Tombigbee, and the upper Alabama Rivers. These are important waterways to both fish and people. Without a plan that takes into account the needs of both, populations of threatened species such as the frecklebelly madtom will continue to shrink and may be lost forever.

Coloration

The frecklebelly madtom possesses the signature keel-like adipose fin on the back between the dorsal fin and tail fin, and displays barbels ("whiskers") like all other members of the family Ictaluridae. This fish is aptly named, for it displays large dark blotches and smaller freckle-like spots on its body over a much lighter background. The flattened head of this scaleless fish can be used like a wedge to unearth small rocks and stones in its search for food in shallow stream riffles. Several of the fins, particularly the pectoral fins just behind the gills and the pelvic fins on the belly, are quite stout and provide leverage as it moves bottom debris. The anal fin, located just behind the anus, and the tail fin are pigmented in patterns that suggest banding, and the dorsal fin is multicolored as well. The small eyes are not used much for sensory input; this fish relies on its touch, smell, and highly developed sense of taste.

The frecklebelly madtom is secretive and little is known about its feeding and reproductive habits. It probably spawns in the spring and deposits its adhesive eggs in well-oxygenated crevices and protected areas of the river. Some parental care of incubating eggs probably occurs. The frecklebelly madtom probably prefers stream-dwelling insects and other invertebrate animals as its principal foods during its nightly feeding excursions.

Neosho Madtom

(Noturus placidus)

ESA: Threatened

IUCN: Lower risk

Length: 2½ in. (6 cm)
Habitat: Under and around rocks in shallow riffles
Range: Rivers in Kansas, Missouri, and Oklahoma

THROUGHOUT ITS range in the south-central states of the United States, the Neosho madtom has experienced considerable ecological changes. The fish's habitat has been diminished by human development, so that it has been forced to survive in denser populations to avoid total elimination.

Water control

Flood control and water supply projects for domestic and agricultural use are a high priority in the states of Kansas, Missouri, and Oklahoma. Most of these projects involve the construction of dams and the modification of stream channels to stabilize seasonal water flow rates and reduce resistance to flow in the channel. The impacts of these activities on stream fishes such as the Neosho madtom are devastating.

Dams create reservoirs that flood stream channels and produce habitat that is completely inappropriate for these fish, both behind the dam and downstream where temperature and flow profiles are dramatically altered.

Also, much of this activity, in addition to deforestation of the surrounding watershed and pollution from agricultural, domestic, and commercial sources, causes soil erosion and siltation in the rivers and further degrades vital living space and water quality. The Neosho madtom relies on clean flowing water free of pollution, silt, and debris, to find its food, to successfully reproduce, and to thrive.

Principal river systems that support the Neosho madtom include the Neosho River, the lower Spring River, and the Illinois River of Oklahoma. These

The Neosho madtom lives in river systems that are important to both fish and people. Unfortunately, the needs of humans usually come before those of wildlife.

are important waterways to both fish and people. Without a plan that takes into account the needs of both, numbers of threatened species like the Neosho madtom will continue to diminish and could even be lost forever.

Typical look

The Neosho madtom has a typical madtom physique. It has the keel-like adipose fin on the back between the dorsal fin and tail fin, and barbels ("whiskers") like all members of the family Ictaluridae. Its barbels are somewhat shorter than other madtoms. This fish displays some dark blotches and smaller freckle-like spots on its body over a much lighter background. The flattened head of this scaleless fish is used as a tool to wedge under small rocks and stones in its search for food in shallow stream riffles.

Several of the fins, particularly the pectoral fins just behind the gills and the pelvic fins on the belly, are quite stout and provide leverage as the fish moves bottom debris. The anal fin just behind the anus and the tail fin are pigmented in patterns that look rather like banding, and the dorsal fin is multicolored as well. The small eyes are not used for sensory input; rather this fish relies on its touch, smell, and highly developed sense of taste.

Secretive madtom

The Neosho madtom is secretive and little is known about its feeding and reproductive habits. It likely spawns in the spring and deposits its adhesive eggs in well-oxygenated crevices and protected areas of the river. Some parental care of incubating eggs

is thought to occur. The Neosho madtom probably prefers stream-dwelling insects and other invertebrate animals as its main foods during its nightly feeding excursions.

Orangefin Madtom

(Noturus gilberti)

IUCN: Vulnerable

Length: 5 in. (13 cm)
Habitat: Rocky, clean river bottom
Range: Upper Roanoke River basin, Virginia

THE ORANGEFIN madtom can be found only in the upper reaches and tributaries of the Roanoke River in the state of Virginia, and is found in close association with a species of endangered darter, the Roanoke logperch. The same human activities that threaten the Roanoke logperch also threaten the continued survival of the orangefin madtom.

Before cities like Roanoke and Salem began to spring up along the river, the orangefin madtom could be found from its headwaters all the way to Albemarle Sound in North Carolina, where the river empties into the Atlantic Ocean. But people's insistence on dominating and over-exploiting natural systems has slowly put a stranglehold on the river's finite resources and forced this fish farther and farther upstream. Urbanization and the resulting deforestation have released tons of silt into the river; sewage has robbed the water of oxygen and

choked the river with vegetation; toxic chemicals have rendered any remaining marginal habitat uninhabitable; and stream channelization as a measure to minimize flooding has turned sections of the river that are critical spawning and feeding grounds into unusable canals.

Water quality

The orangefin madtom is an excellent indicator of water quality. The presence or absence of this fish within a section of stream has been likened to a canary in a coal mine, because loss of the orange-fin madtom is one of the first indicators that water quality and habitat are deteriorating.

Saving this fish from threatened status will require a commitment from many communities along the Roanoke River, particularly those near the headwaters, to "clean up their act." Federally mandated clean water legislation has improved the outlook for this and other Roanoke fish by requiring thorough treatment of sewage and limiting the discharge of hazardous materials, but more should be done.

Color difference

Contrary to its common name, the orangefin madtom rarely displays orange fins. Rather, the fins are more yellow. It has uniformly hued, olive-brown back and sides, and the belly is a pale yellow. The eyes are small and poorly developed and are used primarily to sense the presence or absence of light, as opposed to shape or form. Taste is highly developed to compensate for poor vision. This small catfish has protective spines on the dorsal fin on the back and on both pectoral fins just behind the gills. The fleshy adipose fin behind the dorsal fin extends the length of tail to the base of the tail fin, and gives the appearance of a keel on the hull of a boat. The head is very flattened and allows the secretive orangefin madtom to hide under rocks and in crevices during the day. As with all species of catfish, the skin is scaleless.

During the breeding season in April, the orangefin madtom female searches for a protective and covered space in which to carefully deposit her gelatinous mass of fertilized eggs, usually no more than 75 per female. Depending on the water temperature (warmer water reduces incubation time), the eggs hatch in two to three weeks. During incubation, the male guards the eggs from predators. Using his tail fin as a fan, he drives away silt from the eggs to prevent them from becoming smothered.

The Ouachita madtom is found only in a small portion of the upper Saline River basin.

The orangefin madtom prefers to eat aquatic insects like mayfly, caddis, stonefly, and midge. This fish is not a visual feeder.

Ouachita Madtom
(Noturus lachneri)

IUCN: Vulnerable

Length: 2¾ in. (7 cm)
Reproduction: Egg layer
Habitat: Shallow river pools
Range: Upper Saline River Basin, Arkansas

TODAY, THE HIGHLY threatened Ouachita madtom is found only in a relatively small portion of the upper Saline River Basin (formerly occupying the Ouachita River as well), and is destined to be listed as endangered unless steps are taken to save this fish. As appropriate river habitat is wiped out by human development and activities, this small fish is forced to survive in higher densities to prevent entire populations being eliminated.

The land around the Ouachita madtom's range is primarily agricultural. Flood control in the form of stream channelization to minimize resistance to high water flow also is a priority in the region, and the impacts of farming and flood control activities on stream fishes such as the Ouachita madtom have been devastating. Much of this activity, in addition to deforestation of the surrounding watershed and chemical pollution from agricultural, domestic, and commercial sources, causes and promotes soil erosion and harmful siltation in the rivers and further degrades vital living space and water quality. The Ouachita madtom seeks clean-bottomed rocky streams and shallow river pools. It relies on clean-flowing water that is free of pollution, silt, and debris, to find food and shelter, successfully reproduce, and thrive.

Conflicting needs
The Saline River, a tributary of the Ouachita River, is an important waterway to both fish and people. Without a plan that takes into account the needs of both, populations of threatened species such as the Ouachita madtom will continue to shrink and eventually will be lost forever.

The Ouachita madtom conforms closely to the typical madtom physique. It possesses the signature keel-like adipose fin on the back between the dorsal fin and tail fin, and barbels ("whiskers") like all members of the family Ictaluridae. This madtom can be distinguished from others by two obvious physical differences. Not only is the body of the Ouachita madtom uniformly dark (an unusual trait for

The word *pygmy* means "small," and the pygmy madtom is just that. At just 1½ inches (4 centimeters), it is the smallest of the known madtoms.

a madtom), but the tail fin is quite different in shape and form. The tip is very rounded and the fin extends well onto the top and bottom of the tail, essentially joining with the adipose fin and the anal fin on the belly behind the anus. The flattened head of this scaleless fish is ideally shaped to use as a tool to wedge under small rocks and stones in its search for food in shallow stream riffles and pools. Several of the fins, particularly the pectoral fins just behind the gills and the pelvic fins on the belly, are quite stout and provide leverage as it moves bottom debris. The anal fin, paired pelvic fins on the belly, and dorsal fin on the back are almost entirely clear of pigment and the tail fin is dark like the body. This fish relies on its touch, smell, and highly developed sense of taste.

The Ouachita madtom is shy, and little is known about its feeding and reproductive habits. It likely spawns in the spring and deposits its adhesive eggs in well-oxygenated crevices and protected areas of the river. Parent fish probably take care of incubating eggs. The Ouachita madtom probably prefers stream-dwelling insects and other invertebrate animals as its principal nightly foods.

Pygmy Madtom
(Noturus stanauli)

ESA: Endangered

IUCN: Vulnerable

Length: 1⅔ in. (4 cm)
Habitat: Stream riffles and rapids
Range: Tennessee River Valley

AS THE name implies, the pygmy madtom is the smallest of the madtom group. This fish is extremely rare and at one time was thought to be extinct. Because it is extremely secretive and prefers to venture out of hiding to feed only at night, very little is known about this fish's precise range and specifics about its day-to-day life.

Reduced range

The pygmy madtom is not well-studied and was not even described until 1980. Most likely, in common with most madtoms and other stream fishes, the pygmy madtom has been subjected to multiple insults that have robbed it of acceptable habitat and severely reduced its range. Human activities such as construction of dams for flood control and the generation of electricity are not uncommon in Tennessee. The Tennessee River is one of the most severely altered rivers in the United States. Threats to the pygmy madtom include reduction of water quality because of increased silt and pollution. There are potential threats to the habitat from increased urbanization, coal mining, and also from agriculture. Dams, stream channelization and modification to minimize flooding, and pollution place severe burdens on fish such as the pygmy madtom that have adapted to conditions in clean, free-flowing rivers. The pygmy madtom has been collected from only two short river reaches, the Duck River and the Clinch River. The two populations are isolated from each other, and this separation prevents cross-breeding.

Appearance

The pygmy madtom has the flattened head, long anal fin just behind the anus, keel-like adipose fin on the back between the dorsal fin and tail fin, and whiskerlike barbels that characterize the madtoms. It does have distinctive coloring, being dark brown or black on the top half of the body and pale yellow or white on the lower half.

Presumably, the pygmy madtom dines under the protective cover of darkness and prefers to keep out of brightly lit stream areas during daylight hours. Insects and other aquatic invertebrates probably are the food items of choice for this vulnerable species.

Scioto Madtom
(Noturus trautmani)

ESA: Endangered

IUCN: Critically endangered

Length: 2 in. (5 cm)
Reproduction: Egg layer
Habitat: Swift riffles over gravel and boulders
Range: Big Darby Creek, Ohio

WITH ONLY 19 individuals located when it was first described in 1969, the Scioto (pronounced sigh-O-toe) madtom remains one of the most endangered fish in the world. It occupies a small section of Big Darby Creek in central Ohio, a tributary of the Scioto River, in a rural area just south of the state's capital city of Columbus. Today some experts believe this fish to be extinct. Fisheries scientists take the view that historically the Scioto madtom never occupied a large range within the Scioto River Basin. But today, as pressures on this fish's remaining

habitat increase, the likelihood that a single catastrophic event could wipe out the surviving individuals looms large. These pressures include destruction of habitat and food sources through soil erosion of the surrounding watershed and the siltation that follows, and the ever-present threat of a pollution event, given the site's relatively close proximity to a major metropolitan area.

Little is known
Despite the fact that the fish in Big Darby Creek are some of the most extensively studied in the state, almost nothing is known about the Scioto madtom's lifestyle and habits. This secretive fish is quite small, even for a madtom, and unspectacular in terms of its coloration. The olive or brown and mottled gray background color of the body, which tends to be darker on the back, is covered with many dark specks, spots, and blotches; the belly is milky white with no spots. A prominent dark patch is visible at the base of the tail fin and a cluster of spots forms a darker area at the base of the anal fin, which is located just behind the anus. The dorsal fin on the back and the pectoral fins just behind the gills carry protective spines and are nearly pigment free except for some light coloration that suggests banding. Likewise, the tail fin is lightly banded. The six whiskerlike barbels of this catfish are quite short, but they provide sensory coverage across the snout, mouth, and chin.

Invertebrate eater
Aquatic insects and other bottom-dwelling invertebrates most likely are the favorite foods of the

Scioto madtom. It is probable that breeding takes place in the summertime, with some protection afforded by the parents during egg incubation.

Smoky Madtom
(Noturus baileyi)

ESA: Endangered

IUCN: Critically endangered

Length: 2½ in. (6 cm)
Reproduction: Egg layer
Habitat: Shallow stream riffles over rock, and shallow pools
Range: Citico Creek and Little Tennessee River, Tennessee

THE SMOKY MADTOM was first discovered in 1957 in Abrams Creek, a tributary of the Little Tennessee River. It was later presumed extinct until 1980, when it was collected in Citico Creek. It is only found in 6½ miles (10.5 kilometers) of the creek, and a single adverse event could result in extinction. Threats to habitat include logging, road and bridge construction, mineral exploration, and mining. Pollution in the form of organic chemicals could also be a potential threat, as this has been cited as a possible cause of the unexplained extinction of other madtom species. Efforts have been made to reintroduce the species to Abrams Creek.

Water construction
Flood control and hydroelectric power generation are high priorities in Tennessee. These projects

unexpected. The smoky madtom probably prefers stream -dwelling insects and other invertebrate animals as its principal foods during its nightly feeding excursions.

Yellowfin Madtom
(Noturus flavipinnis)

ESA: Threatened

IUCN: Vulnerable

Length: 4⅓ in. (11 cm)
Habitat: Medium-sized streams in pools and backwaters
Range: Northern Georgia to western Virginia

involve the construction of dams and the modification of stream channels to stabilize seasonal water flow rates and reduce resistance to flow in the channel. Tellico Lake and Fontana Lake, both formed as a result of dams that were built across the Little Tennessee River, may also have hastened the decline of the smoky madtom. The impacts of these activities on stream fish such as the smoky madtom have been devastating.

The principal river system that supports the smoky madtom is the Little Tennessee River. This is an important waterway to both fish and people. Without a plan that takes into account the needs of both, the population of the smoky madtom will continue to shrink, and eventually this fish will become extinct.

Strange looks
This fish has an unusual appearance, even for a madtom. Growing up to 2½ inches (6 centimeters) in length, the smoky madtom is average in size. However, this species is much more tubular in shape, part-

To thrive, the yellowfin madtom relies on clean flowing water that is free from pollution, silt, and debris.

icularly around the head and abdominal region, than other fish in its genus. It has a very blunt snout. Coloration is unspectacular, consisting of a light brown background and numerous dark spots over the head, body, and fins. These spots fuse to form dark regions at the base of the spiny dorsal fin on the back, in the area just behind the gill covers, in a stripe down the middle of the back, and at the base of the anal fin just behind the anus. The eyes are located high on the head and are used primarily to sense movement as opposed to recognizing shapes.

The smoky madtom is highly secretive and little is known about its feeding and reproductive habits. It lives in shallow pools and stream riffles, and like other madtoms, it is thought to spawn in the spring, depositing its adhesive eggs in well-oxygenated crevices and protected areas of the river. Some parental care of incubating eggs would not be

THE POWELL RIVER in Tennessee and Cooper Creek in Virginia, are home to a unique-looking fish, the yellowfin madtom. Like all madtoms, this fish lives in rivers and is threatened by human activities and development within its range.

The yellowfin madtom lives in the pools and backwaters of medium-sized streams. It relies on a habitat of clean flowing water that is free of pollution, silt, and debris to find food, successfully reproduce, and thrive.

The principal river system that supports the yellowfin madtom is the upper Tennessee River. This is an important waterway to both fish and people. However, dam construction activity, particularly from Chattanooga, Tennessee, to Oak Ridge, Tennessee, and from there to the Virginia border, has severely reduced the size of the yellowfin madtom range. As a result, almost all populations within the state of Tennessee have been lost. Most of the survivors live in a Tennessee River tributary, the Clinch River, in Virginia. Experimental madtom populations have been reintroduced into other rivers in Tennessee and Virginia to try to increase their range.

Pigmentation

At 4½ inches (11 centimeters) in length, the yellowfin madtom is larger than most other madtoms. It displays an interesting pattern of pigmentation. A light-colored background is covered with small spots from the snout to the base of the tail. A dark saddlelike blotch on the back over the fleshy adipose fin between the dorsal fin and tail fin, and a dark chevron at the base of the tail make the yellowfin madtom easy to identify. Brown coloration that suggests banding is present on the dorsal fin, tail fin, and anal fin on the belly just behind the anus and, as you might expect from its name, some of the fins show a hint of yellow. The head is flattened to allow access to crevices and other tight places, and the dorsal fin and the pectoral fins just behind the gills are spiny to provide protection against predators.

The yellowfin madtom usually stays under cover during the day and mostly hunts for food at night, although it does sometimes feed during the day. Bottom-dwelling insects are the food of choice. This fish spawns in late spring and early summer by depositing adhesive eggs in a protected area and produces 100 to 250 young per year. Researchers have determined that it reaches sexual maturity after the first year and lives three to four years.

All the madtoms face the same problems as their catfish relatives: pollution, habitat encroachment, and the degradation of their ranges.

William E. Manci
See also Blindcats, Cavefishes, and Catfishes.

Sri Lanka Magpie

(Urocissa ornata)

Class: Aves
Order: Passeriformes
Family: Corvidae
Clutch size: 3–5 eggs
Diet: Insects, tree-frogs, lizards, occasionally fruits
Habitat: Primary evergreen forests
Range: Sri Lanka

THE SRI LANKA magpie is much like the jay in physique and character. It wears light blue body plumage accented by rusty brown wings with black shoulders. The entire head, including the nape, chin, and throat, is an earthy, almost chestnut brown, giving the bird a hooded look. A ring of bare skin around the eye is pinkish red as are the beak, feet, and toes. The distinctive long tail is light blue with a white tip. Like other members of its family, the Sri Lanka magpie has strong legs that allow it to hop nimbly among the branches of the trees where it lives. Its home is the wet forest of Sri Lanka's foothills and lower mountain slopes.

Sri Lanka has two clearly defined climate zones, one wet and one dry. Roughly circular, the island's southwestern quarter is the wet zone where as much as 200 inches (508 centimeters) of rain fall each year. The dry zone wraps around the other three-quarters of the island. Mountains in south-central Sri Lanka account for the great difference. As the monsoons blow from southwest to northeast from May to September, the mountains obstruct the passing clouds, so the rain falls on their southwestern flanks. Little or no rain falls

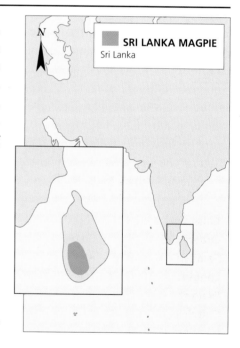

on the northeastern -slopes. From September to May the monsoons switch direction and blow from northeast to southwest. Rain falls on the northeastern quarter of the island, but some also sneaks past the mountains to fall on the southwestern area. Because it receives rain year-round, this

The Sri Lanka magpie is one of many unique animals that lives nowhere on earth except in the wet forest of this island nation.

southwestern area supports a lush tropical rain forest. Many unique animals live nowhere else on earth except in that wet forest of Sri Lanka. Among them is the Sri Lanka magpie.

Ranging through the lowland forests up to 6,560 feet (2,000 meters) in elevation, the magpie works the forest trees from ground level to treetops. It eats any small animals it can catch, including large insects and small frogs. Flocks of up to seven birds may be seen moving through the forest together.

Sri Lanka's wet zone forests have been heavily cut by local people who need firewood and by agricultural developers who remove the native forest to cultivate plantations of coffee, tea, eucalyptus, and other crops. The magpie has shown no willingness to accept the plantations as habitat and the species no longer occurs in many areas where it was once found. This bird is also threatened by the spread of the Asian Koel (*Eudynamys scolopacea*). The Asian Koel is a bird that does not build its own nest, but removes eggs from the nests of other species and then lays its own egg. The Koel egg is then incubated, hatched, and reared by the unsuspecting Sri Lanka magpie. The magpie's breeding success is much reduced because of the removal of its own young from the nest.

Kevin Cook

Maleo
(Macrocephalon maleo)

IUCN: Vulnerable

Class: Aves
Order: Galliformes
Family: Megapodiidae
Length: 22–26 in. (56–66 cm)
Weight: Unknown
Clutch size: 1 egg
Incubation: 78 days
Diet: Insects, spiders, millipedes, other invertebrates, and fruits
Habitat: Lowland forest
Range: Sulawesi, Indonesia

ONE OF EARTH'S most remarkable birds may be lost because people have forgotten a basic principle: given time, life replaces itself. The maleo may not have enough time for people to relearn this basic lesson of nature

Since the beginning of agriculture, people who farm have understood that some portion of a harvested crop must be saved. The reserved portion becomes the seed to plant another crop next growing season. Ranchers well know that they must retain some animals for breeding and only sell off surplus stock. Wildlife management emerged as a profession in response to the excessive killing of animals. Wildlife managers know that hunting and fishing must be restrained so that animal populations can sustain themselves. These fundamental management methods also pertain to collecting specimens, hunting for feathers, and gathering eggs.

The maleo looks much like a peculiar turkey. Its dull yellow beak is short and thick. An unfeathered, pale blue-gray structure known as a casque adorns the maleo's crown. The upperparts plus the chin, throat, and upper breast are a dull black. The belly is white. The maleo belongs to the family of birds known as the megapodes. The name *megapode* means "giant foot." Birds in the family have a very stout, well-developed foot and toe structure that is perfectly suited for life on the ground. Such a characteristic is not particularly remarkable, because many birds have stout legs and feet to suit a terrestrial lifestyle.

The megapodes are notable for their unique nesting behavior. The maleo, in particular, nests more like a sea turtle than a bird.

Enthusiasts who gather the maleo's eggs must leave some behind, or the maleo will perish and the egg gathering will end.

Megapodes do not use the body heat of adult birds to incubate their eggs. Instead, their incubation depends on environmental sources of heat. When not breeding, the maleo inhabits primary lowland forests. For breeding, it leaves the forests for the sandy coastal beaches. Like sea turtles coming ashore from the ocean, the maleos throng to the beaches. After mating they dig pits up to 3¼ feet (1 meter) deep. They lay their eggs in the pits and cover them with sand.

Volcanic hatching

Sulawesi (formerly known as Celebes) is a volcanic island. Pulverized lava forms black sand beaches. The dark sand absorbs energy from the sun during the day. That energy, stored as heat, keeps the maleo's eggs warm through the night. Maleos formerly nested in sandy open ground in forest clearings, where heat from volcanic activity and hot springs would keep the eggs warm. Egg collectors and hunters have virtually eliminated the inland breeding populations of the maleo. Now dogs, pigs, and humans threaten to exterminate the last of the maleos by overharvesting their eggs.

Gathering eggs

The tradition of egg collecting is strong among the local people. Either they have forgotten the principle that some crops must be saved to provide seed for next year, or else they flagrantly disregard the need to allow some maleos to survive. The International Council for Bird Preservation (ICBP) has been working with the people on Sulawesi for several years. The goal of the ICBP is to preserve the maleo as a species but still allow the Sulawesi people to collect some eggs. The entire maleo program has many aspects. It involves regulating the number of eggs taken, incubating the eggs in captivity, excluding dogs and pigs from nesting beaches, and working with the Sulawesi government to allow rigorously controlled access to nesting beaches as a tourist attraction. Additional preservation steps aim to protect the lowland forests where the maleos live most of the year when not nesting. The effort to control egg collecting must succeed if the maleo is to survive.

Kevin Cook

See also Micronesian Megapode.

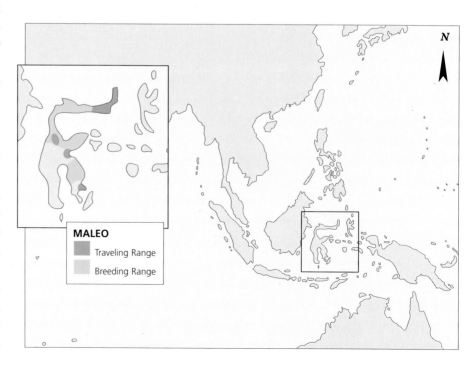

MALEO

Traveling Range

Breeding Range

846

Ibadan Malimbe
(Malimbus ibadanensis)

ESA: Endangered

IUCN: Critically endangered

Class: Aves
Order: Passeriformes
Family: Ploceidae
Subfamily: Ploceinae
Length: 7–7½ in. (17.8–19 cm)
Clutch size: 2 eggs
Incubation: Probably 12–15 days
Diet: Probably insects and some fruits
Habitat: Zones between forests and savannas
Range: Southwestern Nigeria

HIGH IN A PALM tree hangs a peculiar structure. It is an elaborate nest, and flitting in the shadows of the palm fronds, the nest's builder searches for more material. An Ibadan malimbe hops into the sunlight with a long leaf fiber in its beak. The bird's jet black cheek and throat offset the fiery red head, neck, and breast. A black belly, wing, back, and tail complete the contrast.

The bird flies to the nest and busily weaves the fiber into place. Its stout, slightly decurved black beak deftly works the fiber and draws it snug.

When it is finished, the malimbe whisks off to another palm for another strand of fiber.

Unique to Nigeria

Nine species in the genus *Malimbus* make up the little group of weaver finches known as malimbes. They all live south of the Sahara Desert, and one species or another lives as far west as Senegal and as far east as Kenya.

The Ibadan malimbe was first discovered in a garden in Ibadan, Nigeria, and is the only known species of bird unique to Nigeria.

The Ibadan malimbe's preferred habitat lies outside towns and farms. This bird inhabits a zone where two plant communities merge. Ecologists call such areas "ecotones" or "tension zones." In the malimbe's case, it inhabits the ecotone area where the land has traits of both forest and savanna.

Changing savanna

The agricultural potential of these areas has become increasingly important to the Nigerian people. Semidesert conditions limit agricultural development in northern Nigeria; mangrove swamps dominate coastal Nigeria in the south, limiting agriculture there. Inland from the coastal mangrove belt stretches a tropical rain forest. Although the rain forests are periodically cut for lumber products and to open the land for agriculture, the soil is poor and unproductive.

The land between the rain forest and the semidesert offers the best opportunity for livestock grazing and crop production.

As the Nigerian population approaches 90 million people, the nation needs a solid agriculture program just to provide adequate food for its people.

Converting the savanna to cropland and heavy grazing both damage the landscape the Ibadan malimbe needs. Urban expansion compounds habitat loss. Ibadan, a city with well more than a million people, continues to grow, consuming malimbe habitat.

Always rare, the Ibadan malimbe disappeared from its native haunts during the 1970s. Individuals and pairs were seen in secondary forest and urban gardens in Ibadan. Ornithologists urged that research be undertaken to find remaining Ibadan malimbe populations. Once found, the species can be studied so that recommendations for preserving its habitat can be made.

Kevin Cook

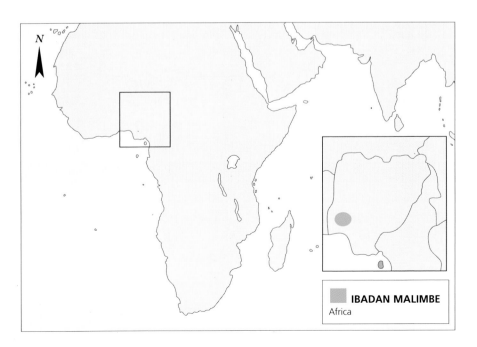

IBADAN MALIMBE
Africa

Red-faced Malkoha

(Phaenicophaeus pyrrhocephalus)

ESA: Endangered

IUCN: Vulnerable

Class: Aves
Order: Cuculiformes
Family: Cuculidae
Subfamily: Phaenicophaeinae
Length: 18–20 in. (46–51cm)
Clutch size: 2–3 eggs
Diet: Small fruits and insects
Habitat: Forest canopy
Range: Sri Lanka

HIGH ABOVE THE forest floor, a bird races through the crowns of trees by hopping from branch to branch. Coming to a space too large to leap, it spreads its wings and glides across the span. The short, rounded wings make a humming noise as the bird sails back into the cover of the tree-tops. It quickly disappears, but a harsh "kok" signals the presence of the red-faced malkoha.

Aptly named, the bird has a large bare patch that encircles the eye and includes the lore, part of the cheek, and extends onto the side edge of the crown. The patch is bright red. Just below the patch, the lower cheek is white. A dark purplish brown color runs from the forehead over the crown onto the nape and sweeps around the neck to the chin and throat. The breast and belly are white, but the back, wing, and long tail are dark brownish black, or black with a little green or bluish sheen. A broad white band runs across the tail tip. The greenish yellow beak is stout and slightly decurved. The wing is not well developed for flying; but the leg, foot, and toe are sturdy. No other bird in Sri Lanka resembles the red-faced malkoha.

American cousins

The malkohas include a group of five species in four genera, all of which live in Sri Lanka, Southeast Asia, or Indonesia. The malkohas belong to the subfamily Cuculidae, which also represents the yellow-billed cuckoo (*Coccyzus americanus*) and the black-billed cuckoo (*C. erythrophthalmus*). Both of these species occur over much of the United States, and they behave much like malkohas. They are birds of the forest, and move stealthily about the canopy. The malkohas and North American cuckoos do not resemble each other superficially, but ornithologists long believed that similar anatomy and behavior indicate their relationship. A revised classification of birds proposed in 1990 separates the New World cuckoos into a separate family and leaves the Old World cuckoos and malkohas in one family.

The red-faced malkoha has wandered to India, but a population has never established itself there. As a breeding species, the red-faced malkoha is a denizen of Sri Lanka's primary forests. These forests include lowland and montane stands within both the wet and dry zones.

From May to September, monsoons blow from southwest to northeast across Sri Lanka. The monsoon winds blow rain-heavy clouds right into the mountains of south-central Sri Lanka. Too heavy to rise, the clouds dump their rain on the southwestern quarter of the island. From September to May, the monsoons switch direction and blow from northeast to southwest. During this time, the eastern and northern sides of the island get most of their rain. Some rain spills over to the southwest quarter and adds to the annual total. Receiving as much as 200 inches (508 centimeters) of rain every year, the southwest quarter is known as the wet zone. The other portions of the island receive 25 to 75 inches (63.5 to 190.5 centimeters) of rain each year. This broad area is called the dry zone, although it is not particularly dry by comparison to desert areas.

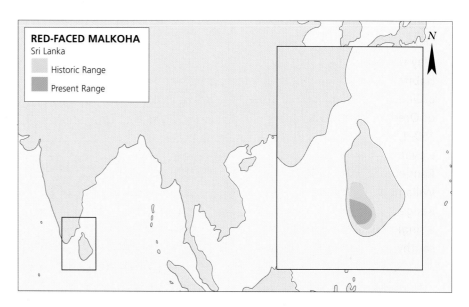

RED-FACED MALKOHA
Sri Lanka

Historic Range

Present Range

Deforestation

Forests occur in both the wet and dry zones. Those in the wet zone are tropical rain forests. The red-faced malkoha inhabited most of the forests in either zone. Agricultural development, especially plantations and firewood gathering, has devastated Sri Lanka's forests. The red-faced malkoha shows no willingness to occupy secondary forest or plantations, so as the forests have dwindled, so has the bird. Human development of land has fragmented much of the forest, particularly in ravines and along streams in the dry zone and a lower montane patch in the wet zone. Usually, considerations such as steep terrain or too much rain determine where the forests survive, because some areas are not useful. The red-faced malkoha survives in some of the remaining forest patches.

The future of Sri Lanka's forest birds probably depends on several factors. First, an alternative fuel source must be developed so that firewood cutting does not exceed a forest's capacity to replenish itself. Second, a system of alternative farming techniques should be used to improve yields on existing farms and plantations, rather than converting all available land to agricultural production. Third, the remaining primary forests must be aggressively protected. Fourth, educational programs about wildlife and habitat must be initiated so that the people of Sri Lanka can learn and understand how important the forests and birds are to them. Such measures must be undertaken if birds such as the red-faced malkoha are going to survive.

Kevin Cook

Nelson's Checkermallow

(Sidalcea nelsoniana)

IUCN: Vulnerable

Family: Malvaceae
Height: 30–50 in. (50–120 cm)
Leaves: Rounded, from 1–5 in. (2.5–12.5 cm) across
Flowers: Arranged in elongate clusters with light to deep pink petals up to 1 in. (2.5 cm) long
Reproduction: Pollination between plants. Hard black seeds have no specialized means of dispersal
Season: Flowering from late May through July
Habitat: Seasonally wet prairies, meadows, and borders of Oregon ash forests, at 150–1,960 ft. (45–592 m) elevation
Range: Restricted to the Willamette Valley and Coast Range of western Oregon, with a single population in southwest Washington state

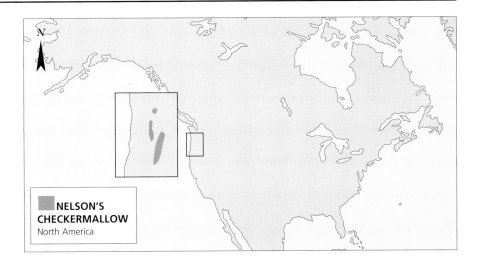

NELSON'S CHECKERMALLOW
North America

NELSON'S checkermallow has one of the widest ranges of any threatened or endangered plant in the northwestern United States. Museum records indicate this attractive relative of the common hollyhock was at one time plentiful, occurring from the southern end of the Willamette Valley to the hills north of Portland, Oregon, a distance of roughly 150 miles (240 kilometers). Over 2 million acres (8,000 square kilometers) of prairie, savanna, and wetland forest existed in this region prior to European settlement, and it is believed that Nelson's checkermallow was a well-represented component of the local flora.

Nelson's checkermallow is an erect perennial herb, with one to several flowering branches originating from the base of the plant. The leaves are rounded, those at the base of the plant are largest and usually have shallow indentations along the margin, while the progressively smaller stem leaves are often deeply lobed. Large colonies of the species, with wandlike stems and deep pink flowers, towered over neighboring wetland wildflowers,

Nelson's checkermallow once existed in large colonies. Destruction of its habitat has severely reduced its numbers.

providing an oasis of pollen and nectar for wild bees and other pollinators during the warm summer months. However, with the establishment of the Oregon Trail in the mid-19th century, farmers, ranchers, and loggers streamed into the Pacific Northwest, and the Willamette Valley was the premier destination.

Soon, much of the Willamette Valley was converted to crops and villages, and today over 95 percent of the land area in this part of Oregon is farmed or covered with cities and suburbs.

Diminishing habitat

Native habitat remains in only a few wildlife refuges, along roadsides and hedgerows, or within old cemeteries, characterized by species such as hairgrass (*Des-champsia*), mannagrass (*Glyceria*), and camas (*Camassia*). Plants that are geographically restricted to the Willamette Valley have suffered the consequences of human progress, and several are currently very close to extinction. Nelson's checkermallow has been particularly hard hit, since it prefers grasslands and meadows that have now been wiped out by agriculture and the drainage of wetlands. Although laws were implemented to protect wetland sites, the damage is largely complete. This formerly widespread native has been reduced to a few tiny, scattered populations.

Habitat fragmentation

Even if we managed to protect all the remaining populations of Nelson's checkermallow, the problems associated with the habitat fragmentation described above will be difficult to overcome. As habitat for the species has been altered, populations have become increasingly isolated and significantly reduced in size and numbers. Small populations are, of course, much more subject to sudden extermination through some unanticipated event.

Pollination

Fewer plants in a patch means less attractiveness to pollinators, and fewer pollinator visits in turn reduces seed output. Nelson's checkermallow has an unusual breeding system called gynodioecy, which means that some plants in a population are strictly female (producing seeds, but no pollen), while others have perfect flowers (meaning they are bisexual, producing pollen and seeds). This system is believed to have evolved to ensure that pollination between plants, which is genetically desirable, occurs on a regular basis. Female plants cannot pollinate themselves, so cross-fertilization is ensured.

Inbreeding

The isolation caused by habitat disturbance places the species at reproductive risk by forcing closely related plants in unnaturally small populations to interbreed. This results in low seed output and unhealthy offspring through what has been called inbreeding depression.

Some populations have become so small and are now comprised entirely or largely of females, that viable pollination has been eliminated. Weevil infestation can also reduce seed crops.

Nelson's checkermallow is protected by law in all public places. The great majority of existing sites are minuscule, however, and such populations can never be considered secure.

Recovery therefore depends on maintaining a series of reserves where large, genetically healthy populations can exist free from disturbance. Plants are currently being grown from seed and cuttings at Oregon State University, with the goal of establishing self-perpetuating test populations on sites where the species has a reasonable chance of long-term survival. Some private nurseries have also inquired about cultivating the species. Hopefully, such public interest in this beautiful native plant will translate into increased sympathy for its unfortunate plight, and a willingness to instigate some protective measures to ensure its survival.

Bob Meinke

MANATEES

Class: Mammalia

Order: Sirenia

Family: Trichechidae

Manatees belong to an odd and unusual order of mammals called Sirenia. This order includes the dugong and the extinct Steller's sea cow. The sirenia have been categorized as being more closely related to the elephants and hyraxes (animals similar to rodents) rather than to other marine mammals such as whales or seals. However, their relationships with elephants and hyraxes are distant enough that none of these mammal groups show any obvious resemblance to their ancestor.

All sirenians are completely aquatic, and their body shape, structures and behavioral adaptations are all oriented toward a life in water. While a cursory examination of a manatee might bring to mind the word *dumpy*, the body is actually fairly streamlined.

Manatees have nostrils placed on the top of the snout, allowing them to breathe without raising their heads above water level. Wide pectoral flippers help guide the manatee through the water and occasionally are even used to hold objects. A large tail flipper pushes the manatee through the water. The tail fin is the simplest way to tell the two Sirenians apart: in the manatees, the tail is a large, round paddle; while the dugong tail has two pointed lobes, similar to those found on the whale or dolphin tail.

All three species of manatee are under enormous pressures from human activities. This is partly due to the large amount of meat a single kill can provide to people. However, a greater threat to their existence is that they live in prime real estate, such as large rivers, bays, and coastal ocean waters. These areas are highly valued by humans, who use them as transportation routes, sewers, and locations for housing and factories. The result is a degradation of the manatees' environment, and frequent interactions between manatees and human-made objects such as fishing nets, motorboats, and dams usually means the manatees come out second best.

Amazon Manatee

(Trichechus inunguis)

ESA: Endangered

IUCN: Vulnerable

Weight: 1,000 lb. (455 kg)

Length: 9 ft. (2.75 m)

Diet: Aquatic vegetation

Gestation period: About 360 days

Habitat: Major rivers and lakes

Range: Amazon basin of South America

THE AMAZON manatee's primary habitat is the large rivers and adjacent lakes of the Amazon basin. It appears that this manatee is found swimming only in fresh water. Although most of its range is in Brazil, it can also be found in parts of Colombia, Ecuador and Peru.

The Amazon manatee differs from its two closely related cousins, the West Indian and West African manatees, in a number of ways. It is the smallest of the manatees, the largest of this species just breaking 9 feet (2.75 meters) in length and weighing 1,000 pounds (455 kilograms). It has light patches on its underside. It is also the only manatee to lack nails on the front flippers.

As is true with many aquatic animals, little is known about the habits and ecology of the Amazon manatee. It is thought to live in small groups of four to eight, which would make it one of the more social of the manatees. Most other species tend to occur in pairs, usually a mother with her offspring. However, the Amazon manatee will occasionally be found in large groups, sometimes numbering hundreds. These groups are probably created by local ecological conditions such as food, temperature, or water levels, rather than any specific social need. Like the other species of manatees, it communicates using high-pitched cries.

Giant plant eater

The Amazon manatee is completely herbivorous. It feeds mostly on sea and river grasses, but will eat most aquatic plants and marine algae. It is even known to graze on shore vegetation that reaches out over the water. A manatee can eat over 30 pounds (13.6 kilograms) of vegetation every day. However, it appears that while a number of manatees may be capable of keeping a short stretch of water free of plants, the high productivity of tropical waters combined with the low productivity of manatees makes this idea unworkable in all but a few places. However, manatees could be used in conjunction with other methods, as manatees are maintenance free

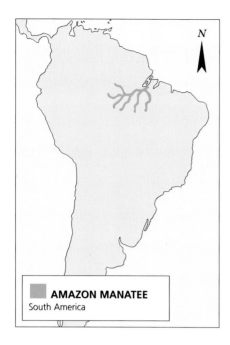

AMAZON MANATEE
South America

riverine habitat by increasing erosion, which increases the silt load of the water. This, in turn, affects the amount of sunlight that can penetrate the water, which can eventually have a destructive effect on the aquatic plant life that the manatee depends on for its survival.

Another problem facing the Amazon manatee relates to its own biology. The slow rate of reproduction in manatees means that reduced populations cannot replace their numbers without many years of protection from further causes of mortality.

Vast range

The Amazon manatee's range, which is enormous and covers terrain that is isolated and frequently impassable much of the year, makes it almost impossible to adequately determine numbers or enforce regulatory laws. Since the rivers in which it lives cross international boundaries, different parts of the same population of manatees may face varying levels of legal protection and enforcement. Since the species appears to make seasonal movements, it is possible that some populations can appear to be under little stress, but periodically become faced with a more intense level of hunting and habitat degradation due to movements into new areas.

One of the most important tasks needed to save the Amazon manatee is determining population numbers and range. Only then can a park or reserve be developed that will adequately protect a population of manatees. These reserves could be the only key to the manatee's survival. A reserve serves little purpose,

however, if it is too small or the boundaries are incorrectly placed to incorporate the entire population of these animals. To complicate this, manatees live in a habitat that is harder to manage than normal, dryland areas. A manatee's habitat can be affected by what occurs elsewhere, and human activity such as mining or development upriver of a manatee reserve has to be carefully managed to avoid adverse effects on the manatee population within the reserve.

West African Manatee

(Trichechus senegalensis)

ESA: Threatened

IUCN: Vulnerable

Weight: 1,200–3,500 lb. (545–1,590 kg)
Length: 10–13 ft. (3–4 m)
Diet: Aquatic vegetation, leaves, fallen fruit
Gestation period: About 360 days
Habitat: Coastal areas, large rivers, lakes
Range: Western Africa

THE WEST AFRICAN manatee looks remarkably like its close relative, the West Indian manatee, and it is possible that the West African species descended from the West Indian species after it crossed the Atlantic some five million years ago. A close look reveals that the West African manatee has a comparatively shorter snub nose and more protruding eyes. Outside of those

and do not pollute the environment; as a matter of fact, it appears that manatee droppings can help to increase the productivity of waterways.

Fasting

The Amazon manatee also appears to be able to fast for long periods, perhaps over half a year. This ability enables it to survive long dry seasons, when water levels can drop over 20 feet (6 meters) and the manatee is forced to live in deep channels where vegetation is scarce. These channels may end up holding large numbers of Amazon manatees during the dry season. Once the rains begin and water levels rise, the manatees spread out again in smaller groups.

Because of the manatee's large size, tasty flesh, and slow movements, it has come under a fair amount of hunting pressure from local hunters and fishermen. As with other tropical American animals, the Amazon manatee is also threatened by habitat destruction. Heavy logging and clear cutting of forests can degrade

differences, however, even experts find it difficult to distinguish between the species. These two species may be more closely related than the West Indian manatee is to the Amazon manatee, whose range it intersects.

The range of the West African manatee is spread out over the west coast of Africa on both sides of the equator. Extending from Senegal in the north to Angola in the south, this range encompasses at least 20 countries. Living both in saltwater and freshwater, the West African manatee may be found over 1,000 miles (1,600 kilometers) up the major rivers of West Africa, and possibly in Lake Chad as well. The manatees found in freshwater feed on many different kinds of aquatic vegetation. However, some saltwater populations appear to feed heavily on mangrove leaves, possibly due to a lack of other available sources of vegetation. The manatees that are found in rivers appear to make long migrations upriver during the rainy season, and return downriver during the dry season.

Threats to the manatee

During the dry season, manatees may get caught in lakes that become landlocked, and some manatees die when these lakes dry up. However, a bigger problem for manatees that regularly move up and down the rivers of Africa is the development of dams built for hydroelectric power, flood control, and irrigation. Manatees are regularly crushed by the devices used on these dams, and the manatee populations are blocked from moving along their normal river

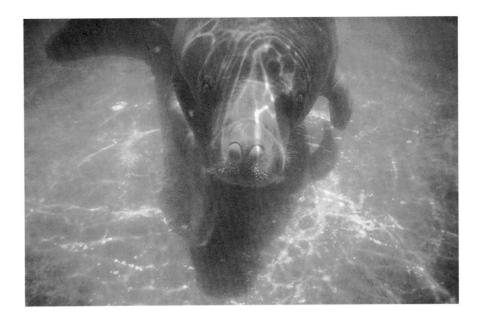

The manatee's tendency to gather in groups during the dry season has allowed people to kill large numbers in a relatively short period of time.

paths by these structures. Manatees trapped upriver from recently constructed dams may suffer when the dams alter water levels. While extensive damming is not yet a problem in many countries, the need for cheap power, flood control, and water during the dry season and in times of drought make it certain that many more dams will be built, and that more populations of manatees will be affected.

The West African manatee is probably the most heavily hunted of the manatees. Some people along the coast specialize in hunting manatees, and traps are the common method of capture. Nets and hooks are also used, as are spears and guns. Accidental capture in fishing nets is another cause of death. These netted manatees are as likely to end up in the pot or the market as purposefully taken ones, and are welcomed as an important source of protein in many areas.

Lack of knowledge

One of the greatest problems in preparing a conservation plan for the West African manatee is the lack of data concerning its numbers, location, and mortality. In most countries manatee surveys have never been performed, and the actual existence of the manatee in an area is frequently determined from anecdotal information. Some wildlife observations may be more than 50 years old, but represent the only published information concerning manatees for a given area. The lack of accurate numbers on the manatee population makes it difficult, if not impossible, to determine how quickly various populations are being reduced. However, there is a general consensus that populations are decreasing, in some cases radically, in the West African manatee's range. Older manatee hunters relate tales of greater past catches, and some areas that were thought to contain manatees no longer appear to do so.

Despite the difficulty in documenting manatee population

declines, a number of African countries that contain manatees have created legislation banning or limiting manatee hunting. Unfortunately, enforcing these laws is difficult at best, given the lack of resources and staffing among local police and conservation agencies. Add to this the acknowledged need for hunting to supplement the sometimes meager local food production, and the problems remain.

International conservation

The West African manatee's survival is closely tied to the development of the countries that define its range. Drought, warfare, civil strife, and poverty create a social environment that contests the importance of conservation—especially for areas that span many countries and require international action. Fortunately, many countries within the manatee's range understand the relationship between successful economic development and a healthy resource base, and have taken strong steps to preserve their natural resources, including

their wildlife. However, without an equally strong enforcement policy and continued vigilance to maintain ecological systems within and between the countries of western Africa, large mammals such as the West African manatee are likely to become additional victims of human poverty and population pressure.

West Indian Manatee

(Trichechus manatus)

ESA: Endangered

IUCN: Vulnerable

Weight: 1,200–3,500 lb. (545–1,590 kg)
Length: 10–13 ft. (3–4 m)
Diet: Aquatic plants
Gestation period: 360–390 days
Longevity: Over 40 years
Habitat: Rivers, estuaries, shallow coastal areas
Range: Florida, the Caribbean, eastern Central and South America

THE WEST INDIAN manatee is probably the best-known member of this odd group of mammals. This is because of its existence around the southeastern coast of the United States, especially the state of Florida, where a good deal of observational work has been done in some of the clearwater streams of that state. Its odd and ungainly features have made it famous among rare and threatened animals, and work on its behalf has led to an extensive conservation effort among professional biolo-

gists and amateur naturalists. The West Indian manatee has two distinct subspecies. The first is the Florida manatee, found around both the Gulf Coast and the Atlantic coast of Florida and adjacent states, as well as the Florida Keys and coastal waters of the Bahamas. The second is the Antillean manatee, which is found down the Caribbean coast of Mexico through Central America, and along the Atlantic coast of South America to below the equator in Brazil. This manatee is also found among many of the Caribbean islands, including Cuba, Haiti and the Dominican Republic, Puerto Rico, and Jamaica.

The West Indian manatee, like other sirenians, is a vegetarian, eating mostly sea grasses and other aquatic vegetation. It appears to require at least occasional drinks of fresh water. Oceangoing manatees quite frequently move into rivers for brief periods, and while at sea can be attracted by the freshwater output from a garden hose. However, some manatees are found near small islands far out to sea, and it is unclear how these individuals survive without any obvious source of fresh water.

Pressures on populations

The West Indian manatee apparently has never been very common around Florida. The principal reason is that manatees are extremely sensitive to temperature. The waters around Florida present barely acceptable year-round temperatures for manatee survival. Manatees tend to migrate to warmer waters when water temperature drops to below 68 degrees Fahrenheit (20

WEST AFRICAN MANATEE
Africa

degrees Celsius). Even so, every year manatee mortality is associated with water temperature drops during winter. Although manatees have been sighted during summer as far north as Chesapeake Bay on the Atlantic coast, Florida can be considered to be the manatee's northern extreme for year-round living.

Interestingly, some human activities have actually led to an increase in suitable habitat for the manatee. This is due to the release of warm water from power plants and factories into rivers and flood channels where manatees live. In winter, manatees often congregate in large numbers around these outlets, basking in the warm flow.

However, human activity has done more harm than good to the West Indian manatee. Hunting has been a constant threat to manatee populations. Although hunting has been regulated in Florida since before 1900 and has been illegal since the early 1970s, people still occasionally poach the manatee, or cruelly use this large, slow animal for target practice. Entanglement in fishing

The West Indian manatee, like other sirenians, is a vegetarian, eating mostly sea grasses and other aquatic vegetation. It appears to require at least occasional drinks of fresh water.

nets and harassment by people have also led to manatee deaths. However, the greatest single human-related cause of Florida manatee mortality today is collisions with motorboats, despite legislation to control boat speeds in areas where manatees live.

The Antillean subspecies is also under pressure from human

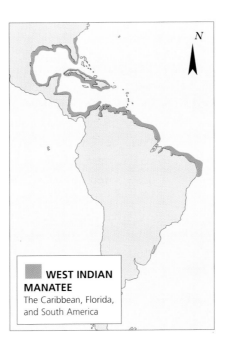

WEST INDIAN MANATEE
The Caribbean, Florida, and South America

activity, despite its large range over the east coast of Central and South America. Although the population has this large range, they are not evenly spread because not all of the coastline is suitable habitat. Much of it lacks shallow waters or ample vegetation. Another reason for uneven distribution is poaching.

The Florida subspecies is one of the better-protected species of rare animals in the world. Three important pieces of legislation were passed in the 1970s protecting the manatee: the Marine Mammal Protection Act, the Endangered Species Act, and the Florida Manatee Sanctuary Act. These acts prohibit killing or bothering manatees. They also impose restrictions on boat numbers and speeds. There are also organizations that are involved in education, conservation, and lobbying for further legislation to preserve manatees. Rehabilitation facilities exist that care for injured and sick manatees and release them back to the wild once they become healthy.

Unfortunately, all this effort may not be enough to save the manatee. The greatest long-term threat to Florida manatees is habitat destruction. Extensive coastal development has threatened them. Salt marshes and sea grass beds are drained, dredged or altered by hotel, homes, and marina construction. These areas are like nurseries for many kinds of sea life. Manatees also depend on the areas for food and shelter. Unless legislation is passed that restricts development along the more critical coastal areas, this threatened animal may yet be edged out of existence.

Peter Zahler

Mandrill
(Mandrillus sphinx)

ESA: Endangered	
IUCN: Lower risk	

Class: Mammalia
Order: Primates
Family: Cercopithecidae
Weight: Males 55 lb. (25 kg); females 25 lb. (11.5 kg)
Head-body length: 27½ in. (70 cm)
Tail length: 3 in. (7.6 cm)
Diet: Omnivorous, mainly vegetation
Gestation period: 168–176 days
Longevity: Up to 40 years or more in captivity
Habitat: Tropical rain forest, thick secondary forest, thick bush
Range: Equatorial Africa

THE MANDRILL AND its close relative, the drill, are large, forest-dwelling baboons. Both share the same environment—tropical rain forest—but the mandrill is larger and more brightly colored than the drill. The mandrill is regarded as being at lower risk, while the drill is endangered because of habitat destruction and hunting.

The mandrill, while often classified as a baboon, looks quite different from other baboons. It is very large, thick-set in body, and fearsome-looking. The male is brightly colored, and several theories attempt to explain the reasons for this. The most probable explanation is that the colors are used as a way to signal their social and sexual status. When angered or agitated, the male's spectacular face of scarlet, white, yellowish orange, and cobalt blue, and its red, blue, and violet rump all intensify in color. Because adult females greatly outnumber the males in their groups, it is assumed that great competition must exist among males to acquire females.

High pitched crowing

Mandrills congregate in single-male groups of from 15 to 50 individuals, called harem groups, which often join with other groups. There can be as many as 100 to 200 animals living closely together. Mandrills are noisy, emitting both deep grunts and high-pitched crowing calls. The complex vocalizations of the mandrill may help to maintain group solidarity in its habitat of dense, dark forests where visibility is reduced.

Primates generally exhibit strong nurturing behavior. Like human babies, mandrill infants need lots of care in the first few years of their lives in order to survive.

A group of mandrills traveling in single file through the forests of western central Africa presents an easy target for native hunters, who have now managed to virtually decimate the population. No valid estimates of mandrill numbers exist, but extinction is possible if populations continue to decline at the current rate.

Smaller females

Females are half the size of males. The female does not possess the same brightly colored features as her partner. Her coloring is less flamboyant, with a gray-black face and a brown-and-black rump. Mandrills usually give birth to one baby at a time.

The female is ready to mate every 33 days, when a swelling is visible between the hardened pads of her rump (callosities) and her tail. Gestation time is not known, but it is thought to be similar to that of baboons (six months). The birth season runs from December to April.

The male mandrill has a very prominent muzzle, with bony swellings on either side of the nose. He also has large canine teeth. The female has altogether less exaggerated features.

Mandrills are well adapted to terrestrial life in the forest. They spend most of their time on the forest floor or at heights of less than 16½ feet (5 meters), and climb into the trees to feed and sleep. They move on all fours, but they walk on their toes and fingers; their soles and palms rarely touch the ground.

Mostly vegetarian

Mandrills eat mainly fruit, leaves, buds, roots, fungus, ants, and termites. Sometimes they raid plantations for crops and palm oil fruits, particularly when food is scarce or at the end of the dry season. When venturing onto local farms they run the risk of being shot by local farmers. It is thought that they are more vegetarian than other baboons, but they have been observed eating small vertebrates, both in captivity and in the wild.

The largest remaining populations of this rare species are probably to be found in Gabon, the Campo Reserve in southern Cameroon, Rio Muni (Equatorial Guinea), and southwestern Congo. Habitat destruction and hunting are the main threats to the mandrill's future survival.

Drill

The drill (*Mandrillus leucophaeus*) is closely related to the mandrill, the main difference being its color and size. The drill is smaller than the mandrill. It is olive brown with a grayish tinge, and it has a deep black face (surrounded by a white fringe), with no grooves on its muzzle. The male drill has a scarlet lower lip, and like the mandrill, the perineum and genital organs are brightly colored in blue, red, and violet. The coloration of both females and infants is much less striking and is not present in the genital region. The male grows a patch of long hairs low on the chest that conceals glands used for marking territory.

The drill lives in lowland rain forest, coastal forest, and on the banks of rivers in southeastern Nigeria, the island of Bioko, and western Cameroon. Although they thrive in similar ecological environments to those of the mandrills, drills are thought to be separated from them by the Sanaga River in Cameroon; thus they occur only from the Cross River in Nigeria to the Sanaga River in Cameroon. In Nigeria the drill is believed to be close to extinction; it is restricted to a small area only 185 miles by 155 miles (300 kilometers by 250 kilometers) in Cameroon.

Drills are semiterrestrial, and group sizes may vary from as few as 14 to as many as 200. Groups appear to consist of single male subgroups of roughly 20 individuals that often join up with other units, although solitary males

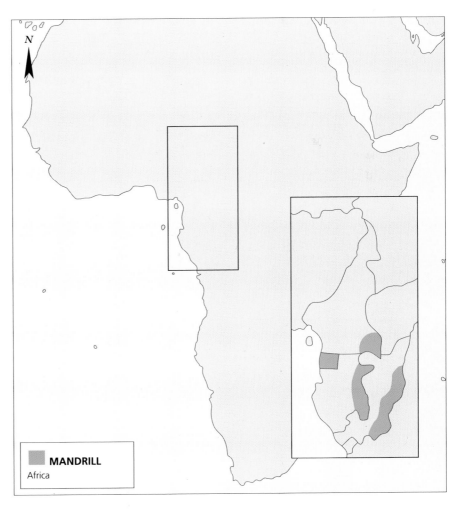

MANDRILL
Africa

have been observed. When females are ready to mate, a sexual swelling becomes noticeable. The length of gestation is probably 168 to 176 days, and the birth season probably ranges from December to April.

Diet

In common with their cousins the mandrills, drills eat fruit, seeds, fungi, leaves, ground plants, ants, termites, and small vertebrates. They have also been observed raiding plantations for manioc and oil-palm fruits.

No estimates of the drill's population exist, but the numbers have declined throughout its range in the last few years. Sadly, it is thought to be threatened with complete extinction. The only area which is known to contain significant drill popula-

tions is Korup National Park in Cameroon. Surveys are urgently needed to establish whether the drill exists in any sizable numbers outside Korup, and to protect it against hunting. Drills are not only being shot while raiding crops, but are extensively hunted

Mandrills live in groups of 15 to 50 individuals and are led by a single male. These "harem groups" will often form close associations with others, establishing a larger clan of up to 200 animals.

for their meat. They are especially vulnerable to hunting because large groups can easily be tracked by listening for their loud cries.

Breeding in captivity

About 60 individuals lived in zoos in 1985, but reproduction in these conditions has been mostly unsuccessful. Only about 25 percent of the animals breed. A successful breeding program is, however, underway in Hanover Zoo in Germany. This highly endangered primate is close to extinction in Nigeria and on the island of Bioko.

Sarah Dart

MANGABEYS

Class: Mammalia

Order: Primates

Family: Cercopithecidae

Subfamily: Cercopithecinae

Mangabeys are large, slender monkeys, closely related to baboons. They are divided into two separate groups: one crested and mainly black (the Albigena group), and the other uncrested and mainly brown or gray (the Torquatus group). Mangabeys are generally restricted to the rain forest of west and central Africa, although two small isolated populations of crested mangabeys are also found in East Africa.

The Albigena group prefers swampy forest and is almost totally arboreal. In contrast to

this, the Torquatus group is often found in primary and secondary forest, spending much of its time on the ground.

All mangabeys have tails that are longer than their bodies, and the females are smaller than the males. Infants are the same color as adults. They share certain habitats with guenons, but their large and extremely strong teeth allow them to eat hard seeds, which guenons cannot eat. They also eat fruit, leaves, mushrooms, grubs, insects, and small reptiles such as lizards and snakes. The mangabeys will also raid crops, making them unpopular with farmers.

Mangabeys live in large groups of 10 to 25 animals, and move around using all four limbs (they are quadrapedal). They are

extremely loud and vocal, and the adult male in particular has a very dramatic call that can be easily heard over a long distance. The female's call, while not as dramatic, is also loud. Both single males and multiple male groups have been observed.

The female's menstrual cycle lasts about one month. Pregnancy lasts about six months, with no evidence of breeding occuring during any one particular season. Gestation varies from 168 days to 177 days. Females are ready to reproduce during their fourth year; males, on the other hand, are not fully sexually mature until the age of six or seven. At age six their canine teeth are fully grown and their voice changes, with the "loud call" being heard for the first time.

Collared Mangabey
(Cercocebus torquatus)

ESA: Endangered

IUCN: Lower risk

Weight: 22 lb. (10 kg)
Head-body length: 26 in. (66 cm)
Tail length: 17–30 in. (43–76 cm)
Diet: Palm nuts, seeds, fruit, leaves, insects, small vertebrates
Gestation period: 164–175 days
Longevity: 30 years in captivity
Habitat: Primary rain forest
Range: Nigeria to Congo

THE COLLARED mangabey is known by several names, including the white, red-capped, sooty or smoky mangabey. It spends most of its time on the ground, foraging in the leaf litter of the forest floor. Its coat is gray, but variations in coloring are found across its range. For example, it has a white collar in Ghana and a red cap in Cameroon.

As with other members of the Torquatus group, this mangabey uses its fingers to bear its weight when walking. It has thumbs that function like our own, and a big toe which stands out from the rest of the foot.

Adaptable

Habitat destruction and hunting in equatorial Africa are causing major disruptions to the lifestyle of the collared mangabey. Logging of valuable timber and conflict with humans over crop raiding present additional threats to its existence.

This mangabey does, however, breed well in captivity, with some newborns being second-generation captive births. It is also more adaptable than some of its primate cousins, showing an inclination to survive in areas that have been logged or converted to agriculture.

Congo has been logging its forests at a rate of 54,000 acres (21,852 hectares) per year. Urban growth has created problems such as waste disposal and air pollution.

Nigeria has already lost 70 to 80 percent of its original forest. It is this kind of abuse to the environment that threatens species such as the collared mangabey.

Sanje Crested Mangabey
(Cercocebus galeritus sanjei)

Tana River Mangabey
(Cercocebus galeritus galeritus)

IUCN: Endangered

Weight: Males, 22½ lb. (10.2 kg); females, 12 lb. (5.5 kg);
Head-body length: 17½–23in. (44–58 cm)
Tail length: 17–30 in. (43–76 cm)
Diet: Palm nuts, seeds, leaves
Gestation period: 164–175 days
Habitat: Rain forest
Range: Uzungwa Mountains of Tanzania; Kenya

THE SANJE CRESTED mangabey was only first described in 1981. No museum specimens exist, therefore, all data comes from live animals. It is a subspecies of the crested mangabey (*Cercocebus galeritus*) and has features similar to another subspecies, the Tana

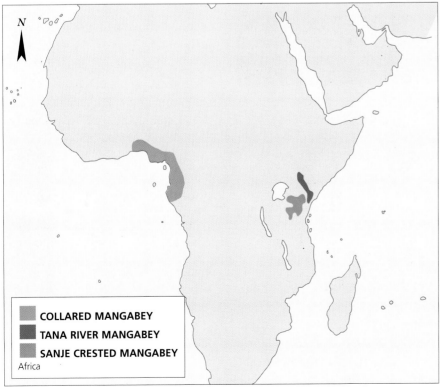

N

COLLARED MANGABEY
TANA RIVER MANGABEY
SANJE CRESTED MANGABEY
Africa

Females mangabeys are ready to reproduce during their fourth year of life, but males are not fully sexually mature until the age of six or seven. Here, a cherry-crowned mangabey (*Cercocebus torquatus torquatus*) holds her newborn.

River mangabey (*Cercocebus galeritus galeritus*).

This mangabey lives in an very restricted area, and there are estimated to be less than 3,000 left in total.

It is protected in the Mwani-hana Forest Reserve, but is threatened by habitat destruction due to timber extraction and charcoal production.

If adequate forest management is not enforced in the very near future, there is grave doubt about the fate of this primate.

Tana River mangabey

This subspecies is found only in small patches of forest that border a 37-mile (60-kilometer) stretch of the Tana River floodplain in eastern Kenya. This mangabey has a fawn and yellow coat, and the hair on top of its head stands up in a crest. Very little is known about this animal, except that it adapts remarkably well to environmental changes. However, as the woodland along the edge of its river is carved up by people, so this mangabey loses

its food supply and the trees which form its natural habitat. The Tana River National Primate Reserve does protect some of these monkeys, but this protection appears to be inadequate in securing its future. There are none in captivity. In the 12 years since the reserve was established, the population has decreased by 25 percent.

Precarious future

The fate of these primates is truly in the hands of the Kenyan people and government. Because the mangabeys share this land with one of the fastest-growing human populations in the world, they are bound to experience more, not less, environmental stress.

Three-fifths of Kenya's land area is semidesert, forcing nearly all of its population into the smaller, more tropical half of the country. As more people are squeezed together in what has become the most industrialized nation in East Africa, pollution increases. More land must be given up to grow food for millions of people. Water pollution from urban and industrial waste degrades topsoil. Even tourism in some of Kenya's game preserves has degraded habitat.

What little is left of Kenya's forests (now 3 percent of the nation's total land area) is disappearing at a rapid rate. This is disastrous for many species, including the mangabey.

Sarah Dart and Gregory Lee
See also Monkeys.

GLOSSARY

actinopterygii: the scientific name for bony fish

amphibia: the Latin scientific name for amphibians

arboreal: living in or adapted for living in trees; arboreal animals seldom, if ever, descend to the ground (see terrestrial)

aves: the Latin scientific name for birds

barbels: a slender growth on the mouths or nostrils of certain fishes, used as a sensory organ for touch

bipedal: any organism that walks on two feet

bract: a leaf at the base of a flower stalk in plants

buff: in bird species, a yellow-white color used to describe the plumage

calyx: the green outer whorl of a flower made up of sepals

captive breeding: any method of bringing several animals of the same species into a zoo or other closed environment for the purpose of mating; if successful, these methods can increase the population of that species

carnivore: any flesh-eating animal

chromosomes: the DNA in a cell's nucleus, containing genes

ciénegas: wet meadow areas

clear cutting: a method of harvesting lumber that eliminates all the trees in a specific area rather than just selected trees

clutch, clutch size: the number of eggs laid during one nesting cycle

corolla: the separate petals, or the fused petals of a flower

cotyledon: the first leaf developed by the embryo of a seed plant

deciduous: dropping off, falling off during a certain season or at a regular stage of growth; deciduous trees shed their leaves annually

decurved: curving downward; a bird's beak is decurved if it points toward the ground

defoliate: to strip trees and bushes of their leaves

deforestation: the process of removing trees from a particular area

diurnal: active during the day; some animals are diurnal, while others are active at night (see nocturnal)

dominance: the ability to overpower the behavior of other individuals; an animal is dominant if it affects others of its own species in a way that benefits itself; also, the trait of abundance that determines the character of a plant community: grasses dominate a prairie, and trees dominate a forest

dorsal: pertaining to or situated on the back of an organism; a dorsal fin is on the back of a fish

ecology: the study of the interrelationship between a living organism and its environment

ecosystem: a community of animals, plants, and bacteria and its interrelated physical and chemical environment

endemic: native to a particular geographic region

estrous: the time period when female mammals can become pregnant

exotic species: a plant or animal species that is not native to its habitat

feral: a wild animal that is descended from tame or domesticated species

fishery, fisheries: any system, body of water, or portion of a body of water that supports finfish or shellfish; can also be used as an adjective describing a person or thing (for example, a fisheries biologist)

forest: a plant community in which trees grow closely enough together that their crowns interlock to form a continuous overhead canopy

fry: young fish

gene pool: the total hereditary traits available within a group; when isolated from other members of their species, individual organisms may produce healthy offspring if there is enough variety in the genes available through mating

gestation: the period of active embryonic growth inside a mammal's body between the time the embryo attaches to the uterus and the time of birth; some mammals carry dormant embryos for several weeks or months before the embryo attaches to the uterus and begins to develop actively, and this dormancy period is not part of the gestation period; gestation period is the time length of a pregnancy

granivore: any seed-feeding animal

guano: manure, especially of sea birds and bats

gynodoecious: designating a plant species in which bisexual and female flowers are produced on separate plants

gynodiecy: some plants in a population are strictly female (producing seeds, but no pollen), while others have perfect flowers; they are bisexual, producing pollen and seeds

habitat: the environment where a species is normally found; habitat degradation is the decline in quality of a species' home until it can no longer survive there

herbivore: any plant-eating animal

herbivorous: plant eating

hibernate: to spend the winter season in a dormant or inactive state; some species hibernate to save energy during months when food is scarce

hierarchy: the relationships among individuals of the same species or among species that determine in what order animals may have access to food, water, mates, nesting or denning sites, and other vital resources

home range: the area normally traveled by an individual species during its lifespan

hybrid: the offspring of two different species who mate; see interbreed

hybridization: the gradual decline of a species through continued breeding with another species; see interbreed

immature(s): a young bird that has not yet reached breeding maturity; it usually has plumage differing from an adult bird of the same species

in captivity: a species that exists in zoos, captive breeding programs, or in private collections, perhaps because the species can no longer be found in the wild

incubation: the period when an egg is kept warm until the embryo develops and hatches

indigenous species: any species native to its habitat

inflorescence: a group of flowers that grow from one point

insular species: a species isolated on an island or islands

interbreed: when two sep-

arate species mate and produce offspring; see hybrid

invertebrate(s): any organism without a backbone (spinal column)

juvenal: a bird with an intermediate set of feathers after its young downy plumage molts and before growing hard, adult feathers

juvenile(s): a young bird or other animal not yet mature

litter: the animals born to a species that normally produces several young at birth

lore(s): the irregularly shaped facial area of a bird between the eye and the base of the beak

migrate, migratory: to move from one range to another, particularly with the change of seasons; many species are migratory

montane forest: a forest found in mountainous regions

mycorrhiza: symbiotic relationship between the roots of a plant and the mycelium of a fungus

nocturnal: active at night; some animals are nocturnal, while others are active by day (see diurnal)

nomadic species: a species with no permanent range or territory; nomadic species wander for food and water

old growth forest: forest that has not experienced extensive deforestation

omnivore: any species that eats both plants and animals

ornithologist(s): a scientist who studies birds

pelage: the hairy covering of a mammal

pelagic: related to the oceans or open sea; pelagic birds rarely roost on land

perennial: persisting for several years

plumage: the feathers that cover a bird

predation: the act of one species hunting another

predator: a species that preys upon other species

primary forest: a forest of native trees that results from natural processes, often called virgin forest

primate(s): a biological ranking of species in the same order, including gorillas, chimpanzees, monkeys, and human beings (*Homo sapiens*)

racemes: elongate clusters of flowers borne on short stalks

range: the geographic area where a species roams

recovery plan(s): any document that outlines a public or private program for assisting an endangered or threatened species

relict: an isolated habitat or population that was once widespread

reptilia: the Latin scien-

tific name for reptiles

riffle(s): a shallow rapid stretch of water caused by a rocky outcropping or obstruction in a stream

riparian: relating to plants and animals close to and influenced by rivers

roe: fish eggs

rufous: in bird species, plumage that is orange-brown and pink

secondary forest: a forest that has grown back after cutting, forest fire, or other deforestation; secondary forests may or may not contain exotic tree species, but they almost always differ in character from primary forests

sedentary species: one that does not migrate

siltation: the process of sediment clouding and obstructing a body of water

species: a distinct kind of plant or animal; the biological ranking below genus; a subspecies is an isolated population that varies from its own species

symbiont: an organism living in symbiosis

symbiosis: two dissimilar organisms living together in a mutually beneficial relationship

terrestrial: living in or adapted for living principally on the ground; some birds are terrestrial and seldom, if ever, ascend into trees (see arboreal)

territory: the area occupied more or less exclusively by an organism or group, usually defended by aggressive displays and physical combat

tubercle: a prominent bump on a fish's spine

veld: a grassland region with some scattered bushes and virtually no trees; other terms are *steppe*, *pampas*, and *prairie*

ventral: on or near the belly; the ventral fin is located on the underside of

a fish and corresponds with the hind limbs of other vertebrates

vertebrates: any organism that has a backbone (spinal column)

weir: a dam or other

obstruction of a stream that diverts water

woodland: a plant community in which trees grow abundantly but far enough apart that their crowns do not intermingle, so no overhead canopy is formed

INDEX

The scientific name of a plant or animal is entered in *italics*; its common name is in roman type. Page numbers in *italics* refer to picture captions.